Dealing with Differences

DEALING WITH DIFFERENCES

Dramas of Mediating Public Disputes

John Forester

OXFORD
UNIVERSITY PRESS
2009

OXFORD

UNIVERSITY PRESS

Oxford University Press, Inc., publishes works that further
Oxford University's objective of excellence
in research, scholarship, and education.

Oxford   New York

Auckland   Cape Town   Dar es Salaam   Hong Kong   Karachi
Kuala Lumpur   Madrid   Melbourne   Mexico City   Nairobi
New Delhi   Shanghai   Taipei   Toronto

With offices in

Argentina   Austria   Brazil   Chile   Czech Republic   France   Greece
Guatemala   Hungary   Italy   Japan   Poland   Portugal   Singapore
South Korea   Switzerland   Thailand   Turkey   Ukraine   Vietnam

Copyright © 2009 by Oxford University Press, Inc.

Published by Oxford University Press, Inc.
198 Madison Avenue, New York, New York 10016

www.oup.com

Oxford is a registered trademark of Oxford University Press

Liberty of Congress Cataloging-in-Publication Data
Forester, John, 1948–
Dealing with differences : dramas of mediating public disputes / John Forester.
        p.   cm.
Includes bibliographical references and index.
ISBN 978-0-19-538589-2; 987-0-19-538590-8 (pbk.)
I. Political planning—Citizen participation. 2. Policy sciences.
3. Mediation. I. Title.
JF1525. P6F67 2009
303.6'9—dc22   2009004890

1 3 5 7 9 8 6 4 2
Printed in the United States of America
on acid-free paper

For Anne
For color and grace,
Laughter and light

Preface

How can we keep today's and tomorrow's possibilities in sight, when so many seem only to see what happened yesterday? Especially in settings of conflict, we find those who say, "We *can* ..." heavily outnumbered by those who proclaim instead, "They'll never ..." and "We can't...." How can we really do better?

I have written two books with these questions lurking in the background, *Planning in the Face of Power* (1989) and *The Deliberative Practitioner* (1999), but this book addresses them head-on and in still greater detail. These earlier books argued that in practice, in a political world, those interested in change or in popular "empowerment" have to learn first, and provide answers and organizing strategies second. More than the first two, and working even more closely with practitioners' accounts of their work, this book shows how to do that, and it shows how we can often do far more, and far better, than we typically think.

It bears repeating that in too many community and policy settings alike, analysis after analysis ends breathlessly with the not-quite-stunning rediscovery, "It's all politics" or "It's all power" instead of beginning there, doing fresh and probing analysis, and asking practically in the settings at hand, "So what? So what can we do now (rather than wring our hands)?" This book addresses this challenge squarely, in diverse settings in which dealing with differences, dealing with challenges of inclusive participation and practical multistakeholder negotiations, matters.

I have had the wonderful good fortune not only to work with bright and engaged students, not only to serve as a community mediator intermittently for many years, not only to have had the opportunity to learn from deeply thoughtful practitioners committed to community empowerment, peacemaking, dispute resolution, participatory research, and more, but to have luckily come upon a way to explore "practice stories" drawn from real cases to begin, at least, to do justice to the wisdom, insight, and political vision of those working creatively in the midst of community and ethnic conflicts all the time. In large part this book reflects a journey taken with the practitioner-interviewees who generously allowed me to explore the challenges of their work by probing their practice stories.

I am grateful for research support in the form of seed grants from the Institute for Dispute Resolution, University of Victoria, and the Clarence Stein Institute for Urban and Landscape Studies, Cornell University. Chapter one revises an earlier essay delivered in honor of John Friedmann's retirement from UCLA; the earlier version was published as "Rationality, Dialogue, and Learning: What Community and Environmental Mediators Can Teach Us about the Practice of Civil Society," in *Cities for Citizens*, ed. Mike Douglass and John Friedmann (New York: Wiley and Sons, 1998). Chapter two clarifies and extends "Rationality and Surprise: The Drama of Mediation in Rebuilding Civil Society," in *Engaging Civil Societies in Democratic Planning and Governance*, ed. Penny Gurstein and Nora Angeles (University of Toronto Press, 2006). Chapter three began as a keynote address to the Environmental and Public Policy Dispute Resolution conference of the Association for Conflict Resolution, MIT (2006); an earlier version (translated by Prof. Laura Lieto) appears in *Critica della Razionalità Urbanistica* (2007). Chapters four and five revise my contribution to Lawrence Susskind et al.'s *Consensus-Building Handbook* (1999). I delivered earlier versions of chapter six as the 2004 Cecil Sheps Visiting Lecture in Social Justice at the University of North Carolina, Chapel Hill, and as guest lectures at the Center for Collaborative Policy, Sacramento, California, and at the Annual Symposium of the Interdisciplinary Ph.D. Program in Urban Design and Planning at the University of Washington, Seattle. Chapter seven began as a keynote lecture at the Safe Communities Symposium in Sydney, Australia, July 2004, and a pithy version appears in the fall 2006 issue of the *Journal of the American Planning Association*. Chapter eight, no less revised, appeared in *Irony and Organizations: Epistemological Claims and Supporting Field Stories*, ed. Ulla Johansson and Jill Woodilla (Copenhagen: Abstrak Forlag-Liber-Copenhagen Business School Press, 2004), and first in the *Negotiation Journal* (April 2004). An earlier version of the conclusion, chapter nine, appeared in *Governance Reform under Real World Conditions*, published by the World Bank's Communication and Governance Accountability Program (Forester 2008a).

For research assistance with interviewing, transcribing, editing, and more editing, thanks, too, to Stephen Atkinson, Nathan Barnhart, Kathrin Bolton, Daniel Forester, Dorian Fougeres, Alison Goldberg, Tanneasha Gordon, Kristen Grace, Nicole Kindred, Brian Kreiswirth, Andrea Kutik, Allison Lack, David Lessinger, Rebecca Liu, Andy Love, Ellen Macnow, Steven Mikulencak, Brad Mueller, June Paik, Linda Phelps, Kathy Seeburger, Christy Tao, Rachel Weiner, and Irene Weiser.

I'm grateful to Peter Adler, Laura Bachle, Sandro Balducci, Lisa Beutler, Frank Blechman, Greg Bourne, David Boyd, Puanani Burgess, Goran Cars, Marion Cox, Benjamin Davy, William Diepeveen, Nathan Edelson, Don Edwards, John Folk-Williams, Tony Gibson, Michelle Greig, Ray Lorenzo, Kem Lowry, Normajean McLaren, Carl Moore, Susan Podziba, William Potapchuk, Iolanda Romano, Dennis Ross, Wendy Sarkissian, Laurence Sherman, Susan Sherry, Gregory Sobel, Shirley Solomon, Lawrence Susskind, Jon Townsend, Karen Umemoto, and Wallace Warfield for their generosity and insights as we explored their practice.

Thanks, too, for comments on related arguments and seminar presentations to Peter Adler, Jennifer Ball, Howell Baum, Robert Beauregard, Howard Bellman, Lisa Beutler, David Booher, Greg Bourne, David Boyd, Xavier de Sousa Briggs, Heather Campbell, Goran Cars, Bayard Catron, Sara Cobb, Bobby Cochran, Grazia Concilio, Jeff Cook, Jason Corburn, Adam Craig, Kieran Donaghy, Christine Duffy, Michael Elliot, John Folk-Williams, Kate Forester, John Friedmann, Boyd Fuller, Flavien Glidja, Rachel Goldberg, Laurie Goldman, Davydd Greenwood, Jantine Grijzen, Maarten Hajer, Phil Harrison, Patsy Healey, Charles Hoch, Judith Innes, David Kahane, Laura Kaplan, Sanda Kaufman, Anne Kilgore, Dong-Young Kim, Deborah Kolb, David Laws, Kim Leary, Soo-Jang Lee, Ray Lorenzo, Kem Lowry, Owen Lynch, Ann Martin, Masahiro Matsuura, Catherine Morris, Connie Ozawa, Lasse Peltonen, Scott Peters, Jessica Pitt, Susan Podziba, Jennie Pry, Jon Pugh, Linda Putnam, Sean Nolon, Ken Reardon, Robert Rich, Henry Richardson, Nancy Rogers, Laura Saija, Tore Sager, Leonie Sandercock, Magid Senbel, Judy Saul, Laurence Sherman, Susan Sherry, Deborah Shmueli, Sarah Slack, Marianella Sclavi, John Stephens, Bruce Stiftel, Gus Stuart, Larry Susskind, Huw Thomas, Jennifer Thomas-Larmer, Karen Umemoto, Gilles Verpraet, Henk Wagenaar, Peter Whitecross, Michael Wheeler, Chris Winship, Dvora Yanow, and Oren Yiftachel. For the cover design, thanks to Anne Kilgore. For the title, and a perpetual sense of possibility, thanks again to Lawrence Susskind.

Finally, too, thanks to Diane Stratton and Emma and David Laws for their graciousness and good spirits, hearth and home shared wonderfully in Amsterdam as the very last draft took shape.

Contents

Introduction: Discovery, Creativity, and Change in the Face of Conflict   3

**Part One: When Parties Conflict, Expect that More Is Possible
                      than Anyone Says**

1. Beyond Promises: Making Public Participation and Democratic
   Deliberation Work   19
2. Cultivating Surprise and the Art of the Possible: The Drama of
   Mediating Differences   37

**Part Two: Respecting Value Differences and Acting Practically
                      Together Too**

3. Exploring Values-Based Disputes   59
4. Dealing with Deep Value Differences in Participatory Processes   77

Part Three: From Venting and Posturing to Learning and Proposing

5. Practical Consensus Building in the Face of Deep Value Differences:
   Negotiating HIV/AIDS Prevention   95
6. Planning and Mediation, Participation and Posturing: What's a Facilitative
   Leader to Do?   111

**Part Four: From Arguing to Inventing, from Presuming to
                      Enabling Action**

7. Making Public Participation in Governance Work: Distinguishing and
   Integrating Dialogue, Debate, and Negotiation   133
8. Envisioning Possibilities: How Humor and Irony Recognize Dignity
   and Build Power   155
9. Conclusion: Transforming Participatory Processes
   Integrating and Transcending Dialogue, Debate, and Negotiation   175

Appendixes   189
Notes   193
Bibliography   207
Index   219

DEALING WITH DIFFERENCES

Introduction: Discovery, Creativity, and Change in the Face of Conflict

"If you know someone's story, it is much harder to hurt them."
BigHart, Sydney, Australia

"Advocacy chooses to stand by one side for justice's sake. Mediation chooses to stand in connection to all sides for justice's sake."
J. P. Lederach (1995: 14)

We can often do much more than we think when we have to deal with differences of power, interests, and values, and this book shows how we can do it. Differences of culture and position, resources and commitments pervade our lives—in public and private—and acknowledging that lets us take the first step not just to wringing our hands, but to assessing when we really can negotiate our differences and when we cannot. Just chanting "power, power, power" won't help us, and neither will sincerely appealing to "dialogue, dialogue, dialogue." So we need to ask, how can we do better than we have, when interests and values, perceptions and perspectives conflict?

This book builds upon practice as well as theory by exploring the accounts of community activists and leaders, mediators and facilitators, educators and consultants who have worked in the face of conflict—through practical and participatory, deliberative and negotiated processes—to find agreements that no one thought possible beforehand.[1] These agreements and accommodations, we will see, need be neither poor compromises nor betrayals of one's values—they can satisfy the interests of stakeholders and gain their pragmatic consent; they need not be romantic, "merely" idealistic, or otherworldly.

In Washington State, for example, local, state, and tribal officials inherited decades of distrust and faced deeply differing views of land and environment, and yet with Shirley Solomon's assistance they began newly promising work together to govern and manage their natural resources, as chapter one begins to

3

show. In Maryland, local and county officials long locked in nasty transportation disputes came to work together in processes designed by Frank Blechman and colleagues, and so we learn in chapter two that we jump from yesterday's rhetoric to tomorrow's possibilities at our own risk. Dealing with differences often means dealing with values as well as interests, with identities as well as preferences, and chapter three explores these issues through four practitioners' work in settings involving racial and ethnic conflicts. Chapters four and five continue to explore deep value differences. In Colorado, we will see, state health officials called for a bottom-up process to address HIV-AIDS prevention strategies, and that meant convening people who'd never been in the same room together: religious conservatives, gay activists, bureaucrats, prostitutes, and local and state officials, among still others with deep value differences. Chapter five examines how Mike Hughes worked across such value differences to build a practical consensus that few had thought possible.

In Hawaii, and on the mainland as well, other mediators and facilitators enable at times the angry, the done-to, the suspicious, and the impatient to learn, as well as to listen, and—more importantly—to move beyond yesterday's posturing and name-calling to create newly negotiated practical agreements, practical commitments to real outcomes that satisfy their interests as well as being collaboratively cogenerated and coproduced, as the examples in chapters six and seven show. In California, after 20 years of political attacks, courtroom dramas, and media condemnations about off-road vehicles on state and federal lands, a mediated process enabled old adversaries to craft new state environmental regulations with promising national implications. Chapter seven examines that story and the lessons of facilitator-mediator Lisa Beutler's practice.[2] Chapter eight continues to explore practice but in a surprising way; in the face of pain and inequality, ambiguity, uncertainty and vulnerability, we shall see, an active sense of irony and humor can provide respect, recognition, encouragement, and actual empowerment. Chapter nine recaps the lessons of the book by giving us practical and detailed advice about the ways that governance processes can integrate inclusive stakeholder participation with expertly informed, mutual gains negotiations.

Beyond Neutrality—to Mediator Responsibility to All Parties

As we shall see, the mediators whose work we examine here make few claims to neutrality but many to serving all parties in a *nonpartisan* way; these "facilitative leaders" work proactively to enable well-informed decisions by parties, so they may level the playing field of preexisting inequalities of information and access to relevant expertise, and more. This is a book, then, about activist mediators, a label that some will take to be a contradiction in terms, but that this book will demonstrate to refer to astute practice responsible to all stakeholders, a practice from which anyone who cares about dealing with real differences has a great deal to learn. John Paul Lederach (1995: 14) characterized this responsibility to all parties insightfully when he observed, "Advocacy chooses to stand by one side for justice's sake. Mediation chooses to stand in connection to all sides for justice's sake."

These chapters will explore a vast middle ground between two extreme and misleading views. On one side, we have a political gullibility that masquerades as realism: because the parties to a conflict talk tough, and have talked tough and acted tougher for years, some believe that no agreements today or tomorrow seem realistically possible. This extreme view replaces political imagination and action with resignation. On the other side, we have political idealism that masquerades as practical judgment: even though the parties have talked tough and acted tougher, genuine dialogue will surely resolve their differences. The first view leads us to squander opportunities and cover our tracks with self-righteous explanations of why nothing's possible. The opposite view leads us to foolishness and false hope, for in many cases no agreements between bitterly divided parties may be possible for the foreseeable future. So we need to chart a middle course—we need to beware of the presumptions of either exaggerated view and instead, very carefully, very practically, to inquire and to learn, knowing that much of what we will hear in any given case can so easily reflect political posturing and gamesmanship, yesterday's outrage rather than tomorrow's possibility. The chapters that follow repeatedly show us cases of deep difference in which, even as little or no practical resolution initially seems possible, practical agreements emerge from real political deliberations: practical accommodations crafted by the stakeholders themselves (and their consulting experts) provide new ways forward. Accordingly, this book is all about making democratic deliberations work inclusively, intelligently, and efficiently—not, as we shall see, as a matter of hopeful idealism, manipulative cooptation, or empty talk.[3]

These chapters will show that these unexpected working agreements—and the processes by which parties who were deeply divided along racial, religious, and environmental lines crafted them—can teach us a great deal about the practical wisdom required to deal with differences in public and private settings alike, in effect, to make democracy work. When deeply divided parties make practical agreements that surprise themselves, we, too, will very likely be surprised. We can then appreciate and reconsider just how *we* have been thinking too narrowly about dealing with real differences of interests, values, power, and more.

This snatching of real possibilities from the jaws of what loomed before as the apparently "impossible" reflects the most evocative, compelling, and useful definition of "planning" that I know: "planning is the organization of hope"—for planning well done helps us imagine our communities as we might really live in them; planning poorly done diminishes our sense of what we can do, weakens our hope, and discourages our action. This entire book tries to show how planners and community leaders might work practically in the face of power and value differences to *achieve* such ends—more just and beautiful, sustainable, and livable places and spaces.[4]

The Practical Agenda

So this book has at least four practical payoffs. First, we explore a lesson about deep value differences that we can paraphrase here and return to in several of the chapters that follow. The lesson in a pithy suggestion goes as follows: parties in conflict may disagree about what the Bible means and what their sense of the Creator requires of them, *and* they may nevertheless agree about where to place the stop signs on the roadway. This simple intuition, we shall see, has important practical and theoretical implications.[5]

Second, we will see that when interested parties disagree about public issues (as is typically the case in any important public policy issue, for example), we do well to think about two often separated concerns together—voice, or inclusion, and effective negotiation as well. We need both to include interested people so they can have their voices heard rather than dismissed and to enable those interested parties to negotiate effectively to satisfy their interests, rather than, for example, to have public officials simply pay lip service to them. We will see that when we try to assure both inclusive or representative participation *and* effective negotiations, we need to understand the sophisticated practice of a widely misunderstood yet deeply political practice that we will refer to broadly here as *mediation*.[6]

Third, we shall see that when interests, values, and power differ, we need practically to distinguish carefully three modes of response that we can roughly call *dialogue, debate,* and *negotiation*. Community leaders and planners, organizers and managers, too, engage in these processes often, but we confuse and entangle and undermine them often as well. The practical payoff arrives when we recognize that each of these common processes involves and requires differing practices, skills, goals, and abilities to accomplish successfully. To promote a dialogue, we must *facilitate* conversation; to promote a debate, we must *moderate* an argument; to promote a successful negotiation, we must *mediate* proposals for action. These three strategies of action—facilitating, moderating, and mediating—produce differing processes that in turn produce quite different *outcomes!* Failing to appreciate these practical differences, we set ourselves up—and set up the people with whom we work—for practical failure as well (cf. Jackstreit and Kaufmann 1995).

Fourth, we see that dispute resolution rarely means just sitting down to make a deal. Instead, skillful and wise practice involves a series of moves, phases, or even stages. Early on, typically, practitioners *assess* a conflict at hand by interviewing affected parties to probe their sentiments, interests, values, uncertainties, vulnerabilities, and, not least of all, their options. Under what conditions might they be willing to explore mediated negotiations while keeping their other options open?[7] After *conflict assessment* comes the work of carefully *convening* parties and their representatives in a safe and supportive venue. After convening comes the initial and then more focused work of *learning*—about each other, about evolving changes in the social, political, or natural environments, and about legal and technical options, options for mutual accommodation or agreement. Only then, after assessment, convening, and learning, might actual *negotiation* or bargaining begin, hardly "late" in the game—for after negotiations can come the work of *monitoring implementation* and possible renegotiation as well. Each of these phases can take many forms; mediators must improvise each of them in each particular circumstance, as the following chapters teach us.

So the chapters that follow explore the drama, the wisdom, and even a peculiar magic of what I will loosely term *mediation*, the daunting work of assisting deeply divided members of public and private sectors to try to come to terms with one another in practical and consensually accommodating ways. By the "drama of mediation" I refer simply to the real anticipations of conflict: the gamesmanship, the anger and fury, the distrust and suspicion, the exaggeration and scheming, the posturing and deceit, the contentiousness and aggression, and the strategy upon strategy attempted to see one's gain and the adversary's loss. Any experienced mediator, like many experienced managers or planners or politicians, knows that very much more than meets the eye and ear matters in public conflicts. Any experienced mediator (again like managers or planners or politicians) knows that community residents will posture no less than developers, that organizers will play power politics no less than aspiring politicians or bankers, that "information" can rarely be taken by anyone at face value, that even heartfelt communications can often be strategic moves as much as sincere confessions.

All this means that experienced mediators need the wisdom to know a bit of what poker players know—and more. To work between conflicting community groups requires any public administrator, planner, mediator, or even volunteer convener to know that first words often differ from last words, that residents' initial perceptions of each other and of the issues at hand will often change as they learn even more about each other and those issues. Knowing how to listen, of course, means knowing that what we hear expressed so emphatically at one time can change, knowing that the table pounding today can, after hard political work, give way to a handshake tomorrow (or after a year). The wisdom of mediators—to try to capture it quickly—reflects lessons and insights learned through many years of working in the trenches of public and private disputes. The chapters that follow try to do at least partial justice to that practical wisdom, in part by asking a bit baldly, "What might planners and public administrators, organizers and managers too, having to work in the face of contentious public disputes *not yet know* that experienced mediators might? What can mediators who've worked for years in the face of deep divisions teach us about public and private differences of interests, values, and power—that can and that might not be resolved?"

Some public disputes will have no possible resolution, to be sure: deeply divided parties may prefer to contest their differences rather than to reach a working consensus or accommodation. Some others will resolve themselves. In between, we find many disputes about land uses, environmental protection, organizational change, public health measures, real estate development, public policy options, and more that community members and public officials alike might handle either *disastrously,* digging ourselves deeper into holes of resentment, impasse, and wasted opportunities, or *productively* in ways that satisfy the diverse community interests at stake. This bears emphasis: we handle disputes every day in our personal lives, and we might learn from personal experience that nothing assures our handling conflicts adeptly rather than poorly. So we can learn from the experience of those who have found productive ways to surprise warring parties, to work with those parties to satisfy their interests in ways they initially thought to be impossible. Here we come not to any "magic" of mediation but to its hard work of assessing a given conflict, convening affected parties, enabling their learning about vulnerabilities, and not least of all negotiating to serve and accommodate their interests. When parties express surprise at agreements they have reached but didn't think possible initially, when they say, "That was magic," they are teaching us an important lesson having little to do with magic and very much to do with the strength of their initial presumptions and convictions: the self-limiting power of their own blinders that the process of mediation helped them to examine and then reach beyond—to achieve previously unimagined gains.

So the drama, wisdom, and magic of the conflict resolution stories that follow concern questions of power and deep value differences every bit as much as the discovery of political possibility in which few parties envisioned many possibilities at all. The chapters that follow, like this introduction, have *no use for* the terms "compromise" or "win-win" or "communication"—for each of these notions confuses us in its vagueness far more than it clarifies.

In an increasingly interdependent world, we will see, both theoretically and practically, that interdependent parties—countries in the global economy or neighboring states or municipalities—need to deal with each other and negotiate their differences. That's the easy part. But needing to negotiate hardly protects anyone from the traps that two realistically wary negotiators can fall into as each tries to protect his or her own interests—as both end up hostage to their own gamesmanship. "Too cute by half," some say. "Bad strategy" or "self-fulfilling prophecy" captures it better; achieving mutually lousy results of hardball negotiations seems all too frequent, but not inevitable.

It turns out that the more parties, the more issues, and the more interests involved in a given dispute, the more that winning versus losing works as a model only for those hoping to be autocrats, not those who have to work or live together. "My way or the highway" doesn't work well over time: today's success comes at the price of tomorrow's reputation and the next day's distrust. So the realities of citizens' and stakeholders' interdependence—their needing to get along, not just on this issue today but on that issue tomorrow—forces all participants to face a new worry and a shared vulnerability: if we can't just act by ourselves, unilaterally, how do we tell when an agreement or accommodation we can reach is as good as we can do, not only for us as a party but for our larger community or relationship over time?

So we face the challenge in any setting of conflict and dispute not to help these neighbors "win" and those neighbors "lose," but to help both satisfy their more important interests and avoid mutually assured demise. Here mediators can help, surprisingly enough. This book shows how they can do that step by step. These essays assess not so much their ideals, their communications, or their values, but instead their hints and tips, clues and cues to how we might deal practically with deep differences in politicized and contentious public and private settings.

Learning from Practice

The chapters that follow do not so much examine the challenges of "dealing with differences" theoretically in terms of the academic literature, "who's published what," or by assessing the intellectual history of disparate conflict resolution literatures. Instead, these chapters work interpretively through narrative analysis by exploring a series of "profiles of practitioners," a distinct, practice-focused form of oral history material I have developed with colleagues over the last 15 years (Forester 1999a, 2006a). These profiles tell us in the practitioners' own words less *what* they have actually done than *how* they imagine and corroborate elements of their own practice. These case-focused interviews seek to address practice, not opinions, to explore performances and flows of interactions, not attitudes or political beliefs. So, for example, our interviews have not asked, "*What did you think about* the threat the mayor made in the meeting?" but instead, "*How did you respond to* the threat the mayor made…?"

Asking, "What did you think about X?" we have found, gets us a theory or speculation; asking, "What did you do when X happened?" gives us a flow of action to consider. Asking what someone thought about a bluff or strategy gives us the considered opinion of a spectator; asking *how* they responded to the bluff or strategy gives us the considered judgments of an engaged actor—and that's what this book's about: the *hows* of dealing with differences of interests, values, and power.

These profiles, drawn from practice-focused oral history interviews, provide no last words on their subject matter, but the richness of the resulting narratives provides a form of internal corroboration. The profiles do not provide technical fixes, of course, but they do provide practical advice, insight, and a sense of both realistic entanglement and possibility.[8] Even if the word *hope* appears no more than a few times in what follows, these chapters teach us about politics as involving not simply distributing goods, "who gets what," but transforming capacities and identities, "who can do what," especially when community members could not imagine such real action earlier. So this book addresses public cynicism and the failure of political imagination in every chapter: the easy cynicism of "There's no use talking to them" and the easy if self-fulfilling cynicisms of "There's nothing we can do." The stories that follow help us to see how we persuade ourselves too easily that little may be possible, and so these stories do generate hope by sharing insights that will allow us to see closed doors as shut perhaps, but yet unlocked.

Consider one of my favorite examples. Exploring a long-standing, bitter environmental dispute in California that Lisa Beutler mediated productively, as we shall see in chapter seven, I wondered as I interviewed her how it could be that so many people might have really wanted to turn around and walk out rather than walk into a room of thirty or more stakeholders so seriously angry with each other. How did Lisa, I wondered, muster the confidence to walk through that doorway to get to work? Her striking answer asks us pointedly and precisely to see "anger" in public disputes less as irrational, interpersonal hostility and more as the expression of serious dissatisfaction with the status quo—so we might take anger as evidence of a real energy and willingness in the room to make the world different, energy and willingness that Lisa recognized as a resource, even an opportunity, with which to work.

Beyond Complaint to Constructive Criticism

So we can move well beyond the glib criticisms of participatory processes. Criticism is not only easy, it's sometimes too easy. We should ask what better proposals the critics really put forward. Do they simply tell us what does *not* work, without suggestions for what might make "the right to the city," for example, more than empty rhetoric? We need to remember the difference between complaint and critical analysis or "critique"—and we should hold careful, critical analysis to a standard higher than mere complaint.

Critical analysis tells us not just that injustice exists, but how and why power plays take place historically and specifically, not simply as the general order of things: how injustice exists changeably rather than inevitably, politically rather than metaphysically—how our lives could have been different. Critical analysis tells us, colloquially speaking, not just what's wrong but also what we can do practically to respond. Complaint, in contrast, tells us what's wrong—unjust, racist, manipulated, sexist, and so on—but tells us nothing new about how the world can be otherwise, how we can change the world, resist injustice, do justice.

So when we read critical analyses, we need to learn how, in the face of power and deep difference, our lives *can be better*, not just to hear once again that who gets what is political, that the ruling rule, the powerful have power, that racism and sexism shatter lives, that environmental justice is widespread. We need neither the promise of good news nor the false comfort of solidarity with the done-to; we need fresh analyses of how diverse coalitions can pursue justice not only in print but in organizing, program building, legislation, and here via dealing with differences in complex social and political settings. We need not more facile criticism of participatory processes—Too messy! Takes too long! Too unpredictable!—but careful analysis of how they can work, and this is one central objective of the chapters that follow.

Evaluation: Calling a Process "Collaborative" or "Participatory" Does Not Make It So

We need to be particularly wary of writers telling us that a process is "participatory" or "collaborative" just because a mayor or city council resolution or a planning director or a community organizer *says* that the process has been—or even was intended to be—"participatory" or "collaborative." Until we as analysts of planning and governance are far less gullible than many of us seem to be today, we will keep rediscovering breathlessly that things did not work out as promised by the powers that be (imagine that!), that significant parties have been left out, excluded, or marginalized (surprise!), and that the supposedly collaborative process has not been collaborative much at all (lip service!). On a used car lot, only the most novice buyers would be surprised that what the salesperson is saying may well have a flimsy relationship to reality. Shouldn't we be at least as skeptical and critical as used car buyers?

Still, discounting as self-serving the rhetorical claims of public officials is the easy part. Should we be any less careful, any less critically attentive, when listening to the claims of developers or community residents, of industrial representatives or well-established (or new) community organizations? Notice, of course, that if we're any less skeptical of the marginalized or "weaker" community members making claims of environmental injustice, for example, we risk buying into the old fallacies of "the noble savage"—to say nothing of being politically presumptuous and morally condescending. So what the affected parties *say*—owners or workers, developers or neighbors or public officials, older residents or new immigrants—is just that: it is sometimes accurate, sometimes fabricated; sometimes insulting, sometimes forgiving; neither automatically true nor false nor insightful nor idle chatter. And even if they *all* say they wish to be collaborative, that in itself does not make their subsequent work collaborative at all. What's said is often more important for what it *does* as a practical performance (making a promise or offering reassurance, for example) than for whatever it *labels*, describes or names.

Evaluating Changes in Understandings, Arguments, and Actions

So analyses of collaborative and participatory processes, as we shall see, must examine how the parties really act, if they enact and reshape relations of interdependence and power. In any case that promises to be participatory or deliberative or collaborative, for example, we need to examine not only the rhetoric of the parties, not just their "good intentions," but the design and conduct of the processes themselves. We need to know not only what parties said, but if they have learned anything, and if they could then act differently to satisfy their and others' interests as a result. We need to know not only what parties want, but what they might offer, threaten, give, take, trade, invent, propose, reframe, and more. We need to know not just how understandings and relationships developed, if they did, and not just how arguments were made, if they were substantiated or refuted or considered by anyone at all, but we need to know who has now made any actual agreements and commitments to real action: who's going to act differently than they would have as a result of the process at hand. We want to know if, as Arnstein suggested 40 years ago, many stakeholders "participated" even as only a very few profited, or did many more do better than that, and if so, how?

If we care about dealing with differences in real spaces and places, then, limiting discussions of participation or collaboration to dialogue and debate, we will see, will simply not do. If we differ about where to have a good dinner—to take what could be an everyday example—we often want not only to talk about it, not only to compare evidence about our options, but to be able actually to go and eat as well. Yet our overly analytic concern with "knowledge" sometimes threatens to limit our vision to seeking understanding and justification, to processes of dialogue and debate, even as action and eating go begging. We risk "participating" all day in those processes of dialogue and debate without ever coming to act more pragmatically on our interests and values.

Assessing Facilitating, Moderating, and Mediating Efforts

So practically speaking, too, when we read about participatory or collaborative processes, we need to know *how* they took place and who structured or led or managed or shepherded them along. To foster illuminating dialogue, for example, we often require the work of skilled facilitators. To encourage serious debate, we often require the work of a skilled moderator. So far so good—for we seem familiar in everyday life with these practices, facilitating and moderating, as they can be done for better or worse. We know what heavy-handed facilitation that closes down dialogue looks like. We know what inept moderation that makes a mess of debate looks like. But *we know much less* about what different skills and what different practical actions encourage successful, mutual gains negotiations instead of prompting mutually punishing lose-lose negotiations: this is the distinctive practical work of mediation, and it differs, we shall see, from facilitation alone, as it differs from moderation alone, even as it builds upon both of those, as the following chapters will show.

If we want to deal better with differences across spaces and places, values and interests, power differentials and institutional structures, we can integrate multi-party negotiation strategies with collaborative and network governance (Susskind et al. 1999, Susskind and Cruickshank 2006, Healey 1997, Hajer and Wagenaar 2004, Sorensen and Torfing 2005). Here collaborative, networked efforts at mul-tiple levels and scales can build upon quite practical mediation and negotiation analysis. Susskind argues compellingly, however, that we must pay systematic, careful attention not just to skillful facilitative leadership, but to the pathologies of ineptly staged multiparty negotiations—to escalation, to gamesmanship and degenerating relationships, to lose-lose traps created by mutual deception, to all of *the failures we risk without skilled mediation assistance.*

Let me be clear: by *mediation* I mean the specific skilled practice of (a) assessing stakeholders' options and initial interests, (b) convening representatives of those parties to present their views and data, questions, and proposals, (c) enabling parties to engage in joint inquiry and learning, and (d) enabling a process of inventing options and formulating agreements that satisfy at least four specific criteria, as follows. These criteria include (1) inclusiveness (including representa-tives, e.g., of environmental quality concerns, among others), (2) maximizing mutual gains efficiency (rather than lose-lose outcomes), (3) stability, and (4) being technically well informed (Susskind and Cruickshank 1987, Susskind et al. 1999).[9] Invoking a frame that seems less potentially misleading than "consen-sus building," Susskind more recently calls such work "facilitative leadership" (Susskind and Cruickshank 2006), and this book assesses the implications of this work—though typically calling it, more simply, *mediation*—for planning, public management, and governance more generally.

To be sure, facilitative leadership or mediating participatory processes pro-vides no cure-all, no panacea, yet as a form of practice it takes a stand toward deep and abiding possibilities in a way that neither facilitation nor moderation does—and it also takes a more nuanced, less simplistically adversarial stance than oppositional or agonistic organizing does. Its precise form, of course, will vary as scales and sectors vary. Nevertheless, mediators typically elicit stories so that diverse parties can recognize what one another takes as relevant, defining, and significant—*and* then those mediators not only go on to ask all stakeholders, "What do you need to know, to learn, that would help you make better deci-sions?" but they also typically go further. They then ask, with the same eye to creative possibilities, now that the stakeholders have heard detailed accounts from each other and have learned more, what kinds of *practical proposals* the parties can offer that both respond to the concerns they've heard from others *and* that will satisfy their substantive interests in place making, in spatial planning, in dealing practically, sensitively, and creatively with their differences.

Distinguishing Related Processes of Dialogue, Debate, and Negotiation

Because public deliberations intertwine at least these three processes of dialogue, debate, and negotiation fostered by the three deliberative practices of facilitating, moderating, and mediating, we now have an initial evaluation scheme to bring to bear as we consider so-called "participatory" or "collaborative" cases. Did we have all dialogue and no negotiation; do some worry that we've had all talk and no action? Did we have argumentation and debate, but neither better understandings nor recognition between parties nor agreements upon action? Perhaps we have action outcomes of poor quality, ineptly informed by available expertise and argumentation (negotiation without well-informed debate)?

So if we refuse to call processes *participatory* or *deliberative* or *collaborative* just because various stakeholders came to public hearings or found themselves represented on planning committees, we might now do better to evaluate cases, concrete outcomes, and the real performance of governance and planning processes. We can do this by neither eliminating nor denying conflict. We need not slide from presuming ineradicable conflict to the self-fulfilling prophecy that engaged parties can do nothing to seek more just and livable spaces and places. We can, this book shows, avoid being hostage to generalities and pay more attention to practical deliberative options, to dialogue, debate, and negotiation as these might not only involve many interdependent and networked stakeholders, but enable collaborative and participatory planning processes to achieve greater justice, greater recognition, and greater efficiency too.

Toward a Collaborative and Critical Pragmatism

This book provides no recipes and no fully worked out theory of dealing with public and private differences. But we might call the perspective that underlies this analysis, though, a "collaborative and critical pragmatism," for it suggests a stance toward conflict and dispute that stresses public learning, recognizing differences of interests, values, and power, the power of asking good questions, and always anticipating structured biases related to ethnicity and culture, race, class, gender, and more.[10] These chapters provide no "ten-step method" to deliberative democracy, but they provide many warnings about the ways planners and public administrators—and citizen activists and community leaders too—might make a hash of "participatory processes."[11]

These chapters warn us that we stand to lose as much by jumping to conclusions, prematurely assuming power differences to be irreconcilable or nonnegotiable, as we do by naively assuming such differences might not matter. These chapters presume no perfect understandings to be possible, assume no ultimate triumph of the force of any better argument, and certainly offer no reason to wish to avoid the conflicts that plurality, diversity, and difference inevitably produce. These chapters should help us to take spatial, political, and community conflicts seriously, to understand better their accompanying gamesmanship and traps, as well as their hidden possibilities, and our opportunities to live well together with them too. Dealing with our differences well or poorly challenges us in our homes and neighborhoods and workplaces, and in our legislatures and international relations as well. The chapters that follow take us into complex and messy, daunting yet hopeful conflicts involving our land, our health, our public policies, our religious beliefs, and our many areas of deep difference with one another. We shall see that we can do far more together than we often think. If we're going to be critical about differences of interests, values, and power, let's not begin by tying our hands and presuming that there's little we can do—let's instead examine, critically and practically, all the avenues we have to rebuild and transform the messy, politicized world we share. The next nine chapters begin to do just that.

Part One

When Parties Conflict, Expect that More Is Possible than Anyone Says

CHAPTER ONE

Beyond Promises: Making Public Participation and Democratic Deliberation Work

Let's begin with a practical overview. As the daily news tells us, when our diverse interests and values conflict in public life, we fall too easily into the pathologies of "us" and "them." Our community and political leaders rarely help as they preach civility but practice contentiousness. "Civil society" turns out to be not so civil after all. So we need to understand better—if we, as diverse citizens, immigrants and neighbors, developers and others, hope to live together—how we might really speak in many voices, care deeply about our many interests and values, and still come to deal with our differences peacefully and effectively, honoring our values and satisfying our interests rather than going on the attack.[1]

We can address these challenges of daily democracy, what some call "democratic deliberation" and "public participation," dealing with our differences in civil society, by learning from those in the trenches: community and environmental mediators and facilitators working in the face of complex, public-private disputes. Because these practitioners act in between conflicting parties all the time to seek peaceful, timely, and productive working agreements, we will take their stories as windows onto the practical political world of making democratic deliberations work. Because these *mediators* deal every day with diverse and passionate parties at odds with each other, their experiences can teach us not only about culture and class, politics and identity, but about dialogue and learning, leadership and emotional sensitivity too. Questions of power, of course, remain ever-present, ever a challenge, presenting both potential obstacles and sources of opportunity as well.

We will see that mediators' accounts of their work can teach us about five challenges that call for practical action and theoretical insight at the same time. These challenges involve (1) how we recognize and may respect our differences, (2) how we design participatory processes, (3) how rational our democratic deliberations may be, (4) how nonneutral or activist planner-mediators can be, and, finally,

(5) how we can protect space for real acknowledgment of loss and inequality, even for traumatic memory, in our real deliberative conversations, dialogues, or negotiations in civil society.

Beyond the Impasse of *"He* says…" but *"She* says…"

To live together amidst differences of lifestyle and culture—or to listen to each other across differences of religious commitments and political ideologies—is always a precarious achievement, an ongoing struggle, not a natural fact. No natural process guarantees that diverse voices will respect or even inform one another instead of becoming just so much shouting and noise, or worse. No historical chemistry guarantees that citizens, or noncitizens for that matter, will recognize each other's diverse, multilayered identities or take seriously each other's political arguments.[2]

At times, though, advocates of multicultural, pluralistic civil societies can get stuck in their own celebrations of inevitable difference, inevitable conflict. We can celebrate voice, but we should not forget that *voice* means something practical: it means not just "words" but making real claims on others, claims typically for respect and resources, claims that can not only be bogus or inflated or exaggerated or manipulative or self-serving or oppressing, but threatening or insulting or abusive or hectoring.[3] The developer claims that her project will alleviate the housing shortage. The neighbor claims that it will change "the character" of the neighborhood. The environmentalist claims that open space will be lost to the greedy. A student asks if issues of race and racism really lurk under the surface here. Does simply recording each view enable "participation" in any meaningful sense? Hardly.

We can celebrate voice without thinking that every claim is as sound or worthy of respect as every other. More directly, recognizing a *speaker* as a human being worthy of respect does *not* require us to be gullible, to buy or "respect" whatever they say. This simple distinction—respect the person but question his or her claims—frees us from the traps of thinking that our obligations to respect difference somehow must keep us silent or agnostic in the face of conflicting constructions of social reality. The theoretical glitz of what Robert Beauregard has called "postmodern weightlessness" has at times led us too easily to replace politically critical hope with ordinary resignation; in the name of a facile tolerance ("Well, that's what *they* believe!") we slide into a deferential yet complaining cynicism.[4] We risk, it seems, forgetting that practical political claims—the drinking water is safe, the politician speaks for the community, the species will survive, the company has fixed the leak—can be more *or less* justified, can be *tested* critically. That means that political claims can be, roughly, humanly, more likely to be *true or false*, which means, either "sound" or, in Harry Frankfurt's sense, "bullshit," which he takes to mean, "showing a lack of concern for the truth."[5] So if we know that political claims make rhetorical demands, that they are fallible, not "last words," we can then imagine participatory processes as negotiated learning processes, not just as impasses of "He says..." but "She says..." in which simultaneous claims to respect stop us cold from resolving the differences at hand.

By shrugging our shoulders or weaseling away from these problems of distinguishing critical discourse from myth making, then, we risk blinding ourselves. We risk confusing the hype or advertising of self-promoters or demagogues with the real possibilities of a vibrant and deliberative civil society. So in a world where everyone does not look just like you, in a plural, diverse civil society, we risk treating the likely truth of political claims as merely a matter of taste or subjective preference—for some, a local matter, and for others, a systemic product of power; for some, a fleeting particular, and for others, a scientist fact; for some, the property of educated elites, for others the property of a ruling class, and for yet others, the property of every locality's local knowledge (Corburn 2005). When anything goes, critical thinking about real future possibilities will be among the first casualties.

Now these issues of critical political argument and truth seeking—systematic political criticism and moral realism—can involve heavy philosophical lifting. But we can take a lighter approach instead and follow the late Wittgenstein (himself a deep critic of systematic philosophy), who once remarked that philosophy could be taught by telling jokes. In that spirit, we might consider the story of the postmodernist patient who is (also) taken too far by the view that "reality's socially constructed." Hearing a life-threatening diagnosis that she does not like, she responds, "Well, doctor, I see—but couldn't you just touch up the x-rays?"

This joke's "on us," unfortunately, for in this glorious age of rhetoric and discourse, "textuality" and "postpositivism," we face the constant danger of becoming this pathetic patient. The joke itself is literally pathetic: full of the pathos of the patient's hope and terror, the evasion promised by killing the messenger, the plea masking the tougher hint that sometimes the truth hurts. But the irony of "touching up" the x-rays also conveys, of course, the deeper sense, too, that human possibilities are not just constructed at whim—that we really can learn, in some objective ways, about our future possibilities and our real vulnerabilities. We really can learn about our own prospects, for better and at times for worse—whether we are using X-rays or counting housing starts, exploring workplace safety conditions or air and water quality.

So this simple joke addresses the possibilities of our learning together, after all: we learn that our deliberations must address possibilities, not just who said what; we must examine proposals to inform hope, not simply catalogue differences of opinion to justify doing nothing; we must do more than air complaints about power and ambiguity and even tragic limits—so we can learn how to face and resist power, to create meaning and beauty, ambiguity and all, as we live in a tragic (inevitably limited) world of conflicting goods and obligations, as finite, real people.

So to celebrate vibrant and diverse cities, a thriving and just civil society, we need not find any philosophical truth machine, an ethical pasta machine with which to crank out "right answers." We face another more practical challenge: how to imagine and put into practice a *deliberative democratic politics* that actually recognizes and respects plurality and difference ("Yes, he says this and she says that") while being no less practically committed to *learning and acting together*—the challenge to imagine and practice a politics that helps us to clarify critically the truth of our possibilities for human betterment, helping us to *listen, learn, and act*—even as we know full well that some people along the way will be lying through their teeth (whether out of fear or out of greed).[6] We can call such critical listening, learning, and acting in theory "a critical pragmatism," and now we can turn to examine what it looks like in practice (Forester 1993).

Learning from Practice: Creating Deliberative Democratic Spaces in Civil Society

We can begin to learn about these possibilities by exploring the reflections of three practitioners who have often faced these issues: dealing with differences and the need to act together, dealing with different constructions of reality and human need, and dealing with differing senses of strategy. Community and environmental mediators deal not only with neighborhood disputes, but also with the legacy of racial and ethnic conflicts. They deal not only with legal rights to land, but also with the meaning and identity-shaping significance of place and space. They deal not only with issues of discrimination, but with the legacies of racism, not just getting their hands dirty with the messiness of practical agreements, but with the inevitable incompleteness of human understanding and acknowledgment. They deal with unique particulars and more general principles, too, as engaged and potentially critical pragmatists, not as abstracted social critics. Dealing with large-scale land use disputes at the provincial level and complex ethnic and class-based disputes between neighboring jurisdictions, such mediators shape the participatory processes and the broader civil society in which we live. Their work provides us with a natural laboratory, a series of deliberative experiments, that can teach us about the challenges of reconstructing our diverse cities, our civil societies (cf. Fung 2004, Fung and Wright 2003). If we listen closely, we can learn about the character and the requirements, the contingencies and the possibilities, of dealing with our differences in a democratically deliberative way.[7]

Regional Land-Use Planning as a Deliberative Exercise

Listen first to Gordon Sloan, a Canadian mediator who facilitated an ambitious, eighteen-month-long land-use planning process for Vancouver Island. He describes the early stages of that process this way:

> The Commissioner—who is Provincial, or in U.S. terms, in a state agency—announced that rather than simply recommending to the cabinet what land use he saw for the area, he would rather that people negotiated over the uses on Vancouver Island, and he invited people to negotiate in some way. He...was swamped with over a thousand briefs, letters, faxes, and representations. What his office did was to begin to organize those into more or less like-minded perspectives. What we distilled out of that were fourteen different points of view: distinct enough that it wasn't possible for any one of them to speak for another. That was really our test: How can you gather people around a table in a totally *inclusive way, but still be effective?* (emphasis added).
>
> We had local government, provincial government, forest employment, the forest manufacturers and managers, the big companies, an aboriginal presence, conservation, outdoor recreation, general non-forest employment, tourism, mining, agriculture...All of those people were at the table.

From Assessment to Convening via "Orientation"

So how did Sloan go about this, more practically? He continues,

> How do we have them vent their anxieties in a way that's at all productive, when it might also fuel the fires? What's productive is for me to do an orientation on a Sunday-Monday with the green side of this problem and then on a Wednesday-Thursday with the brown side of this problem.
>
> They're *each saying exactly* the same thing about the other. That's a piece of information that they should know. It's handy to be able to tell them that, when they

say to you, "You'll be able to trust what we say, but there's no way you can trust anything *they* say."

It's great to be able to say to them in response that, "You won't believe this, but they used *exactly* the same words to describe their view of *you*."

They're amazed. "They did? *They* don't think *we're* accountable?" They discover that there are all kinds of assumptions that one value system makes about the other that have to be debunked.

Accommodate, Not Compromise

But more than debunking is involved, Sloan says, as parties begin to specify further their own real interests to inform their negotiations:

There's a lot more going on here than just teaching them communication skills. Macro-wise, they're just getting a bunch of information. They're finding out about what the process might be like, getting a sense of the great big circus they're getting into—because this thing lasted a year and a half, and any long multi-party public policy process is like that. There are survival skills one needs, to be able to get through it. So, there's the information component, and that was a big deal.

Secondly, there's a communication skills and negotiation component that they just scratch the surface of in a day and a half, but that's important. Thirdly, I think they *begin* to crystallize their own "interests." They don't know that yet, because they don't know what "interests" are. But they begin to retreat from positions that they take about the land base, and they begin to identify specific areas of need, desire, concern, fear, aspiration, expectation—what I would call "interests"—that they've got to be very clear on by the time the negotiation gets rolling.

They do that by way of the exercises in the training session, and through the discussions that are going on. They're beginning for the first time to think in terms of, "What do we really want to get out of this?" rather than, "What is our opening gambit going to be?"

You want to dissuade them off all that. You want to persuade them to disclose to everyone at the table—and persuade everyone else to disclose to everyone at the table—what they're really there for, because you want to *build solutions together* that *accommodate, not compromise*, the interests of everybody.[8] *That's* the objective. So they begin to get a sense of that. I say, "begin" because it's a long process, but it happens, and it happens early.[9]

Sloan summarized his thoughts about these early stages in this way:

These training sessions did begin to allay some of their apprehensions about the process and also increased their level of recognition of others and others' levels of recognition of them—it was really interesting. Looking back on it, it's quite surprising to me that that was happening, because we'd never done that before.

But since then, in several large things that I've done or am now working on, I've insisted upon some element of what I like to call "orientation." Nobody wants to be "trained," but "orientation" they can live with. And so we call them "orientations," orienting each sector to the process. That was a major hallmark of the success of how this negotiation went.

Now, this mediator is no judge delivering a verdict, no technical expert rendering an opinion, no bureaucrat implementing regulations. Instead, he and his co-mediator had to try practically to "deal with differences" in civil society—differences here regarding land and resource use, environmental and economic issues. Even this brief excerpt, though, illuminates the practical challenges confronting many of those hoping to make participatory governance processes and, more broadly, democratic deliberations work.

We learn immediately about the problem of representation. In months of preparatory work of conflict assessment, these mediators worked to constitute fourteen "sectors" to "sit at the table." They had not just to ask, but to answer, the questions, Who are the relevant members of "the community" here, the affected members of the polity, and how are they (here, in fourteen "sectors") to participate? If citizens are to heed Oscar Wilde's warning—when he quipped that the problem with socialism is that it takes too many evenings—what scheme of representation will be both fair and workable?[10]

Learning

We see, too, the challenge of dealing with the parties' *unexamined* presumptions, with their fall from the theorists' grace of perfect information and full rationality. We see each party as a righteous adversary—convinced not only that they live in a zero-sum world where "more for them" means "less for me," but that in the face of such difference and intransigence, little practical agreement seems likely at all.

But we learn here, too, that even if—and perhaps *because*—information is poor and minds are not omniscient, that the parties can and do actually learn about one another. As Sloan had put it, suggesting the parties' own surprise,

> They're each saying *exactly* the same thing about the other. That's a piece of information that they should know...
>
> It's great to be able to say to them, "You won't believe this, but they used *exactly* the same words to describe their view of you."
>
> They're amazed. "They did? *They* don't think *we're* accountable?"

And so Sloan teaches us, "So they discover that there are all kinds of assumptions that one value system makes about the other that have to be debunked."

The deliberative learning that goes on, as such assumptions unravel, does not seem limited to learning about others, as difficult as that may be. For we get a glimpse here, too, of the parties' learning *about themselves,* their own learning about "ends" and "means" together. So we learn that somehow the parties, "begin to crystallize their own interests…They begin to retreat from positions that they take about the land base, and they begin to identify specific areas of need, desire, concern, fear, aspiration, expectation—what I [Sloan says] would call 'interests.'"

This exploration of parties' "interests" retreats and advances at the same time: it retreats from a strategic position based on an earlier, rough anticipation of the "us against them" discussions at hand, and it advances, too, toward a more particular, finer grained view of what's really at stake and possible in this multi-stakeholder process of negotiation together.

So the parties here learn about one another and about their own evolving priorities as well. In addition, Sloan tells us, the parties—and we too—can come to understand the enormous practical distinction between jointly beneficial solutions that *accommodate,* that satisfy, diverse interests and mere *compromises* that sacrifice those interests. That distinction, of course, is part of the classical promise of dialogue, and democratic politics too—not mere bargaining about who gets what but social learning about who we are, not compromising ideals but transforming what we can really do, not self-sacrificing but jointly gaining, not disintegrating speech into personal attack but creating new and mutually beneficial options, new ways of going on together.[11]

Lastly, this brief excerpt teaches us not just about the semantics of *training* and *orientation* sessions, but that some processes of preparation, introduction, orientation, or training can enable participants to do better *in their own terms*—to be more familiar with the process of learning before negotiating, to develop strategies and skills to satisfy their values and interests, and to learn more than they already knew about others, about the changing political environment, about their own interests, and about possible outcomes they might really achieve together.

"Mediators" like this one, Sloan teaches us too, are hardly neutrals. Committed not to specific outcomes or specific parties' interests but to the generative quality of these deliberative conversations and mutually crafted agreements (Forester 1999a), these practical democrats shape not only representation, but the parties' preparation, their perceptions of each other, the ways they listen and speak, and the creativity of the agreements they might reach. Like other midwives of a deliberatively democratic civil society, as we shall see, these mediators have no end of practical judgments to make, and we can learn from their practice.

Conservation, Recreation, and Class: Ground Rules and Anger

We turn now to a second brief excerpt from the account of another environmental mediator, the late Gregory Sobel, recounting a conservation-recreation dispute that involved local and state regulatory authorities, off-road vehicle users, and defenders of a threatened bird habitat. Sobel tells us,

> There were a lot of discussions. First of all, in the mediation itself there was extensive and candid discussion of the parties' interests and concerns. This was in plenary session so that all the concerns were aired, including the concern of the state agency representative and including the very angry response from the local people who were pushing for the more flexible approach. They felt that this was heavy-handed regulatory government behaviour, a "command and control" approach to problem solving, and that it wasn't recognizing the realities on the ground...So there were very strong feelings.
>
> One way to handle that was to try and let all of that be expressed and then work through it. I have a pretty high tolerance for what might appear to be confrontational statements and positions. I believe it's very important for people to be given a safe place to express all of their feelings, including their strong negative feelings, including their feelings of injustice, of oppression, which arose in this case.

Sobel hardly seems to be describing a unique case. Local people perceive "heavy-handed" government behavior and have "very strong feelings" that officials or community leaders would dismiss at their own risk. Convening parties, Sobel teaches us, involves far more than merely inviting them to the same meeting. So how did Sobel create "a safe place" for the expression of those "strong negative feelings"? He goes on:

> We did some of this in plenary session, because I think that there's a place for some of that airing to occur with all parties present. There's a strong value to everyone understanding the depth of the feelings of the other players and the reasons for those feelings, what gave rise to those feelings.
>
> There's an important part of the process which is *storytelling*, where each side gets to tell their story in their own way, and the other folks listen to the story without interrupting. Hopefully they then have better insight into the other side's *perspectives* and the reasons for their perspectives.

He continues and speaks to the mediator's practical challenges here:

> There are limits, and when there's passion, as there often is in these cases, I view it as the mediator's job to set those limits. One of the ground rules is that the parties cannot abuse one another. One of the mediator's jobs is to keep parties focused and on track.

A bit later he extends these thoughts:

> There are limits of how far I, as mediator, will allow them to go in personalizing their presentation by saying, "*You* did this to me."
>
> But frankly, I try to err on the side of allowing a great deal of that kind of expression all together at least once. Once it's been done, once together, or maybe twice, then usually I'll encourage the parties not to continue to harp on their strong negative feelings, but to move on.
>
> Sometimes they need more airing or venting, and sometimes they have things they need to say that they can't say in front of the other parties. All those sorts of expressions can take place in private caucus.
>
> I believe that it's very appropriate and useful in a couple of ways for parties to be able to say, "This is why I'm angry."

Why? Sobel suggests,

> It's useful information to the other parties, and it's helpful to the person who's expressing it to be able to feel heard on those issues. It's often necessary to have that kind of communication to clear the way for more dispassionate problem solving. But a mediator's got to make a "judgment call" about how long to let that go on. You've got to make a judgment call about when it becomes *destructive.*

So Sobel amplifies and extends several of the points we have just considered. In the participants' storytelling, they may be able to listen in new ways, to recognize issues, reasons, and motives that they do not already know about, so they can actually learn about one another: "Hopefully," Sobel tells us, [the parties] then have better insight into the other side's perspectives and the reasons for their perspectives."[12]

Sobel also tells us that emotion and passion have an important place in the dialogues and debates, the conversations and arguments that animate public disputes and controversies. Like leaders and managers, activists and planners in many organizations, Sobel and other mediators work in between parties who often have "very strong feelings," "very angry response(s)," and no shortage of "confrontational statements and positions."[13]

Most importantly, though, Sobel does *not* tell us that parties must leave these emotions "at the door," as if "strong feelings" and emotion had no place in deliberative public discussions. Quite the contrary, Sobel teaches us that recognizing these feelings—anger, fear, suspicion, confrontational moves—and not denying but pragmatically "working through" those feelings are both possible and crucial: "Sometimes they need more airing or venting, and sometimes they have things they need to say that they can't say in front of the other parties. All those sorts of expressions can take place in private caucus."

But here we learn, too, about one of the critical roles of any intermediary, community leader or manager, for example—and, by extension perhaps, of those hoping deal with differences or promote deliberative democratic discussion more generally: creating *"a safe place* to express all of their feelings, including their strong negative feelings, including their feelings of injustice, of oppression." Here we see the subtle and deeply political problem of setting limits, creating "ground rules" to protect parties, to ensure safety, and to "keep parties focused and on track."

We see, too, that even after evoking and establishing such pragmatic ground rules, the mediator must still make "judgment calls" about how to enact and apply those rules, how to interpret the needs of some parties to express anger, the needs of others perhaps to be protected from intimidation, how to interpret parties' needs to develop trust that they will have a real chance to be heard, that they will be able to say what they will without disruptive interruption, dismissal, or disrespect. There are no gimmicks here. Community leaders and planners, activists and managers all need to improvise in real time and space, in each particular case here—to improvise in a way that combines the sensitive awareness of each person's words and tone and even posture with an astute responsiveness, too, to the encompassing norms, obligations and principles of the institutional settings, the "context," at hand (Forester 1999a).

These judgment calls, encouraging some and discouraging others, worrying about timing and inclusion and safety and time to rest, can serve the control of the mediator or facilitator, but they can do more too. Carefully encouraging expressions of anger, Sobel suggests, can help many parties to learn, as well as enabling the expressive party to "be able to feel heard on their issues." But he says more practically, too, "It's often necessary to have that kind of communication to *clear the way* for more dispassionate problem-solving," if the group is to continue to make progress on the issues before it.

Land Use, Ethnicity, and the Shape of Deliberative Rituals

We can build on the reflections of these two practitioners by listening to a third who speaks, at somewhat greater length here, of dealing with ethnic and environmental conflict, land-use planning, and Native American claims. Shirley Solomon tells us of a series of meetings she facilitated in Skagit County, Washington, to bring together local, county, and tribal community members and planning staff to discuss growth control, jurisdictional relationships, environmental protection, and their sense of space and place. She begins:

> We used a talking circle, with different people opening the circle. For the very first circle, I asked Bill Johnson, who's one of the tribal leaders, to open the circle. Then, just a few minutes before the thing was to start, Bill disappeared.
>
> Oh God, I was...wondering, "Now when is Bill going to re-appear?"...because I had a schedule to maintain—but...he finally arrived.
>
> What he had done was to go off and find a cedar tree and take a bough from the tree, in ceremonial fashion, to use in this circle. Also, he'd found a particular rock, and he talked to people about what he did and why he did it and what the symbolism and the significance of it all was. That really set the tone and the tenor for the initial sharing. That was then carried forward by others who used their own symbolism and used their own orientation. But we immediately created a very special space, in that initial introductory event, if you want to call it that.

Solomon goes on, speaking to the cultural differences she perceived:

> What you had here was essentially two worlds, two cultures. People will say though, "Well, hell, you know, I mean that's nonsense, because Indian people here have been around white people for a century or more. They run their governments. Their governments look very similar to any other form of government. They know how to conduct meetings. They do Robert's rules, all these things....What are you talking about, two worlds?"
>
> But the fact of the matter is, an Indian world view is fundamentally different from a western world view, and the structures that we brought with us are those that have been super-imposed over Indian peoples, like it or not. By now you've got a real and pretty hefty callus that has built up. If you want to shape-shift things, if you want to shake them around and have different outcomes, then you've got to come at it differently. You've got to allow that which is not much prevalent, in the way we do things; you've got to allow that forward.

She gives us an example that teaches us both about culture and about apparently "neutral" meeting procedures:

> There's one piece that just brings tears to my eyes every time I hear it. It's Bill Johnson, who you have to sort of bend forward to hear, because he doesn't articulate, he doesn't move his lips, in a way that helps you hear very easily. But what he said is, "In those meetings where it's Robert's Rules of Order, I know that I either have nothing to say, or what I have to say counts for nothing."

It just pierces me every time I hear it. That is, by and large, the world for Indian country and Indian issues. There is not the opportunity to bring forward who and what they are in totality, so what you have are what are derogatorily termed, "the thousand year speech," where an Indian person will stand up and talk about what and who they are, how they see things, what has happened to them, and people "turn off" because "the thousand year speech" is an attempt to gain standing and status, but it's in an environment that is unsympathetic. It's "out of order," so to speak. It's not part of the agenda, but it is a valiant and courageous attempt on the part of that particular Indian person, taking on the role of spokesperson, to let all these uncaring others hear just something that is different. But it's ineffective.

In our case the intent was to get more familiar. That was the whole and sole purpose of the undertaking. How did we get people to not turn off? It involved the whole notion of collaborative learning.

Solomon concludes,

There's a wonderful image related to this. I've never seen this, but I've heard several people talk about it. There's a temple in Japan someplace that has a garden. The rocks are arranged in such a way that one has to walk all the way around in order to see every aspect of it. The principle is that no one individual could possibly know all that there is to know about anything, about this piece of art, let alone anything else. So in order for the larger truths to be revealed, all the voices—that are part of whatever it may be—need to be present and need to be heard.

Solomon's account echoes several points of our other practitioners, but it adds fresh insight as well. Like the other mediators, Shirley Solomon faced the problem of beginning with adversarial presumptions and working to enable productive and collaborative relationships. Like Sloan and Sobel, too, she suggests that in complex disputes, the parties and the facilitators alike have much to learn from one another's stories about their possibilities and opportunities:

I was surprised at just the history the vast majority of people had there…The county commissioner characterized his feelings differently from a tribal leader, but you began to see the similarities and the common ground—or not the common ground, but *the opportunity* to find the common ground.

She tells us more, too, though. Her sense of the action in this meeting focused on a structured process that encouraged both a common focus upon the participants' shared *place* and upon personal expression, actual listening and mutual recognition, the discovery of common ground and the exploration of future options.[14]

In a moving passage, she echoes the voice of the tribal leader, Bill Johnson, who finds that conventional, presumptively neutral "ground rules" of meetings can be exclusive, dismissive, and humiliating: "In those meetings where it's Robert's Rules of Order," he says, "I know that I either have nothing to say, or what I have to say counts for nothing."

In one moving, if brutal, sentence here, this tribal leader reveals both the beauty and the violence of speech—of action understood as deeply, even constitutively, expressive, revealing, and communicative. He shows elegantly the subtlety of what academic theorists crudely term *disciplinary power* and *systematic distortions of communication*.[15] He tells us that the seemingly innocent ground rules that structure conversation and agendas in participatory processes can be as important and as culturally biased as the content of any given conversation. Not only does the content matter, we learn, but so does the stage on which we interact and speak together, the institutional setting of expectations and norms that provide what we might call the "social infrastructure" of public deliberation.

By contrasting the "talking circle" with meetings structured by "Robert's Rules of Order," Solomon tells us about a good deal more than the disciplining power of agenda setting that privileges linear argument and punishes emotional expressiveness. She asks us to think more creatively—if we want to do better than using "Robert's Rules"—about designing better processes, and to appreciate more sensitively, then, the subtle ritual structuring of so much participation, the ways that the simplest structures of talk shape speakers and listeners both, shape the spaces we inhabit, the ways we are able to listen, the respect we give one another, the relationships we are able to reconstruct, and the historical memory we rebuild together (Forester 1999a).

Solomon, too, like Sloan and Sobel before her, tells us that deliberative encounters require *safe spaces*. Creating these spaces—in talking circles, at meals, in small groups, in informal time-outs between formal sessions—will in turn require shared expectations and "ground rules" that will assure, even if they cannot guarantee, the participants that they will count, that they will all be heard, and that they will all be able to express their concerns, their anger, their pains, and their hopes together.

These deliberative spaces and the rituals that shape them should be evocative, Solomon suggests: they should encourage not so much strategic argument but more detailed accounts, more instructive explanations, richer and so more revealing story telling.[16] By enacting ground rules to show participants that each person will be taken seriously here, that every speaker has "standing and status," these practical deliberative encounters not only dignify the participation of members and provide an initial measure of respect and recognition, but they enable those present actually to listen, learn and act together in new ways too.[17]

But make no mistake. Solomon, Sloan, and Sobel create these processes not to erase conflict, not to make friends of historical enemies, not to deny deep differences—but to enable more than the talk, talk, talk of business as usual, to enable a new exploration of strategies to address materially the pressing interests at stake.[18] By bringing participants together across lines of interests, class, ethnicity, and gender, these deliberative conversations can begin practically and substantively to *bridge differences* of experience, stereotype, established relationships, and conventional expectations.

By evoking deeply felt concerns and senses of possibility, interests, and emotions, these processes of dealing with difference, these deliberative rituals, can cultivate a partially shared political imagination, or, as Solomon put it, "collaborative learning" rather than legalistic argumentation—a cogenerated practical judgment instead of doctrinal persuasion. As we shall see, these processes often encourage more dialogue, less debate, more learning, less pontificating, more practical negotiating, less grandstanding.

Solomon's work also suggests that these participatory processes and social rituals required *planning* of a quite special character. Like other community and environmental mediators, she had to pay attention and be committed both to enhancing the deliberative democratic spaces in which parties could meet and speak *and* to promoting the welfare of those parties. How can this be done more generally? The practice of skilled facilitators and mediators can show us how, in deeds, step by step, in the following chapters. This imaginative and practical vision requires the political and ethical sensibility not of experts or autocrats, not of judges or bureaucrats, but of what we might call critically reconstructive "civic friends"—*not* ordinary friends, to be sure, but civically imaginative, politically critical friends caring about real outcomes.

Notice, of course, that Solomon does not provide us with anything like a "theory" of participation. She suggests, "For the larger truths to be revealed, all the voices—that are part of whatever it may be—need to be present and need to be heard." As she does so, though, she is hardly being literal, as if she were arguing either against convening representatives of large groups or calling for some grandiose ideal conditions; she is instead calling our attention again practically to the ways that deliberative structures might narrow agendas, exclude participants, discount perspectives, "discipline voice," "distort communication"—or do very much better than that.

Conclusion

So Gordon Sloan, Gregory Sobel, and Shirley Solomon provide us with windows onto the larger world of dealing with differences, organizing participatory processes in not so civil "civil" society. If we look closely through those windows, we can learn about real possibilities of dealing with real conflicts of interests and values, cultures and commitments. These three practitioners give us neither recipes nor technical fixes, but approaches to consider—perhaps even these six practical directions and challenges that the remainder of this book will explore in every chapter:

I. We see that conflicting neighbors and community leaders, politicians, developers, and others make claims not just seeking interests and utilities but expressing identities. Shaped by privileged or painful political histories, citizens come with no shortage of presumptions about Others, about "enemies" and adversaries. Nevertheless, participating together, these parties can *listen to and learn about* one another and their collective possibilities, and community leaders and planners, mediators and facilitators, and managers in many settings can help or hinder that learning. The theoretical issues of "identity politics" take a practical form in such cases: here we face what we might call "the problem of the practical ethics of listening or recognition."[19]

2. We see that pragmatic "ground rules" for meetings, conversations, and negotiations in civil society can *provide "safe spaces"* in which citizens can deliberate together or, alternatively, might leave us with more typical public hearings that too often prevent dialogue, humiliate participants, and reward hyperbole. In carefully crafted participatory processes structuring not so much debate as participatory research and inquiry together, citizens can tell their stories and listen too, surprise one another and themselves, teach and learn from one another, and come to imagine and actually negotiate new possibilities together. We can call these issues, "the problem of political process design."

3. Looking far beyond grudging settlements, community leaders and public managers, planners and mediators can shape processes that explore and seek to capture "joint gains"—*mutually beneficial agreements* rather than lose-lose compromises, mutual gains that take maximal *advantage of the parties' differences in priorities*. Here mediators know to ask the seemingly counterintuitive questions about the ways parties can not just resist each other's demands but actually also help each other—precisely because several of their practical interests and priorities will differ, perhaps even being irrelevant to each other. We can call this challenge, "the problem of moving from lose-lose compromises to mutual gain agreements."

4. We see that conflicting parties with little trust and ample antagonism come together with limited information, various assumptions and presumptions, and that they can *learn about value, about "ends" as well as means,* about "the facts that matter." They can "crystallize their interests," retreat from earlier positions, clarify what's at stake in the cases at hand. Initial resignation, "There's no way…" can give way to new appreciation of issues, new ideas about surprising alternatives, new working relationships, and practical and "collaborative learning." We can refer to this cluster of issues as "the problem of participatory research informing action" (or deliberative rationality).[20]

5. We see that although conflicting parties can listen, learn, and act together, doing so is anything but a natural achievement. Practitioners who hope, in real time in real settings, to enable historical adversaries and community members to deal with their differences have a host of practical "judgment calls" to make: how to *intervene to prepare* for negotiations and conversations with "training," organizing, or "orientation"; how to *respond to inequalities* of citizens' knowledge, skill, and other resources; and how to *pace and shape conversations* and apply whatever "ground rules" are at hand. We can call this, "the problem of capacity building and empowerment," reaching far beyond what mediators recognize as the fiction of neutrality.[21]

6. We see that neighbors and developers, immigrants and tribal members, community activists and church members—all—can bring painful histories to the table, and so the question of how to respect deeply felt traumatic memory in conflict resolution and democratic deliberation remains anything but clear. Sloan, Sobel, and Solomon warn us about either dismissing those histories, asking that they be "left at the door," or allowing them to "become destructive," preempting practical discussions and deliberations from going forward today. We can call this, "the problem of trauma and *working through*"—an essential challenge confronting anyone seeking to foster real empowerment and transformative learning.[22]

These problems—assessing identities, designing productive and fair processes, replacing compromise with mutual gain, learning together, capacity building and empowerment, and enabling transformative learning—represent practical and theoretical questions to face both for all those hoping to create any actual participatory process and for each of the chapters that follow. As we will now see, these challenges arise in diverse settings in which we try to deal with differences, and our responses, our practical answers, are hardly deep-wired: we can do better, or worse, and so the practitioners whose work we shall now explore have a great deal to teach us.

As a practical matter, if we care about dealing with differences in participatory processes and civil society, we need to understand both the risks and the real possibilities we face—and not just have "critical" theories tell us that "power" is everywhere, that "better" is an empty or self-serving social construction. The abiding challenge of any useful and critical theory of governance, public management, or planning, then, must be to articulate a critical pragmatism: to help us to be activist realists, not resigned cynics, to bring imagination and insight to bear on the real problems and possibilities we face, to keep real hope alive. The following chapters explore how we can do that in the face of deep differences of interests and values, power and resources too.

Chapter Two

Cultivating Surprise and the Art of the Possible: The Drama of Mediating Differences

"What I always tell people is, 'Whenever you get to the table, you still are surprised, because you never can anticipate really fully where people are going to come from.'"

Thom (1997)

Challenges of Interdependence

In community settings as well as in workplaces, in the United States and in many other countries too, the contested goals of "inclusion" and "participation" can mean, in part, dealing with differences—differences of culture and class, interest and ideology, values and identities. When we are not all the same and yet have to come to terms with one another—when we are interdependent—we as community members often struggle to learn not only to understand our many cultural, economic, and political differences, but to build bridges so we can work together in and across our multiple subcultures too. So here we will address these challenges in complex disputes that have not only involved bargaining over differing economic interests but required reconciling deeply differing social and cultural identities as well. We shall see, as we explore several disputes involving land use and transportation issues and value conflicts over abortion and sacred sites, that planners and activists, organizers and managers in many other contexts too have much to learn from experienced intermediaries' skills and insights, stories and strategies.

Cultivating the capacity to mediate such disputes, we shall see, provides no panacea, no technical fix, for the challenges of sustaining plurality and difference within our localities, encouraging not only mutual respect but local community building and practical cooperation as well. When our basic commitments to land or quality of life come into conflict, mediation processes and deliberative practices become not less but more relevant—a potentially important source of practical strategies that can complement legal and legislative action (Susskind and Cruickshank 1987, 2006).

Skepticisms of "Just Talk?"—and Political Cynicism

Yet in a world of conflicting interests—to build or not to build, to "protect" or "develop" the land, to invest here or there—many seem skeptical of solutions that depend on the "mere talk" of dialogue or deliberation, of facilitated or mediated processes. The rhetoric and presence of diverse deep differences in our cities or our workplaces challenge both our hope and cynicism: can we imagine in the face of our differences that we can or can't work and live together? For all the rhetoric of multiculturalism and diversity, respect and dialogue, defenders of civil society appear to know much more about "how to talk the talk" than they do about "how to walk the walk" (Fung and Wright 2003, Sandercock 2003a).

We see these challenges in everyday life, for example, as a friend might say about another acquaintance, "There's no use talking to her; nothing's going to be possible"—even when a great deal might really be possible—and the result, we sometimes suspect, is that our friend may just have set him or herself up for failure. Too often, when many of us face differences of values or religion, culture or class, race or gender, a deceptively simple realism seems to blind us by suggesting, "No, we can't really act together with them; they'll never listen; they'll never talk to us about the real issues here."

In community or political settings this familiar skepticism can easily become a seductive cynicism, a practical failure of hope. This threatens not just our friends and acquaintances, but our lives as members of any democratic polity or civil society more generally (Dryzek 2000).

As a matter of everyday life and ethics, our skepticism of others can lead us to miss real opportunities when they're right in front of us: we fail to build informed relationships and suffer the consequences needlessly. As a matter of practical negotiation, we often split differences, settle grudgingly for both-lose outcomes rather than creating substantially better-for-both, mutual gains (Susskind et al. 1999).

As a matter of identity and respect, instead of building mutually respectful relationships, we often presumptively dismiss and feel threatened by differences, even if we know that resentment, of course, is like taking poison and hoping that the other person dies. We are so easily tempted to take "value differences" literally that we miss real practical opportunities—where we might put the stop signs—behind what we take as irreconcilable abstractions ("The natural environment must be protected!").

These problems of everyday politics, ethics, and negotiation of differences have been encouraged, in part, by three widespread presumptions that blind us unnecessarily. First, struck numb if not dumb by cultures celebrating technical expertise and scientific experimentation, we often think about *analysis* and even *rationality* in ways that devalue our emotional sensitivity, expression, and actual responsiveness as merely idiosyncratic, less practically important than our "knowing the right answer" about what might now be done. In the name of being right, doing right suffers.

Second, just as we see consumer preferences changing easily in contrast to apparently more fixed, pious appeals to "bedrock" religious traditions, we often think about "interests" as ever-negotiable but "values" as tied to fixed "identities" somehow immune from transformation in times of conflict and political negotiation.

Third, often being captured by our ideals as much as we espouse them, we often think of "deep value differences" presumptively and automatically as differences we cannot negotiate, practically speaking, at all.[1]

So we need to look carefully at the work of skillful intermediaries to learn how they may have had surprising successes in particular cases as they have faced strong emotions, identity conflicts, or deep value differences, in just those situations in which many of us, community activists and leaders, planners and public managers, for example, might well—left on our own—have thrown in the towel. Looking at such cases, we might really ask, of both these intermediaries and our fellow organizers or public managers as well, "What could they have been thinking?" What were the intermediaries thinking that *helped them* to achieve surprising results—and what thinking might have led the rest of us, though, in exactly the same situations, *to give up too soon?*

Learning from Practice When Interdependence Matters

Why focus here on the practical work of *mediators* of public disputes? Routinely working in between conflicting interests—public and private, communal and religious—mediators can serve us as "canaries in the mine," especially if we want to learn how both to manage tensions in our diverse communities and workplaces and to improve community and public deliberations. So mediators can teach us about handling the inevitable conflicts of interdependence: when parties cannot simply satisfy their interests unilaterally—when neighboring communities can hardly avoid dealing with each other, for example. But more too: mediators know how disputing parties so often can fall into—but also might escape—the traps of producing poor compromises, what we can call lose-lose agreements, as suspicious neighbors or employers or developers are so easily tempted to escalate demands, to exaggerate data, to posture, to hide their interests, and more. Mediators will also, we shall see, help us to think more carefully about settings that involve differences of "values" as well as of interests, differences of identity as well as differences of goals and preferences.

When facilitators and mediators who work with conflicting parties produce surprising results—"We never thought an agreement like this would be possible!"—they can show us possibilities that we, too, will find surprising because we hardly yet understand how those results were achieved at all. When the community leaders or activists or developers in disputes tell us that they themselves been surprised—the actual parties who know their problems better than anyone presumably!—we, too, as readers may well be surprised ourselves, and we can learn a good deal as a result (Nussbaum 1990, Forester 1999a, 2006a). Iris Murdoch put a part of this beautifully once, when she said of learning from good practice, "Where virtue [good practice] is concerned, we often apprehend more than we clearly understand, and we *grow by looking*" (Murdoch 1970: 31).

So if we look closely at facilitators and mediators—we, too, will *see* that they can teach us that our bodies reach where our intellects often do not: that actual practice can and has led theory, that our good intentions can get us so righteously stuck, that our "analytic understanding" in all its realistic and well-informed glory can persuade us that nothing's possible when trying, sketching, playing, even taking walks and sharing meals can really show us that a great deal's possible after all.

When we listen to experienced mediators, we find that they speak again and again of finding possible outcomes that none of the parties first thought possible. We might recall that T. S. Eliot wrote of poetry as a "raid upon the inarticulate," and so we may come to see that mediators work every day in the face of conflict to "raid the impossible," to bring back working agreements across boundaries of suspicion and distrust, culture and commitment, differences of race and class and gender—agreements that no one first thought possible (Susskind et al. 1999). This daily and practical drama of intermediaries' work can teach us about outcomes (and practices) that we never thought possible, and the surprises we discover can teach us not just about new possibilities but about our old expectations, our old ways of thinking that won't pay off, old ways of looking that have blinded us to what we really can do (Schön 1983, Lewicki, Gray, and Elliot 2003).

We can explore these questions—assessing in particular, what the mediators were thinking—in two parts by working with excerpts from their "practice stories," excerpts we can take not as histories of cases but as windows onto the world of their practice.[2] In the first part we consider the insights of two practitioners who find mediated and facilitated multistakeholder processes always closely intertwined with issues of power and emotion in public disputes.

In the second part we consider three short stories. Mediator and consultant Frank Blechman recalls facing officials' fears of explosive comprehensive planning meetings in three counties (Blechman 2005). Mediator Stephen Thom, recently deputy director of the U. S. Department of Justice's Community Relations Service, reflects on a case involving identity conflict in a California land use dispute. Then we return to another provocative account of Blechman's that involves deep value differences between abortion rights opponents and advocates.

Finally, the conclusion suggests lessons we can learn from these intermediaries' practical and anticipatory (and so theoretical) thinking too. We will ask what these practitioners can teach us about recognizing and even cultivating possible working agreements that others might so easily see as impossible.

I. Listening to the Mediators

Let us begin with two practitioners who summarize the promise of mediated participation in a world of power and emotion. The first suggests why traditional zero-sum hardball might not work anymore—and why he came, and we might come, to take mediation and practical consensus-building processes seriously.

Frank Blechman, political consultant and planning consultant, worked for many years at the Conflict Clinic at George Mason University. He tells us,

> I've spent most of my career as a conflict generator...
>
> Conflict generating is fundamentally the process of raising an issue to visibility and forcing public polarization so that fifty percent plus one will land on your side: It's essentially the opposite of consensus building processes, although it uses all the same fundamental skills: Understanding where people are coming from, how far they're willing to move, getting people to feel comfortable so that they're willing to reveal information that they initially withhold, all of those...
>
> Sam Rayburn is alleged to have said, "Any bill that passes by more than ten votes wasn't strong enough." Now that's the ultimate statement of the virtue of non-consensus: That if in fact you only need fifty percent plus one to make policy, then in fact getting more votes than that means you gave up more than you had to.

But in many of the public issues that we face today—because we have empowered, over the last generation, so many people to obstruct so effectively—fifty percent plus one is not enough, sixty percent plus one is not enough, seventy percent plus one is not enough, so that indeed you need to get closer to ninety percent plus one in order to actually carry out policy.

And at that point, the skills required to get fifty percent plus one have to be re-tuned toward a different objective—and it may be a hundred percent minus one or it may just be ninety percent plus one depending on the scale.

But most of the work that I now do falls more into the ninety percent plus one to the hundred percent minus one than the fifty percent plus one range.

Now, this is an almost confessional statement of a practitioner's own evolution from being an adversarial, win-lose conflict generator to a more collaborative consensus builder, and his transformation has nothing to do with idealism, but everything to do with pragmatism and power. Fifty percent plus one is no longer enough, he argues: in many situations of ongoing interdependence, it doesn't work; the society and polity has changed, and implementation—getting anything done—becomes the hostage of many parties' abilities to be obstructionist. Still, he suggests that many of the skills, "understanding where people are coming from and how far they're willing to move," remain very much the same for the consensus builder as for the conflict generator!

So far we have a direct account of self-interest: if you want to get something done, pay attention to those who can block or delay or obstruct you. But many situations are not so straightforward and unambiguous. The second story suggests that there's no talking about mediated participation without also talking about suspicion and anger, humor and irony. So listen to a facilitator who thought she'd lost it in a contentious meeting in a small town's land use case. Michelle Robinson Greig—now a planning consultant with Greenplan, Inc., recounts what she did, and so, perhaps, what we might sometimes have the presence of mind to do:

There were a couple moments in the meeting when things became hot. There was one I remember really well—when a woman in the front of the room became really enraged about attorneys, and she said,

"Well, you know, the problem is that the town just tries to do something, and then somebody tries to stop it, and then it all goes to these attorneys, and they just keep fighting each other and everybody just keeps spending money on these attorneys."

As she was speaking she rhymed off all the major issues in the community like the shopping mall and the franchises…, and she touched every button in the room.…I could see every person in the room rising up behind her, you know, filling with rage.

And I thought, "Ohhh no," I felt I was going to lose control of the meeting.

But when she stopped speaking, I just…sort of lightly made a joke, and I said, "What should we do then? Should we shoot all the lawyers?"

And everybody just burst out laughing, and the moment was kind of salvaged.

But I think…it's necessary to have a sense of humor about it, and to be mindful of everybody in the room and respectful of everybody in the room, and whenever somebody put something negatively, I would just try to find a positive idea there. I'd try to turn it around to a positive suggestion.

So someone would rant and rave about something, or somebody became angry about…houses being built in cornfields—they really didn't want to see that—and I said, "Well then, what do you suggest?" and since they had said something about a land trust in the course of talking, I picked out that idea and I said, "So, are you saying it would be good if we had a local land trust that could try to protect some of this land?"

And they said, "Yes"—you see?

So it was really a question—whenever anybody spoke negatively—of trying to turn it around into a positive suggestion, or just coming back with, "Well, what would you like to see happen?"

You know? "What would you like to see happen?" And that set the tone for the meeting, and really had set the tone for our organization as a whole about what we're trying to do, which is find positive solutions. (Greig 1997)

Here we see a wonderfully rich but precarious, contested, and critical moment in which we find a public discussion of land use possibilities confronted by legacies of anger, not just one person's but widely shared anger too; we see a group about to turn on an easy target, a common enemy (lawyers!); we hear an experienced practitioner worry and wonder if the discussion was heading irretrievably south; and we then see more than her handling the anger rippling through an audience too.

We see part of the promise of skillful mediation here, not in comedy but in the quickly linked recognition of anger and the proactive request for proposals. Greig responds sensitively, not dismissively, in a pragmatic and empowering way: her sense of humor and irony acknowledges and then reaches beyond anger and frustration to ask practical questions of what might now be possible. So her humor and recognition are both serious and freeing; they evoke in a gentle yet persistent way a sense of next steps, a sense of hope. "Okay," Greig says, in effect, "we don't want to spend all our money on lawyers, so now what? What do you propose? What can we do?" This moving toward proposals, she suggests to us, is what mediation's all about: searching for practical strategies generated *not by the mediators or facilitators* but by the contentiously divided and diversely interested community members themselves.[3]

II. From Practical Cases, Practical Lessons

So consider now three short accounts of disputes involving bitter transportation arguments, housing and tribal values, and myriad abortion-related issues. We come to see more clearly both the political and ethical challenges of mediation as well as real practical lessons for the rest of us who work or live all the time with public or community conflict, ethic and cultural differences, or differences of deep value commitments.

*Antipathy, Distrust, and the Baggage of the Past: County Comprehensive
Planning in a Contested Corridor*

Frank Blechman tells us of his practice as a mediator working with county governments in a busy East Coast transportation corridor:

> We were asked by one of the counties to help them consider how they ought to do comprehensive land use planning…in their part of the…corridor.
>
> Part of their concern was that this is an area which is somewhat more blue collar, a little bit tougher—a little less civil—than you have in other parts of the county: there was a lot of bitterness that the other parts of the county had been getting better service, and there was a feeling that there was no way to open up traditional citizen participation without getting completely out of hand and getting explosive.
>
> And so they asked us: could we propose a process, do process design work, give them advice on how they might proceed with comprehensive planning?

Here's a planning process that had been stymied by fear and evasion, by the threatening difficulties of "traditional citizen participation" and a sense of incompetence in the face of meetings getting "completely out of hand," "explosive." Here's an allusion to missing "social capital" in the form of missing trust, norms, and networks: trust that others at the meeting won't explode, norms that they needed a process design to suggest, networks that the convened parties could begin to form (Briggs 2008).

So what happened? Blechman continues, "We said, 'Would you be interested in considering a process which integrated what you're doing with what's going on with the adjacent jurisdictions in the corridor?' And they said, 'You are out of your mind.'"

Now this might quite reasonably be a point at which many community leaders, public administrators, or planners would pack their bags and look for more promising problems to address. Planners, for example, have been trained to see the impacts that the counties have on one another, but they're often not trained to know how to proceed when they've made a proposal and the key officials respond by saying, "You're out of your mind."

So let's follow Blechman's story:

> We said, "Well, let's take a look." We then went out and interviewed about a hundred and thirty people, roughly one-third business, one-third citizen-activist and political types, and one-third governmental officials.
>
> We then constructed four focus groups representing slightly different geographical areas, but each mixed in terms of those three sectors. And we then constructed, out of those focus groups and out of the interviews, a team of fourteen people who represented all of the jurisdictions and all of the sectors—who then formed a negotiating group to discuss a process for integrated planning.

He goes on: "That group, through us, then presented the proposal for a pretty dramatically different kind of process to the planning agencies in two of the counties and to the county council in the third—and it eventually won approval for that new process, which is now beginning." Now this was so far "just" the beginning, and Blechman recognized the enormous amount of hard work remaining to be done, but he also usefully reminded us of what had been accomplished too. He tells us:

> Now, this was a consensus building process in the sense that county officials believed initially they could not sit in the same room with each other—but ultimately they sat down and came to an agreement about how the process ought to work. It included the county official who said, "I don't think I can sit in the same room as those people."
>
> Obviously, this is not the same as building a consensus on comprehensive planning, land use, transportation, environmental management, growth and so on in the corridor, but it's clearly the first step.

Now, we will go beyond that first step in a moment, but we should not lose what we can already learn from this beginning. What might planners and other community leaders see happening here?

First, those hoping to convene the interested parties—those facing the contentious situation, facing deeply entrenched and passionately divided interests—were not stopped cold by the officials' visceral skepticism: "I don't think I can sit in the same room as those people." This wasn't a coolly reflective, intellectual skepticism they heard that said, "Pretty dubious." This was, "You're crazy to think about getting all these people together, getting us together with 'those people.'"

Second, we see that from the point of officials' initial worries about cooperation, the process built upon careful representation and "a negotiating group" that discussed, recommended, and then gained official approval and mandate for a process that few people thought possible, that had been dismissed as "crazy."

Third, we see here a deceptively simple—but politically complex—process of learning via interviews. Blechman later suggested how much more than information such crucial "interviews" can produce. He tells us,

> While I love doing surveys...I know that for purposes of conflict resolution surveying absolutely is no substitute for personal contact. Interviewing is partially information gathering, but it's sixty percent relationship building. You are introducing yourself and inviting people to trust you.
>
> It's a negotiation in itself. And if they trust you, to share information with you, and you treat that information with the respect that you promise, it's then not a very large leap to say, "Now, will you trust me to put together a meeting where you won't get beaten up?"

So interviewing and asking questions, he suggests, can reach far beyond information gathering—and here we see not just qualities of sharing information, manifesting respect, earning trust, building relationships, but all of this then in the service of convening conversations, "a meeting," in which parties' fears of aggression, antipathy, distrust, and disrespect can be overcome in the pursuit of practical learning, real productive negotiations and actual, not idealized, civic deliberation (Reich 1988, Dryzek 2000, Forester 2006b, Yanow et al. 2006).

We need not make too much of this first story—but we can take as simply worth exploring further this achievement of cooperative and officially mandated results in the face of its earlier dismissal, a dismissal not by cranks but by the officials and well-organized participants with local knowledge, those most centrally involved!

But let us turn now to cases involving conflicts over identity and deeper value issues.

Challenges of Identity in Land Use Planning

In Southern California a developer wanted to build 100 or more new homes. Local Native Americans opposed the project because the land in question held an ancestral burial ground. Political officials were worried about still other constituents—as we hear from our next practitioner—neither Anglo nor Native American, but Asian American (Thom 1997). Stephen Thom of the federal Community Relations Service begins,

> When the Mayor and county supervisor found out that somebody neutral with the experience that I've had working with Native American issues was available, the mayor immediately asked me to come into a private meeting with him. In his mind there were multiple parties, and he couldn't figure out what their position was, and he wanted to know, could we assist? He was more than willing to sit down and work with the parties, and he wanted to…begin to get a representative body that could enter some constructive forms of negotiations.
>
> So that's when we entered into a series of public meetings. Our role initially was to talk to many of the tribal members in the area. In those meetings, what I attempted to do was to go over…what the developer was proposing, and what the city was permitting the developer to do—acknowledging that there was a sacred burial ground, and acknowledging that the developer would be flexible and try to be respectful to the Native American interests—but the Native American interest needed to begin to grapple with what they felt they wanted to accomplish—what they felt was sacred and religious and respectful.

Here we have a mayor interested in a negotiated solution, not just in pushing through the formal permitting process. But the mayor, we hear, unsure both about the real issues and about the parties, turned to a mediator experienced with tribal issues for help. Thom continues:

> The tribal members wanted to try to keep the ground from getting excavated. They wanted to try to set that land aside so there wouldn't be development on it, and they also had an interest of seeing that whatever was built around complemented the intent of the tribe's use, historically, and demonstrated a respect for what their burial ground would be…So the picture started clearing up.

At this point, the picture may be clearing up, but we could easily enough worry about impasse, legal suits, and traditional political power. Negotiated outcomes don't appear all that promising when one party says, "Let's get the shovels," and another says, "Don't touch the land—it's sacred."

We seem to have all the signs here of what might easily be an intractable conflict involving identity issues.[4]

So what happened? Our mediator, Stephen Thom goes on:

> Meanwhile the veterans' administration was looking for land, and there were veterans pushing the city to get some kind of a veterans' home, and they were a third

party coming into the picture. The city was very interested, and the county was very interested, in having a veterans' home because there was a military base in that area—a large constituency so that the home made political sense to the supervisor and to the city to support.

Now the picture's getting more complicated, and he goes on:

The developer owned the land. The developer was asking and trying to get permission and permits approved to do the building.
  The city and the county were leveraging, "We'd like a veterans' home," and the Native Americans were leveraging, "You're on a sacred burial ground."
  So you really had three agendas.

So far, our assessment of the conflict, viewed from the outside, might be as follows: a new housing development versus a veterans' home versus a sacred burial ground; it still doesn't look very promising. But Thom tells us that at their actual meetings they discovered more:

Now—what was really interesting was that the Native Americans loved the idea of having a veterans' home there, because what that did for them was that it gave the land respect for the elders...
  They liked the concept of having a living place for elderly people that would be respectful to their property, and they felt that the veterans would accomplish that. So the veterans and the Native Americans began to talk, and they began to agree—that they supported each others' agendas.

How did that happen? Had representatives of the parties not met face to face, they might never have discovered this much. Thom explains,

A (Native American) leader had evolved who basically tossed out a couple of concepts that he felt were important. One was setting aside five acres, and a second was building a Native American memorial on that site which would complement a veterans' home and would give some tribute to those Native Americans that participated in America's wars. That became the hook: the Native Americans gravitated to this concept because it was so reverent, respectful of Native Americans, and it so well complemented the veterans home, and it gave tribute, like no other tribute to Native Americans in this nation.

From there, he continues, the negotiation started to take shape:

The developer had to consider whether to get a permit. He had no objections to building a veterans' home and giving twenty-two acres of land for that purpose.

He had no objections to giving some land…to the Native Americans, if that be what they wanted—he was flexible on that—so long as he got to build on the balance of the thirty something acres and build, I think, a hundred twenty homes.

What happened was that the city and the county had very clearly stated that a veterans' home was going to be a clear criterion for allowing the permission for the development. One of the commissioners on the State veterans' review board—who was, I think, of Native American ancestry—had indicated clearly that if the town hoped to gain State approval and hoped the State would come and bring money and build the veterans' home, it was going to have to come in unified with the Native Americans as well as with the veterans. So the leverage was all set for reaching some accord.

So here, a dispute that we could easily have seen initially as irreconcilable—as a dispute to excavate or not, to leave the land untouched or build new housing on it—no longer seems hopeless. We began with images of marketed land versus sacred land, the clash of one group's interests, or perhaps even ways of life, against another's, and now we sense possibilities that might satisfy the interests (and perhaps the ways of life as well) of each of the apparent adversaries (cf. Fuller 2005).

But even more important, we see our own earlier expectations of irreconcilability refuted, and so we find ourselves surprised to see new possibilities we had not imagined. We might find ourselves less cynical, more curious now, and needing to understand better how our earlier practical assessments of likely impasse could have been mistaken. We need to ask seriously, "What were we thinking? Why might *we*, ourselves, so easily have *missed* encouraging and achieving such mutually beneficial outcomes? Why might we so easily—and simplistically—be ready to presume irreconcilability?"

We see here again a "drama of mediation"—and, of course, of negotiation more generally: we start with conflict and apparently irreconcilable interests that have little to do with each other, and we wonder how in the world these parties will ever stop living at cross-purposes, and then skillful negotiators and mediators, organizers and managers can sometimes come up with results that no one expected. We need to explore how these dramas can work: how at times our own comfortable "realism" about struggles of power, interests, and identity can keep us presumptuous or blind (or both), keep us from finding options and possibilities that really do work for the people involved (Forester 2008b, Heifetz and Linsky 2002, Kolb and Williams 2003). So we need to explore, once more, how skillful mediators might snatch possibilities from the apparently impossible, and how community leaders, public managers, and planners working in the face of multiple and conflicting parties might do just the same. If we can learn how our initial presumptions hold us hostage, how our initial socially constructed assessments preempt our learning about real possibilities, we can learn to approach future cases more critically, not less, with more curiosity and less presumption, as skillful practitioners here show us how to do.

Making Progress When Little Negotiation Seems Possible

Let us turn now to a third story, a third drama of negotiation provided by Frank Blechman (2005). We might come to see, in the wonderful words of Russell Norwood Hanson, that "there's more to seeing than meets the eyeball," that there can well be more going on in a case than we expect, and that when our expectations too quickly narrow our vision, we need to learn to see more, we need actually to learn to learn, to know that we don't know what we need to know, even though we are now confident in what we think we do know (Hanson 1961: 7).

As we'll see, Blechman's account first appears to be full of apparent contradictions: he seems to disavow the promise of "agreement," but he tells us of agreements reached nevertheless. He speaks of nonnegotiable issues, but then points toward evidence of real and productive negotiated agreements. Let's listen closely to appreciate what he really says:

> The program I work with does not start from negotiation theory. Indeed it starts from the premises that: the conflicts that go the longest and cause the most damage are rooted in non-negotiable issues, in race, class, gender, religion, nationality, deeply held values, and that those deep rooted issues, therefore, will not be resolved by negotiation, and that the end product of a resolutionary process is not, therefore, an agreement.
>
> That creates a somewhat different framework for what we do.
>
> So the end product, often, is an understanding. Parties come together, parties who are deeply divided; they join in an analytical process, and they go away not having agreed about a damn thing but having come to understand their own situation and the other people's situation better.

So far, we have an appeal not to any negotiated outcome but to improved understanding, and of course we should want to know what any such "understanding" might be good for: if some parties gain control and resources while others gain "understanding," we might worry about just what they're understanding![5]

Still, understanding our own situations and those of others with whom we must interact might certainly be goods in themselves, but of course there's more to it. Blechman continues:

With that understanding they act unilaterally in the future in ways that are less conflictual, more constructive for each, and in fact they may find that while they can not get within a shred of agreement on issue X, they in fact have dozens of issues A, B, C, to J on which they *can* cooperate—many of which are essentially negotiable.

How can this work? Listen a bit more, as he goes on:

I'll give you a classic example. A few years ago, the pro choice and pro life forces in this state, which is heavily Catholic, had really gone to war with each other, and the state police were proposing to go to the legislature seeking new authority to interpose themselves to prevent violence.

There was a meeting arranged between leaders of the pro choice and the pro life forces who immediately agreed that it would be very undesirable if such legislation was passed and that they should jointly oppose it on a variety of free speech grounds.

Now here we have an agreement prompted by what both parties take perhaps for different reasons to be an external threat: increased intervention by the state police. But their discussions produced more, Blechman tells us:

As the discussions went forward they discovered, not entirely to their amazement, that they also shared strong common interest in increasing health care for at risk teenagers and pregnant teenagers—and they also wound up forming a coalition which voluntarily proposed a set of rules for how they would picket each other to sort of lower the risk of violence, thereby forestalling the state police proposal.

Simultaneously they formed a coalition in the legislature to increase state funding and support for prenatal health care. That coalition, despite all the wars and despite all the interventions of groups like Operation Rescue from outside the State coming in, has held up and for many years since it has succeeded in increasing state funding for health care even at times of budget cuts. And that has, at some level, improved the civility of debate.

Now, on the fundamental issue of abortion, needless to say, the two sides did not convince each other and did not agree, and if the purpose of bringing them together was to seek common ground on that issue, they might never have come together, and my guess is that it would have failed. But, bringing them together in a different context made it possible for them to identify very constructive things that they could do.

We have a great deal to learn here, for Blechman alerts us to distinctly different practical outcomes and to how we might achieve them. First, he tells us, two adversaries that have been involved in deeply and fundamentally value-defined, bitter, and at times violent, conflict have somehow found ways to agree practically:

a. On steps to resist legislative support for increased police power;
b. On steps to develop rules for picketing to lower the risks of violence at demonstrations;
c. On steps to improve healthcare for at-risk teens;
d. On steps to form a coalition to lobby the legislature for prenatal care funding; and
e. On ways to improve the level of adversarial debate, of "civility," at a time when anti-abortion protests were increasingly characterized by the intimidation of women at clinics and an escalating rhetoric tantamount at times to the incitement to violence.

But these substantial outcomes are still not what's most important here, as surprising and counterintuitive as these agreements between archenemies might be. The far more important lesson for community leaders and organizers, planners and mediators alike follows: "if the purpose of bringing them together was to seek common ground on that issue, they might never have come together...But, bringing them together in a different context made it possible for them to identify very constructive things that they could do." Here, Blechman suggests, looking for agreement on the core issue would have led to failure. That's the easy and obvious—but seductively self-fulfilling—conclusion drawn by the political realists who say, "Of course, they'll never agree!"

But Blechman teaches us a still more important and practical lesson. If we failed to bring the parties together at all—because they so obviously and realistically could not agree on the core issue—*that narrow realism, too, would have been a source of failure* and missed opportunity. Again, "bringing them together in a different context made it possible for them to identify very constructive things that they could do."

Now here we started with nonnegotiated "unilateral actions": what parties do on their own, uncoordinated with others, and we have the suggestion that their "understanding," far short of any agreements, might lead these unilateral actions to be less adversarial and more constructive for each party. In such a case, again without any explicit and reciprocal agreements, parties might produce nonnegotiated but mutually fruitful "joint gains" (Axelrod 1985, Winship 2006).

But what follows these nonnegotiated, more mutually constructive actions in Blechman's account is even more interesting: honoring the assumption that on certain issues no agreement—not a shred—will be possible on a central, defining, "focal" issue, still, he suggests that "they may find," they may discover—clearly having not approached one another with this understanding or this expectation—that there may be "dozens of issues on which they *can* cooperate."

But here, of course, we're back to the possibilities of actual negotiation freshly discovered in a bitter setting in which no negotiation at all seemed possible on an overarchingly dominant issue. So what we can come to treat—so realistically, it seems—as a dominant and defining issue, we now see, can paradoxically be a blinding one. We think we see the central issue, it looks nonnegotiable, and we draw the implications for action: Let's get out of here; let's not waste our time and resources trying to do the impossible. But Blechman suggests that this apparently reasonable rationale, "Nothing's possible," hides the real possibilities we have. We risk confusing our obvious disagreement on a central issue with the potentially negotiated agreements we might reach, the outcomes we might yet achieve on many other important issues.

So Blechman shows us that thinking about "agreement" too early on can not only be hopeless, but worse: focusing on the impossibilities of "core issue" agreements can actively disempower us. We don't just set ourselves up for a fall, but we keep ourselves ignorant, narrow-minded, and uninquisitive: we ignore opportunities right in front of us.

So Blechman, like Thom and Greig (Forester 2005), teaches us a striking lesson about our presumptions of others who seem to cherish deep and "fundamentally" different values from our own. The realists—our friends who say, "It's no use talking; they fundamentally disagree"—are being earnest yet far too literal and, so, unfortunately, too superficial as well. As a result, these so-called realists are likely to miss many real opportunities that grow from conversations that are in deed possible—even when a "deeper" central negotiated agreement on a core issue like abortion is certainly not possible.

So we have at least one punch line from this third story: "agreement" can at times be a deceptively simple, inappropriate early goal of dispute resolution or participatory processes, and our perception of "no possible agreement" on a central issue, our own negotiation realism, can lead us to miss real opportunities. So this is all a story about realism that can become a blinding cynicism despite the best of intentions. We're thinking about deep differences on a key issue; we really do think no agreement's possible, and we're both right, narrowly, and wrong, more practically. We might be happy to learn eventually that we've been wrong, but we'd be even happier to recognize and act on our real opportunities in the first place!

Conclusion

These accounts suggest that skillful and wise intermediaries—and planners, organizers, and managers like them—can surprisingly at times snatch real possibilities from the jaws of impossibility. How, we should continue to ask, do they raid the impossible when others think the game is up? What lessons do they suggest that community leaders, planners, and others need to learn in situations of complex public and private disputes?

Experienced mediators seem to know that in contentious disputes there's always more going on than meets the eye, that parties always care about even more, sometimes much more, than they say or announce or defend as a matter of public posture. So, they suggest, as community leaders, public officials, planners, or citizens we should be very careful about tying our own hands with the political rhetoric of those who seem to be adversaries. To put this more bluntly: in a globalizing world of increasing cultural diversity, we need to listen more carefully both to—and, every bit as important, *beyond*—"the words"! In socially, economically, and politically diverse settings, of course, engaging with and far beyond the spoken word enacts recognition and respect, listening and learning too. Listening merely to "the words" is hardly listening at all, of course, so we need to be less gullible, and less self-satisfied in our political realism about what can't be, so that we can be more curious, more critical, and more creative as we find opportunities that others have presumed not even to exist (Forester 1999b, Menkel-Meadow 2001).

These mediators have their presumptions too, though. So they expect that in times of conflict, stereotypes and fears will often focus parties' attention in limiting ways, so that parties will need to and can in fact learn new things. As parties facing differences in complex disputes, for example, we often come to realize that there's more that we need to find out, so we can come to learn, first, and act as best we can to achieve our ends, second. In a globalizing environment, our increasing need to negotiate cultural, social, linguistic, and religious differences means practically that we have to presume less and learn more—in real time, no matter how well we are "prepared." Being prepared will mean, in part, being able to pay attention and learn.

These skillful mediators assume that parties can surprise one another with new information, gestures, offers, disclosures of self, and more that can enable them—enable us all—singly and together to act in new ways as they and we learn from and respond to one another. So after initial assessment comes convening. After and through convening comes learning. After and through learning, negotiation that takes advantage of mediation assistance then becomes possible.

So these mediators presume that in the first place, initially and practically, conversation matters more than *and must precede* any agreement, as we saw in all three cases. In many settings in which participation or inclusion matter, then, this means we must resist the urge to bargain too quickly, to look for fast and simple deals, simply to trade and exchange rather than allowing ourselves to talk and to listen and probe, to inquire and to find new ways to avoid the stereotyping that ends up making us blind, self-righteous, and less informed, rather than perceptive and more insightful.

Furthermore, these astute mediators know, too, that when disputes take win-lose or zero-sum complexions, then complications—additional interests to negotiate!—can actually help. We look stuck, but more information and more concerns, new relationships and news of environmental change can get us unstuck, as the role of the veterans played in the second case. Additional complexity—additional facts that matter, additionally relevant details or stakes—can save us from our own "rush to interpretation," our own preemptive, presumptuous "realism" that blinds us to possibilities we really have (Coles 1989). This can sound easy, but it makes personal demands that are not always simple: we need to tolerate ambiguity and complexity, to take seriously beliefs unlike our own, to respect ways of organizing the social and cosmological world that are unlike what we know. Community leaders and organizers, public managers and planners who can appreciate difference in these forms will help cultivate diversity—and cooperation—in communities and workplaces rather than run from it or suppress it.

The mediators whose work we have explored assume that dispute resolution involves not only knowledge and broad value claims and commitments—not only differences over epistemological and ethical claims—not only words but small offers, reciprocal gestures, the sharing of information, and the building of trust that we saw in the richness of interviewing practices. Here reassurance and respect take shape not so much in words but in tone and body language, in eye contact and posture, in the minute ritual performances of the ways we break bread and share meals, not in verbal promises or flattery.

More precisely, these mediators' practice tells us to focus less on contradictory words, less on conflicting arguments, less on general and abstract knowledge and value claims, and more on the specific tone, style, and conditions of conversation and dialogue—the practical, expressive character of others' and our own ways of speaking and listening. So in environments of diversity and plurality, citizens and planners alike must not only think differently but act differently: we must not dismiss but really take advantage of a cup of tea here, a walk on the site there, the diverse conventions and rituals of meeting and listening, talking and eating, walking and working together through which we can usefully learn about one another. The work of inclusion and participation happens not only in words but in deeds together as well.

Finally, these mediators presume in the face of conflict that when parties typically and inevitably care about much more than they say, those parties will also have to manage multiple, conflicting, and ambiguous goals, responsibilities, and obligations—and that, as practical people, many of these parties can and will improvise, innovate, and cooperate practically to serve their own interests, to solve shared problems, and to build new strategic working relationships (as the abortion opponents and advocates did) in unforeseen and unimagined ways. So, too, as they face increasingly diverse and interdependent relationships, community members and activists, public managers and planners alike will come to appreciate that our many differences are not just issue defined but are far more complex and ambiguous—and that very complexity and ambiguity can provide us with real opportunities, as well as with obstacles, in our work together.

So this analysis makes few claims for mediation as any general technical fix. Instead, drawing from thoughtful mediators, we can learn about the ways our own presumptions can often hold us captive, learn about our own gullibility and cynicism, our failures to inquire critically and to act on good judgment, our own failures of imagination and hope. In situations that can look to the facile realist's eye quite irreconcilable, these mediators teach us, we can at times, surprisingly, discover cooperative, consensual outcomes in the shadow of looming impossibility. All this we can explore, as the next chapters make clear, even as we face contentious and seemingly irreconcilable value differences.

Part Two

Respecting Value Differences and Acting Practically Together Too

CHAPTER THREE

Exploring Values-Based Disputes

When we face public controversies, they rarely turn up in neatly organized forms with "economic interests" over here, "political values" over there, a "communications issue" here, a "cultural matter" there. The same is true when we care about our schools or our neighborhoods, our health or our safety, our abilities to have work or to get to work, among the many public policy and place-based debates and disputes affecting us all. In all of these settings, we may rightly feel that we have both deeply felt values and quite practical interests at stake at the same time.

Yet we seem to know much more about settling controversies over interests than we do about resolving those that challenge our values. When interests clash, we bargain and negotiate. But when our values conflict, then what?

We begin to explore this question here by identifying crucial themes that characterize values-based disputes—those of history and identity, loss and grief, respect and recognition. We turn next to explore the reflections of four practitioners, two who provide glimpses into larger negotiation processes and two who reflect upon carefully organized deliberative retreats. We draw tentative lessons from these practitioners and conclude with a series of questions that we must explore further—if we hope to improve our public deliberations when value claims and differences come into play.

Values-based disputes, as we will see, pose not only the familiar challenges of assessing interests, but special challenges of recognizing—and respecting—value systems or cultural histories, religious traditions or ethnic memberships—or all of these, as they help to define, or even constitute, any particular dispute. Notice that we speak of *satisfying* interests or wants, but *cherishing* and *honoring* values.[1] Not doing well where we have interests, we may feel regret. Sacrificing cherished values, though, we grieve and try to work through our losses. When an interest of ours takes a hit—when our car becomes unreliable, for example—we try to compensate; but when a cherished value takes a hit—say, our place of worship is attacked—*we* feel attacked; a part of our identity feels assaulted. So when disputes involve values, we should not be surprised that we often have to come to grips with questions of identity, as well as with interests.

Appeals to values in a dispute also seem more substantially ambiguous than appeals to interests do. Wanting control of acreage, for example, seems far clearer than characterizing the "sacred" nature of the land. That deeper ambiguity of value claims, we will see, has implications for the kinds of respect demanded of us, as facilitators and mediators and stakeholders too, and for the ways that we might design processes of conversation and storytelling—processes of facilitated dialogue and mediated negotiation both—rather than engage in the more familiar and seductive, but equally problematic, processes of moderated debate.

To see what these themes can mean in practice, we turn to several accounts of skillful practitioners' work in the face of messy value and identity-based disputes. These will involve race and community relations, county and tribal government issues, Arab-Israeli negotiations, and state government regulation of Native Hawaiian homelands as well.

Local Disputes and Long Histories

Let's begin with the reflections of mediator-facilitator-consultant Wallace Warfield. Warfield tells us about work with a small city's officials, police department, and black community representatives after a controversial arrest that involved police claims of "interference with the duties of an officer" and community claims of "excessive use of force." Warfield had been asked by the assistant city manager for help—as many might guess—in the form of a relatively quick fix. Discussing the longer and deeper facilitation that he ultimately designed and led, Warfield at one point tells us,

> So let's come back to the original event: the Police Department wants the black community to isolate the event that took place—with the arrest and the disturbance—from the history. Of course, the police chief becomes increasingly frustrated because he says [to community representatives]: "Why are you calling me a racist? Why are you dredging up all this other stuff that happened ten or 15 years ago to deal with this situation?"
>
> But in the minds of the black community, you can't separate out an event that happened to your cousin last year, to your uncle the year before, to your friend two years before that...

Yes, the political culture in the United States is an individualistic culture, but for people who have been disenfranchised as a group, they think about solutions as group solutions. So they articulate their values as a group value—not as an individual value—because the individualistic nature of the political culture of the United States has not worked for them: so that's how they articulate and frame their views. So you're talking about two groups of people who don't even talk in the same language.

He goes on:

This comes back to what I was saying about strict neutrality in mediation, which tries, artificially, to build parity between groups, where there is no parity—or, in this particular instance, it would in all likelihood try to get the black community representatives also to focus on the event—because by focusing on the event, you thereby fashion a resolution tailored to that particular event—but not to the ambiguity of where they're speaking from.

Then Warfield tells us pointedly, "As an intervener, I don't choose to do that any longer: I'm not going to play that kind of role." And he says,

In these situations I find myself becoming the cultural role interpreter. I will tell stories, or use metaphors. I find that whites in positions of influence and power will say to me: "Well, you're like us"—it's a benign co-optation: "You're more like us than you're like them." And I say: "No, I'm not. Let me tell you stories about what happens to me, a so-called successful black man in America in a year like this."

We have just a snapshot here, but Warfield raises several significant themes we should consider. First, we see the classic question of problem boundaries—the question of one party's wanting to "isolate the event...from the history," and so the problem of recognizing or leaving aside, perhaps respecting or, alternatively, dismissing, "that history," as unspecified as that may initially be. Let's leave aside for the moment the presumptions that make it possible for a police chief, or other community leader, to ask in apparent surprise, "Why are you dredging up all this other stuff that happened *ten or 15 years ago* to deal with *this* situation?" In a values-based dispute, it seems quite clear, 15 years ago can seem like yesterday.

Second, Warfield suggests, not only may some parties identify as part of a salient "group"—racial, religious, and so on—but, as he says, "they articulate their values as a group value, not as an individual value, because they find the individualistic nature of the political culture...has not worked for them." Here, Warfield goes on suggest, the black community might wish to resist focusing just "on the event—because," he says, by doing that, "you thereby fashion a resolution tailored to that...event—but *not* to the ambiguity of where they're speaking from."

Warfield is telling us that something quite significant would be missing in the eyes—and the hearts—of the black community, if a resolution simply focused on this discrete event: there's an "ambiguity" to recognize, he suggests, a lived, felt, multilayered experience of multiple meanings, an inherited and still actively lived ambiguity of "where they're speaking from"—a history that makes an expressed claim to recognition and respect, which other parties and "third parties," too, ignore at their own risk. Just think, for example, how easily a compliment from 10 years ago can be forgotten, and how easily someone's humiliating remark from the same time can be remembered.[2]

Third, Warfield points to the subtle but important judgments about process design that facilitators and mediators have to make in such cases. The police chief and the city manager want to settle a dispute about an arrest; the black community sees the arrest as just one, however important, instance of a patterned history of indignities and humiliations, making the chief, some say, "a racist." How can the facilitator here recommend a process and scope of discussion broad enough not to be seen as just doing the city's bidding and narrow enough to have a promise of achieving tangible and timely results?

Last but not least here, Warfield tells us not only that in the face of such a dispute he doesn't find a strictly neutral mediator role helpful, that he's "not going to play that kind of role" any longer, but that he has come to "find himself becoming a cultural role interpreter": now facing parties with such disparate value and cultural orientations that, as he puts it, they're "two groups of people who don't even talk in the same language."

"I will tell stories, or use metaphors," he says, and then he immediately makes clear that he's not telling those stories, or using metaphors, for entertainment. Told, he says, by "whites in positions of influence and power" that "You're more like us than you're like them," he replies, "No, I'm not. Let me tell you stories about what happens to me, a so-called successful black man in America in a year like this."

Now, in the face of such differences—of assumptions of "us" and "them," of event and history, of felt disenfranchisement and power, of some wanting to get on with business today and others wanting historical justice at last—why does Warfield turn to stories and metaphors? Certainly it seems, faced with the stunning presumptions of "You're more like us than you're like them," his stories might be pitched to help the parties see in new ways, to help the parties reframe understandings, to help the parties come to see one another's interests and values both in new ways, to help them to explore those palpable ambiguities of where they're both "speaking from."[3]

Without Stories, No Reconciliation

Let us now explore several of these themes as they arose across the United States, 60 miles north of Seattle. With funding from the Ford and Northwest Area foundations, Shirley Solomon convened a four-day retreat of Skagit County officials and Swinomish tribal leaders, along with, as she put it, "several mayors, key policy staff people, executive directors from the port and public utility district, and other activists and community leaders"—all of whom were concerned with governance and value questions ranging from land use planning through jurisdictional authority and sovereignty (Solomon in Forester and Weiser 1996).

Solomon saw not only conflicts of interest here but deep value differences too, as she put it, "essentially two worlds, two cultures." "We'd done a lot of convenings and gatherings," she tells us, "and by and large one always gets into 'my view versus your view,' and 'my needs versus your needs,'" and so this time she hoped to convene a "talking circle," the "Skagit Fellowship Circle." She contrasted her view of public governance as usual with her hopes for the retreat in this way:

> As a woman, I've had great resentment, over time, to the way in which conversation and dialogue has been just obliterated from the way in which we conduct our business. The whole relational aspect of our work has been neutered, just sterilized, I think. There's no opportunity to do anything other than to speak to the topic at hand. Our public engagement processes are just criminal in my mind. A public hearing, for instance, is just an abomination—because it requires people to indulge in hyperbole: You've got two minutes to speak, and you've got to be as rash as you possibly can in order to make a point. There's no opportunity for discourse.
>
> That is what we were trying for in this fellowship circle: thoughtful discourse, where I had the opportunity to tell you something about me, the way I see the world, the way I think about things, and you not being in "rebut mode"—where you're sitting there poised to say, "Yes, but…" or poised to use what I am saying as a way of making your own point better—but instead to really see my world, see things from the vantage point that is mine and mine alone.

Now, we will return to the seductive time and place of that "rebut mode," but Solomon suggests that when worlds and cultures collide, when fabrics of values in addition to discrete interests pull in different directions, facilitators need to do far more than to set the stage for rebutting arguments, for my view versus yours, my needs versus your needs.

Solomon, like Warfield, sees that history matters here—and not simply as a record of events. She had asked guest speakers to present historical background material to inform the group's deliberations. She warns us that infinitely more than information's at stake here. She's inviting speakers, but she has one eye on fury and another on possibilities of reconciliation. She says,

> It's very delicate because, again, you're dealing with a great power imbalance, great loss, great change, guilt, fury, lots of things. I mean there's a cauldron under this that you're trying to help release in a way that doesn't just blow you all to hell, but starts the siphoning off of all this torture and pain.

One afternoon began with an archaeologist, who was then followed by a community college professor speaking about white settlement. Solomon continued,

> From the way people asked questions, you could just see that the archaeologist was mesmerizing, with people becoming engaged in that story and beginning to think about what life was like there for those people…The professor was just a little abrasive, so he was harder to deal with for the participants—but the story he told is a story that needs to be told: when white settlement occurred, the environment of Skagit County changed dramatically. There had been spruce marshes and cedar marshes, and all those ancient, ancient, ancient trees got cut down, and the area was drained and diked, and it became farmland—that brought prosperity to those who moved in and usurped Indian land, and it brought extreme dislocation to those who were displaced.
>
> That's a story that needs to be conveyed. It needs to come out—it's the history of the place—and it's in the recognition and the appreciation of that, that reconciliation occurs.
>
> Stories have to be told in order for reconciliation to happen.

Solomon appeals to history and stories, though, no more for an ideal of reconciliation than for the pressing practical reasons of not being blindsided. She says, "There's all this underlying stuff that just hasn't been adequately spoken to…and…if you don't take care of all this…, it comes up and catches you time and time again at times when you least expect it." But this has consequences, of course—as Warfield taught us too—for the strategies of intervention she imagines:

> So then, if we go through the political deal making that attends so much of the mediation that I have been exposed to, all you're doing is band-aiding the stuff

again. It's a power play and you're herding and corralling and co-opting and doing all the stuff that I no longer want to be a part of. But the fellowship circle…is to me a way of attending to the needs of the future—perhaps by healing the wounds of the past and releasing all the energy that has gone to attending to individual pain or collective grief, or to power politics or to the Alinsky style of organizing—which I certainly have followed for much of my career.

Warfield warned us of the *institutional* pressures to get on with business—city officials' wishes to focus on the event and not be held hostage to an ambiguous history—and he not only spoke of resisting those pressures but working with revealing stories and fresh metaphors, too, both helping to shape new under-standings and future strategies as well. Solomon strikes similar chords; she no longer wants to ignore the "underlying stuff," to herd and corral and co-opt, and she, too, asks us to consider the dignifying and respecting, healing and redemp-tive role that personal stories can play. One of her starting points, even touch-stones, she explains, was the felt reality of "place": "What we were trying to do here was, again, to deal with 'place,' place as the common denominator, place as that thing so that you would set aside some of your own personal stuff and think bigger, think more collectively around the good of the order, i.e., the good of your place."

She continues,

So then we had the personal stories: How I came to be at this place and what this place is to me. We…asked people to bring a slide or two or…something that would speak to either, "This is how I came to be in this place," or "What this place means to me."

Some people brought slides. We interspersed them. We took pains from our standpoint to make slides that spoke to the full range of experience…

So up the slides went; we'd just hold the slide and start asking questions: "What does this evoke? What is this of? Do you have any relationship to whatever's being portrayed there?"

That was just a tremendous session. We scheduled it for a couple of hours, and it just went on and on and on and on and was just wonderful—very painful, very funny, very revealing…

Solomon tells us that one slide of an Indian family in a hops field showed one of the children wearing what looked like a uniform:

I said, "You know, that uniform looks very much like the uniform that I wore when I was in boarding school at the convent. I wonder what that kid's story is," and we just got talking about what the boarding school experience had been like.

That led to just an enormous amount of very, very painful information—not of my own, of somebody else's. I just asked the question, but then someone was telling about the Indian boarding school experience.

These stories, Solomon suggests, knitted together history and pain and personal experience in ways that seemed to alter the meaning of place—and the interdependence of all the residents in that place—for everyone present. She says,

> There were big time dislocations. There was a lot of opportunity for questions, "What was that like?" "I don't know anything about that." "What happened?"
>
> So there was a sort of social learning and collective sharing and the opportunity to bear witness to what had happened. There was the necessity for those who are of the group that hold the greatest power to sit in place and be with this. Most times, it was, "Oh well, it wasn't my people," or, "Oh well, I just moved here."
>
> Well, that's true, but that's...not the history of it. This is part of who these people are, and irrespective of whether it was you, your ancestors or somebody else entirely, it's part of their story in this place. It's part of the ethos of this place...what this place is all about.

But then Solomon reminds us she's not interested in a traditional history lesson; she's interested in setting the stage for parties of two worlds, two cultures, of deeply rooted and deeply differing value systems, to continue to learn about one another and one another's issues without simply falling into "rebut mode," into my argument versus yours, my problem versus yours. So she says,

> What you're hearing in these stories is one person's experience. The setting and the forum are not designed to debate issues or to change opinions on things, but really just to get a feel and a sense for somebody else's experience. It's a gift. It's a window into somebody else's life, how they do things, what has happened to them, how they've processed it.

Solomon was willing, she says, to start small but nevertheless to set the stage for consensus building and collaboration:

> Everybody's not tracking in the same way, and reconciliation is something that takes a lifetime. What we were trying to do here was pierce the skin, the crust that holds everything at the status quo. It's like a pie really where you have to break the crust to relieve the pressure. Some steam comes out and so on and so forth, but you also want some left, so that there's some dynamic energy.

These are fundamental differences, and no matter how many times you sit in circles, no matter how many times you experience greater understanding and trans-formation, the fact of the matter is that I see things fundamentally differently from the way an Indian person sees things. I always will because I am not an Indian person.

But now, what we are trying to do…is to find an overlap where we are identify-ing commonality, where there are places that there is an overlay of interests, and where we can start small: to do this "crawl, then walk before you run" routine— where you're developing some habits of working together in a different way, where you begin to see the opportunities that collaboration may offer.

So Solomon searches for an "overlay of interests," for beginning to see the opportunities of collaboration, but she warns us that if we don't attend to deeper, "underlying" issues of experience and worldview, we'll be continually blindsided. Even as she noted the practical resolutions that the fellowship circle members made public about resource protection strategies, the legitimacy of tribal gov-ernment's concerns and future cooperation, Solomon pointed to what she might have done differently. She says,

> In hindsight, I would have continued to staff it in a more substantive way, if I'd understood how fragile all this stuff was.
>
> I think you've got to nurture and squire, and nurture and squire, maybe forever, you know? It's not that people are reluctant. It's that there are too many other things on the front of the plate. It's also atypical behavior; it's not institutionalized behavior this way. But no one is reluctant—it's just not their mode. It was as if people felt, "Create the setting, and I'll come"—that kind of thing.

Nurture and squire, as she puts it, and anticipate the forces that pull in other directions, the forces, some enabling, some obstructing, that shape place-making deliberations, our coming to see "our place" in fresh and new ways. Solomon lays down an institutional challenge. Clashes of worldview and value are not automatically and preemptively irreconcilable: create the setting, she tells us, and people will come.

So, she's suggesting, we need to understand better how our more ordinary public processes can punish rather than encourage thoughtful deliberation. We need to protect time and space for stakeholders' stories that can be agonizing and angry, painful and revealing—possibly enabling movement toward healing and reconciliation too. We need to understand, surely, that speaking about "place" can be speaking about identity and interests and values all at once. So Solomon warns us of the temptations of falling back into the "rebut mode," *and* she asks us to imagine other conversational, deliberative forms and processes like the fellowship circle that she's tried here. There's action to take, she suggests: the listening, learning, and careful and sensitive "nurturing" required to create fresh institutional forms and new deliberative processes of dealing with our differences.

Israelis and Palestinians and the Narrowing of Internal Debate

Let us turn now, to continue to pursue these themes, to a quite different contested place, one certainly characterized by deep historical and value differences. Let us move from Skagit County to the Middle East, from Shirley Solomon and before her, Wallace Warfield, to Dennis Ross, best known perhaps as President Clinton's Middle East envoy.

I had asked Ross how his work had changed over the years, particularly in regard to his side meetings with parties. He answered in a way that was unremarkable, but quite revealing too. He began,

> The one-on-one relationships were not dramatically different—that I came to pretty naturally. From early on I began to develop these side relations, forged in very informal settings, with both sides, pretty much wherever I was working.
>
> What was instinctive for me was to realize that the formal part of negotiations or mediation is just one necessary part of a larger process, because there are certain times each side has to be able to put something on the record. They have to do it.
>
> That's the formal part—because positions that are adopted are usually adopted as a result of a lot of pulling and hauling by whomever you're talking with in any mediation.
>
> So for example, when the Palestinians came to a position, it came after a lot of internal debate. Or when we were negotiating with the Soviets, their position came after a lot of internal debate—much like some of our positions came after a lot of internal debate.
>
> So those positions—since they went through a process—they had to be presented. If you tried to pre-empt that—or avoid that—you were building the need for them to do even more of it.
>
> So you had to allow the formal part of this process. That was critical—to say what the position, the outcome, was—not to air the laundry about what the debate was, and the position often was the lowest common denominator position.

What is most familiar here, of course, is the sense of formal and informal aspects of a negotiation process. Formally, "each side has to be able to put something on the record." Ross says, "They have to do it"—and his argument seems to have at least three parts: one concerns respect ("each side has to be able to put something on the record"); another concerns a kind of procedural legitimacy ("since they went through a process"); and a third more pragmatically concerns escalation (doing "even more of it").

Because this "lowest common denominator position" reflects a hidden history "of a lot of pulling and hauling," Ross suggests that the result has been hard won, and that in itself deserves a degree of respect. He implies that ignoring that process might easily be taken as dismissive, though, and he's emphatic about the dangers of preempting or avoiding what the parties "had to present": you risked "building the need for them to do even more of it."

But none of this is as striking as the double vision that Ross suggests. Contrasting the generative but hidden richness of each side's "internal debate" to their formally announced "lowest common denominator," Ross acknowledges clearly how much more concerns and interests and threatens and drives and animates the parties in that barely out of view "pulling and hauling"—in that "ambiguity of where they're speaking from," as Warfield had so precisely put it.

Notice that the double vision here also calls for a practically demanding doubling of respect—one that mediators need to practice far more deliberately than many members of the general public may: Yes, I hear your emphatic position and respect it fully as the product of your own internal debate—*and*—not only that, I respect you enough, too, to care, and wonder, about the broader fabric of concerns and values, fears and threats, options and possibilities that might very well come to matter to you as well.[4]

So Ross continues, less surprisingly than instructively:

> So you don't fight that position, but you also realize that you don't get anything done with that. So you have to create discussions away from the table. You have to create forums or settings that are informal—non-committal, exploratory. You have to do that—to get anywhere.
>
> So, almost always, we would set up the meetings and then—let's say, with the two heads of delegation—I'd say, "Why don't we go off for a chat?"

So, Ross says, you don't take the argumentative bait, you "don't fight"—but recognize and respect—the lowest common denominator, and he adds, "but you also realize that you don't get anything done with that"—there is, after all, a pragmatic agenda here about reaching negotiated agreements.

So mediators face the challenge, Ross also suggests, following Warfield and Solomon, to create new institutional spaces, new norms of conversation and interaction, that will help get things done, discussions "away from the table," forums or settings that are "non-committal" and "exploratory," he says, but all this still taking place in the shadow of the formal process—and, as Carl Moore following Robert Axelrod (1985) beautifully puts it—all this done to enlarge the shadow of the future too. Those shadows matter, of course, for these conversations could hardly be as "noncommittal" or "exploratory" in the glare of the light of more formal sessions.

So we have here the curious, if also common, situation in which earlier internal debate narrows positions and hides important interests and values from view and yet demands a mediator's formal and perhaps even public respect and recognition, even while the mediator very well knows what more gullible observers do not, that "You don't get anything done with that," with the public or official announcements of each side's positions or demands, their "common denominators."

Just this much might suggest that when espoused values conflict—the sanctity of the land, the quality of the environment—then debating those proclaimed values may be just the wrong thing to do: that might be not nearly as helpful as trying to understand and acknowledge "where those values are coming from," not contesting them as too vague, too ambiguous, too internally contradictory to be considered seriously, but really exploring them, seeing how many different things they can mean practically, precisely because of all their ambiguity!

So Ross helps us to see what experienced mediators know—and what observers and disputants themselves sometimes come more slowly to learn: the parties' righteous presenting claims simultaneously are and are not what the dispute at hand is really about. He went on, "Or sometimes before the meetings, I would get us together and say, 'All right, look, I know you each have to do what you have to do, but among the three of us...'"—since I knew these guys, whether it was the Israelis and Palestinians or the Israelis and Syrians."

So, Ross continues,

> This is where I learned, I think, over time—to do more preparation: I'd do more to prepare...in advance of the meeting—more preparation with the other guy, with one of their advisors, just the two of us.
>
> So with Tarasenko, before Baker would meet Shevardnadze, we began a practice where we would meet before their meetings. We would sit down, and I would say, "All right, let me tell you what we want to get done at this meeting, and I want to hear what you want to get done..."—and then we'd see where there was a kind of convergence.
>
> Increasingly the informal took on different forms...

Ross gives us another example:

> Later on in the negotiations with the Israelis and Palestinians, or with the Israelis and the Syrians, I would have lots of separate discussions even when we had the process on going. There were times...for example, with the Israeli/Syrian negotiations...at the Wye Plantation in Maryland...before we would start, the two heads of delegation and I would get together over the weekends.
>
> We would meet formally Monday through Thursday, because Friday, Saturday and Sunday was treated as a Sabbath. But...over the weekend,...I'd bring them over to my house. We'd sit out on my deck, and we'd have conversations about what we'd try to get done.
>
> One of the really tragic things about this was that when there were four bombs in nine days, we had just worked out, at my house, a breakthrough in security arrangements. It didn't come in the discussions down at Wye.

We should not take this story to make a case for meeting with Israeli and Syrian negotiators at our homes on the weekends—but to highlight the several parallel conversations and processes potentially taking place within "the same" larger value-charged conflict and dispute. Ross takes pains, here, to contrast his low expectations of discovery and invention, exploration and interest-analysis in the formal process to what he could learn in less pre-scripted dialogues—in part because the formal process was so easily held hostage to what Solomon called the "rebut mode" of "my needs versus your needs."

So Warfield, then Solomon, then Ross all suggest that when we face value- and identity-based disputes, we need to mine stories, not sharpen debates, and we need soft structures and safe processes that will enable less posturing, more revelation, more surprise. We may need to recognize the winners of each party's previous "internal debate," but even more we need to listen and learn about the values and interests behind those narrower common denominators. So, they all suggest, too, we need to respect both what's so righteously said in the moment, even as we also respect the stakeholders enough to know that they care about far more—they're interested in far more—than they've presented for each others' initial benefit.

Warfield, Solomon, and Ross all tell us to take the ambiguity of value positions as an *invitation* rather than an obstacle to conversation. They also tell us to take dialogue as a search not only for "understanding" but for significance, as a search for value, for stakes, for interests—so this is a matter of ethical and not only epistemological inquiry—just as it also helps them to enlarge that shadow of the future by asking the abiding practical questions that some dialogues may skirt: "What don't we know that we need to know? What will happen if we do nothing different from what we have done before? What can we do now?"

Surprise and Discovery

Consider finally, now, the kinds of discovery and surprise that these contested value and identity-dominated processes might produce. In Hawaii, Puanani Burgess had been asked for help: in the face of public acrimony, bitter distrust, and years of conflict between Native Hawaiians, the staff of the Department of Hawaiian Homelands, and the Board Members of that department, could she make enough peace so that these three entrenched and angry groups could do real land use planning together? Her response involved many of the themes we've broached: lengthy careful preparations with the parties, careful attention to their roots and their stories before ever turning to their demands, and a retreat she designed so that the stakeholders might all speak, listen, learn, and understand—and also then be more able to act together.

After lengthy preparation and interviews with the stakeholders, Burgess convened a daylong retreat to see if deep hostility and suspicion could give way to future cooperation. In the morning, the twenty-two participants—homesteaders, department staff, and board members—had not spoken about their issues; instead, in an exercise that Burgess calls "Guts on the Table," in a ceremonially dignified, if not sanctified, process, they had spoken about the stories of their names and so their family roots, their communities, and so their conceptions of place and identity, their gifts and capacities, and more.

In the early afternoon, then, the twenty-two drew maps for one another of the land they cared so much—and had differed so bitterly and publicly—about. They were no longer drawing maps based only on yesterday's assumptions; they now drew maps that incorporated what they had heard and learned from each other in the morning sessions.

The results, Burgess suggested, were quite striking. Some staff expressed surprise, for example, that the some of the Native Hawaiians were willing to talk about what trees they might grow. Some of the Native Hawaiians realized, for their parts, that the staff would, after all, consider allowing ranching in particular places—and so on. Burgess tells us,

> But most of the insights were, "I'm so surprised—we have more agreement than I ever thought we had"—because, before, they always had been talking to their

disagreements. They had always been talking to the things they didn't like about what was said, and who said it...—all the things that you cannot ever take back and cure.

And so having gone around that, not having dealt directly with the issue at hand, we found all this agreement—because none of our processes dealt with, "What did the Department do, that you didn't like, community?" and "Department, what did the community do, that you didn't like?"

There was none of that—none of those questions. Yet, at the end of the day people said, "I think that many of the issues have been resolved."

Some said, "They may not have been resolved, but I think I can talk it over with you. I still may have a problem, but I think I may have a way to talk about it with you."

Burgess summed it up this way: "That was my end point....The major thing that came out of this was that they agreed to plan together. So people from the agency volunteered, and people from the community, and they sat together, to do this planning, to do this map. So, they got their wish. They got what they worked for."

I had asked her, "Was this what you had hoped for, for the retreat?" She said, "This was more than *I* thought would happen. This was more than *they* thought would happen. This was more than they *ever* thought would happen."

This dispute had pitted Department staff with general state mandates against residents intensely identified with their land. Burgess tells us not only that the process produced more than the parties "ever thought would happen," but that the process had helped them talk and listen differently than they always had before—not now "always talking to their disagreements," "the things they didn't like about what was said, who said it... all the things you cannot ever take back and cure"—but now "having gone around that," she says, "at the end of the day people said, 'I think that many of the issues have been resolved.'"

We have a tale of three institutional stories in Burgess's account—a tale that resonates with the insights of Warfield, Solomon, and Ross as well. First, there's a history and legacy of value conflict in which the stakeholders have beaten each other up. Their disagreements take center stage; they have responded to and rebutted each others' claims; taking back anything said in the heat of a moment isn't easy through the press or the rumor mills; each is all too aware of what the other wants to do that they don't like—and no one's bashful to say what's wrong with what the other wants. We can call this institutional form, broadly, "debate," adversarial business as usual—disagreement, argument and refutation, claim and counterclaim, and often escalation, not the least being the escalation of grudges and resentment.

Second, though, we hear each of these practitioners taking pains to create new institutional spaces, newly improvised deliberative processes of a second kind. Here we have seen appeals to ambiguity not as a muddy swamp but as a lush garden; we have appeals to history not as a mere backdrop but as a living fabric of commitments and fears, a living fabric of group members or believers seeking honor and respect; here stories reveal not quaint vignettes but humiliations and indignities, values and interests, facts and details that matter deeply to the parties. We can see these storytelling spaces as institutional spaces of "dialogue," and we need to see such dialogues as expressing both meaning and significance, bridging epistemology and ethics, fact and value, articulating both "what they, the stakeholders, mean" and "what matters deeply to them," what they're claiming to be so and what they value as parts of their own identities too (Herzig and Chasin 2006, Yankelovich 1991, 2001).

Third, of course, these practitioners all warn us that the rebuttal mode of debate can at times do more harm than good—promising clarity but delivering escalation, promising an elusively "neutral" moderation but producing little substantive learning, less capacity, and still less in terms of strengthened relationships. Instead, Warfield and Solomon, Ross and Burgess show how much we need to learn about others through informal, improvised, even indirect, processes of dialogue and exploration, and they teach us about what these nonrebutting deliberative conversations and discourses might then make possible: mediated spaces of participation and negotiation in which stakeholders (1) can move beyond their stereotypes and presumptions, (2) can recognize and learn about each others' values and interests both, and (3) can inquire together to invent options for mutual gain—can explore the "what if we did...?" questions—questions that they can ask, though, only once parties come to recognize and respect one another differently than they had before.

Conclusion: Further Questions

When disputes heat up, when values and identities come into play, public officials may find the moderated debate of public hearings to be the most familiar model of dealing with differences that they know. Fostering and moderating debate, the public officials and their staff seem to remain neutral. Escalation and recrimination seem to become the fault of hotheads, as if poor process design played little part. But our practice stories here suggest, to the contrary, how formally moderated *debate* can so easily threaten to preempt and even damage considered attempts at public deliberation—undermining both facilitated multistakeholder dialogues and mediated negotiations too. To do better work on value- and identity-based disputes, then, we need to refine the ways we convene action-oriented conversations and deliberations, learn and inquire in them, and assess and reach outcomes in them too.

On Convening

In value-based disputes, as facilitators face stakeholders' skepticisms about "What's even discussable here?" and their skepticisms about the prospects of even convening in the first place, facilitators must convey the double truth that doctrinal disputes can continue even as practical cooperation can also be possible. So in specific cases we need to explore together how we can keep our deep disagreements about what "God" requires of us, even as we might still come to agree about where the stop signs should go.

Facilitators of value-based disputes can help parties develop useful ground rules and rituals of meetings. Meals and site visits, small group processes and problem-solving groups, for example, can build relationships of mutual recognition of one another's roots in their distinctive, particular places and histories.

On Learning and Inquiry

We see that the complex histories of these disputes include deep differences, the "pulling and hauling," as Ross put it, on all sides. These histories—hardly past—now have great significance for the ways parties imagine their present and future.

Skillful facilitators express respect not only for what is proclaimed and strongly felt but also for what remains possibly to be discovered and created. These facilitators respect table-pounding now and simultaneously the stakeholders' real possibilities of continuing to learn, caring for more than they can possibly say, being able to create, as Burgess put it, "more than they ever thought would happen."

On Producing and Assessing Outcomes

In value-based disputes, these practitioners suggest, we must pull back from academic argument, from *debating* values claims in the first place. Facilitators of values- and identity-based disputes might then distinguish and disentangle deeply felt, if not always very expressible, value differences from more practical options that can address and satisfy the interests of the parties at hand. Our political and academic institutions train us to treat disputes as fuel for debate. We need to resist that training and instead encourage, model, and experiment with dialogical and negotiated alternatives that might produce real mutual gains for adversarial stakeholders.

We might think more here about how musicians settle disputes in a performing trio or quartet—and less about how poker players play their hands. With no shortage of strong and deep feelings, when musicians differ about the almost inexpressible, they seem to debate less and play and listen more: "Let's try it this way," "What if we played it like this?" They might teach us about dealing with deep differences: sketch and suggest, probe and explore more, rationalize and argue less.

Lastly, because we compensate for losses of interests but grieve and work through losses of cherished values, we need now to extend Solomon's insight—echoing both Warfield's and Burgess's reflections—that "stories have to be told in order for reconciliation to happen." We need, too, to gauge success, to appreciate reconciliation or accommodation in cases of deep difference as practical accomplishments, not as rosy and romantic ideals.

To develop these practices further, we will need to study dispute resolution practice in the face of values-based disputes quite a bit more closely than we have. Warfield, Solomon, Ross, and Burgess all suggest that a great deal *can* be done—and that we need to pay attention, for business as usual squanders our political possibilities. Facilitators and mediators can respect and yet not be stopped cold by stakeholders' skepticisms about compromising or negotiating values. Those facilitators can hold open and create new possibilities of understanding and recognition, new possibilities of relationship and collaboration—and they can do this, in part, by cultivating the insight and revelation, the fresh vision and recognition that richly surprising, place-based stories can bring into the world. Puanani Burgess expressed this capacity lucidly once when she remarked, "Humor and stories are the most critical parts of my practice. They allow people to go into deep water without being so scared..." (Forester 2004c: 228).

"Humor," she went on, "is a way of showing you can see deeply." That sense of humor, of irony and perspective taking has very little to do with being funny and still less to do with jokes, but everything to do with the capacity for creative imagination and multiple vision: the vision to see that parties can differ very deeply, perhaps even irreconcilably, on doctrine *and* that they might also figure out together how, now, to treat each other with respect—and how to live on the land in peace.[5]

CHAPTER FOUR

Dealing with Deep Value Differences in Participatory Processes

This chapter explores the intriguing difficulties and the potentially crippling obstacles that disputes presenting deep value conflicts force us to confront. In the next chapter we turn to an extended examination of a fascinating case involving HIV/AIDS priority setting in Colorado, and we conclude with lessons for community planning and public management, dispute resolution and participatory practices more generally.

When values conflict, public participation does not have to collapse into ideological or moral bickering, or worse. It turns out that a little healthy skepticism and a lot of inquisitive pragmatism can go a long way to help. Even if dealing with deep value differences seems so often so futile to many people, we can and often do manage our value differences in ways far better than through avoidance or stalling, sniping or fighting.

Why do value conflicts look so special? Our values seem intimately connected to who we think we are, or to aspects of the world we cherish—whether they involve the sacredness of our land or our water or the sanctity of life or private property. As the last chapter suggested briefly, *values* seem to run deeper than *interests* in the following sense: when we give up one interest, getting our grocery shopping done quickly, for example, we often try to make up for that by gaining on another interest, getting our purchases less expensively perhaps. But when we give up something we value, a unique historic building, let's say, we often feel that we've given up part of ourselves—and that's often very difficult, very threatening, hardly compensated by some gain somewhere else.

Because values seem connected in this way to our identities and not to simple choices of this good versus that one, this benefit versus that one, they appear inherently personal, subjective, developed as a matter of tradition and socialization, hardly easy to change by simple persuasion, rational argument, or even bargaining.

No wonder, then, that we find the public deeply skeptical about reconciling value differences, coming to terms with their subjectivity, and overcoming their intractability: for if persuasion, rationality, and bargaining can't get someone to budge from a *value position*, what in the world can ever be done when values conflict?

In this and the following chapter we explore this problem and provide a way to face these challenges, first by assessing several popular misunderstandings of value conflict, and second by listening closely to—and learning from—practitioners who have handled deep value conflicts successfully.

The more we mystify value differences as ultimately personal, subjective, irrational, or intimately spiritual, unfortunately, the more we pull the wool over our own eyes, the more we will misunderstand what value differences involve. The more we presume that value differences are so personally subjective that they are virtually beyond discussion, the less likely will we be even to *try* to discuss such differences. The more that our own rhetoric of "deep" and "fundamental" value differences presumes unbridgeable chasms between people with differing values, the more likely we will be to wring our hands, and the less likely we'll be to look for practical ways to live together, acknowledging and honoring rather than fearing, recognizing rather than shunning, understanding rather than obfuscating whatever real value differences we may have. Deep value differences deserve serious attention, to be sure, but our common ways of speaking about those differences—with the labels *fundamental, essential, unbridgeable,* for example—can often just make our problems worse, not better.

One of the most surprising results of mediators' work in the face of value differences, though, involves the transformation of parties' strong presumptions—that the others' value systems are so radically different that "We'll never be able to work something out with them"—to parties finding themselves astonishingly enough crafting real, productive, and satisfying agreements. In British Columbia, for example, facilitated negotiations between Canadian First Nations and nonnative parties, including government, interest groups, and industry, created an innovative community development trust fund in the face of long-standing conflict and mutual suspicion (Dale 1999). In the United States, where community conflict over abortion rights has led to escalating hostility, polarization, and, at times, deadly violence, the Network for Life and Choice has used facilitated dialogues to explore common ground, build trust, develop respect, and even formulate collaborative action projects in some cities (LeBaron and Carstarphen, 1999). As many facilitators and mediators take pains to remind us, these processes involve no technical fixes, not rocket science but deliberative skills of practical judgment, sensitive exploration of issues, persistence, and creativity. Dealing with value differences takes not only the vision to look well beyond our initial presumptions to future possibilities, but the deliberative abilities to listen and learn too: the abilities to probe both fact and value together, abilities that community members valuing inclusion and respect can refine and practice as they learn to deal with their differences and so govern themselves (Gutmann and Taylor 1992, Gutmann and Thompson 1996, Forester 1999a).

But how can stakeholders and mediators work practically, sensitively, and effectively when disputes involve deeply differing views of the world? When not just wants and interests differ but much more basic perspectives as well, what can the parties—and the mediators and facilitators, planners or managers working with them—really do? They can do a lot, it turns out, and we can begin to appreciate how much is really possible by assessing mediators' actual practice in such cases.

Value Differences and Public Skepticism: Mediation Snake Oil?

As soon as we begin to think about public discussions of value differences, though, we get into trouble. In colloquial terms, *value differences* seem to be so personal and so passionately espoused that they seem irreconcilable. If one person believes that all land is sacred and another believes that all land is a potential commodity to be bought and sold on the market, what kind of resolution can there be? Because many people understand that changing a person's deeper values involves not just changing his or her preferences but changing who the person is, changing his or her identity, the public skepticism about resolving value conflicts seems reasonable enough. Still, that skepticism can not only encourage an "I told you so" resignation—"They'll never even talk to us"—but it can easily mislead us too; it can easily hide practical solutions from our view. As we will see, even in the face of deep value differences, many practical resolutions may be possible, even if—or indeed because—asking parties to change their fundamental beliefs is often *neither* necessary nor relevant to settling the dispute at hand.

But value differences do often appear irreconcilable to the public eye, and so when mediators come on the scene and begin talking about "negotiation," "joint agreements," and "consensus building," anyone who's still awake rightly begins to get suspicious. After all, if the value systems are irreconcilable, and this mediator is talking to us about reconciliation, agreements, or compromises, then either we're being sold "a bill of goods" or someone's going to get hurt—and in either case, we're likely to be poorer for the experience. So we might wonder, "If I participate in consensus building, will I be pressured to compromise my principles? To betray my commitments, my integrity?" When value systems are at stake, public suspicions of morally dangerous compromises seem both reasonable and quickly forthcoming.

Similarly, any politically astute community members who feel their cherished values to be contested will be suspicious of mediators' claims of neutrality. That much hardly requires cynicism. Who in the real world is neutral? Who's kidding whom? So when the values involved concern the sanctity of life or land, traditions or the environment, mediators who speak of respecting all viewpoints equally may seem more like political spin doctors with no values at all than helpful, somehow "neutral" dispute resolvers.

In such cases, mediators start out with two strikes against them, almost before they open their mouths. They can talk the talk of accommodation and respect for the other and mutual gain, but many in the public often hear "accommodation" or "compromise" as "induced betrayal." If mediators point to the possibility of compromise, many in the public will begin to feel resentful: "Betray my values? Who the hell are you? Why can't you take me seriously? No thanks!"

Mediators who speak in this way of "public compromise" may mean well, but they practice poorly. Failing to recognize the intimacy and immediacy of the parties' commitments to their "values," these mediators begin with a procedural solution: a problem-solving process that they believe (sometimes rightly) they can implement, but they may unwittingly antagonize the very people with whom they wish to work. Sometimes they don't even know they've done it: "I'm just suggesting a *process!*" a prospective mediator might say. But environmentalists or tribal members or neighborhood residents hear it quite differently: "This mediator wants to plug me into his or her process, as if I'd negotiate about anything and just give away my grandparents' land. They're not taking me seriously, the hustlers—they're presuming that I'll just sell out whatever I believe in. They don't get it."

Not surprisingly, when government officials similarly try to promote mediated-negotiation processes, they can run into these same suspicions and problems. What they propose as an apparently "neutral" and unbiased mediation or consensus-building process, the public can interpret as anything but neutral. That public of both doers and done-to often has little love for government, little trust in city hall, and certainly no inclination to assume that officially sponsored dispute resolution processes will be unbiased. Will those processes really be indifferent to the interests of the politicians, the prerogatives of government agencies, and official pressures for budget cuts that often mean displacing costs onto neighborhoods? "'Neutral and unbiased,' ha!" the public will often think.

In a contentious political world, any public with half an eye open will be right to worry that processes of compromise might just mean fancy-looking deal making. The noble language of "public involvement" and "stakeholder participation" hardly persuades affected citizens that narrow bargaining will not preempt broader, real participation and substantial public learning about issues and options. A history of government secrets, planners covering up decisions already made, ineptly handled communication between decision makers and affected publics—all this has bred a public cynicism, and a political realism, that easily preempts a critical and creative democratic imagination, the civic capacity required to recognize, learn from, and act well in the face of value differences.

So mediators, conveners, and disputing community members alike have their work cut out for them. When apparently deep value differences are at stake, they begin not with respect and public confidence, but in the glare of public skepticism and moral suspicion.

Threatened Interests versus Threatened Values: Different Strategies Required

So public distrust of mediated participation has been fed, ironically enough, by the vague language of officials, planners, and dispute resolution practitioners themselves—especially when deeply held value differences seem to be at stake. Too often, many differences between what people care about—their apparently evolving, subjective interests—can take on a very different, and, practically speaking, apparently more intractable complexion as more deeply secured "values" or relatively fixed "commitments" or worldviews. Too often, for example, to dramatize or emphasize the seriousness of a concern we may feel as participants in public, we may present what we want, desire, or prefer—our preferences—as far less subjective, far less changeable than they are, and so we present them, intentionally or not, as more firmly rooted "needs," precommitting ourselves to the severity of our wishes. Although differences in preferences can often seem manageable, differences in deeper needs often seem harder to reconcile without someone getting hurt in a more serious way.

Similarly, when people have different interests, they might negotiate to come to a mutually agreeable accommodation. But when values conflict, those disputes seem less amenable to fair resolution—and so more sensitive deliberative strategies are required. When threatened with the loss of several of our interests, as the last chapter suggested, we ask if gaining on some other interests can *compensate* us. But when threatened with the loss of cherished values, we feel morally compromised, betrayed, damaged, or sold out. Wrecking our trusted car may have put a dent in our possessions, but the insurance company might compensate us adequately for our loss. Wrecking structures we value deeply, though—a trusted marriage or the health of a loved one—changes not just our possessions but the constitution of our lives and so can hardly be "compensated." So we speak of "making up for" the loss of a possession, but we speak of "mourning" and "working through" the loss of a loved one.

So the stakes here, of course, are not semantic but strategic and involve our practical expectations and options. Faced with another's demanding preferences in a negotiation, we will try, as parties, to devise a counteroffer; but faced with deep value differences, we must respond differently, for a counteroffer proposed too quickly can appear to devalue, to fail to take seriously, what the other parties care about deeply. What can seem to us as a quick, even simple counteroffer can offend and humiliate the other party, fuel their resentment and distrust, and escalate our conflict further, making our job of negotiating successfully even harder as we undermine our possibilities of problem solving together.

Now sometimes none of this will matter. When you exaggerate the depth of your needs and I respond as if you're strategically misrepresenting or exaggerating in just that way, we have old-style positional bargaining. This may not be pretty, but through small steps, listening and learning, probing for diverse interests, inventing and improving upon mutual gain options, we can resolve our differences effectively and efficiently. That's the easy part.

Value Commitments, Recognition, and Respect

But consider what happens when you're *not* exaggerating the depth of your value commitments, but I'm still responding as if you *were* exaggerating and misrepresenting those deep concerns. You're presenting cherished values ("Four generations of my family have farmed this land; it's who we are..."); but I respond to them as if they're just fabrications ("Look, there's lots of other land you'd like..."). The result: you will very likely feel disrespected, humiliated, insulted, and, not least of all, very angry. This is unlikely to help us solve our problems together.

And vice versa, of course: if you treat me as if I'm lying precisely when I'm telling you about what's really important to me, when I'm even partially revealing who I take myself to be, I'll feel disrespected, offended, and humiliated, and I'll be angry. Mix the attempts to express deep values on either side with suspicions of misrepresentation insinuated by the other side, and you get the recipe for the explosions we too often see. The result: increasing cynicism about the capacity of anyone—especially government or outsiders with ready-made techniques—to resolve disputes involving deep differences of value, and diminishing trust that anyone involved in public disputes will listen respectfully and take value differences seriously.

But we can face another trap here: you *do* indeed misrepresent your desires as deeper needs, but I'm gullible, and I treat your representations as deeply tied to who you are. This combination threatens to bias our resulting agreements in ways that hold them hostage to the initial deception. If your demand for complete control (of the institution, land, process, etc.) is really *not* nonnegotiable, as you have righteously claimed it to be, we are likely to *miss opportunities to generate mutually satisfying options.* We'll miss those opportunities just because we are really willing to negotiate, to trade, more than we have so far, but your posturing combined with my gullibility prevents us from *both* gaining further by trading: "It's nonnegotiable!" you bluff, and I affirm your posturing, "I hear you! Okay"—and we keep each other stupid, sealing ourselves off from exploring options of further negotiation that we would *both* have preferred. We congratulate ourselves about being tough bargainers, feel that we did as well as we could have, and both, unfortunately, miss real opportunities that we had before us, opportunities that grew from our differences, our willingness to "trade"!

Here's an example involving political conflict and educational administration. I remain thunderstruck to this day at the words of a University of California, Berkeley, administrator who, after several weeks of incommunicado-like silence, readily agreed to meet with striking students and explained his lack of previous telephone contact with the student leaders with the stunning, "But they *said* their demands were 'nonnegotiable'!" That combination of posturing by the students and literalism on the administration's part here took a great toll, weakening the university's credibility and public support, rupturing faculty-student relationships, and damaging students' education.

Practical Traps and Possibilities

Let's consider these problems of posturing, obtuseness, and missed opportunities more carefully. Let's say that stakeholders Perez and Jones find themselves face to face in a contentious public process. Perez wants to build housing units and says that without such already overregulated property rights, our economy will revert to the Stone Age. Jones thanks Perez for this self-serving insight and insists that he stop destroying the environment that is home to us all. And so on: in public meetings we see hundreds of variations of such confrontations of radically differing claims. How might their interaction unfold? The following presents four elemental possibilities:

1. Perez might just actually be expressing deeply held values, and Jones might actually respond as if Perez is really doing that. This is just one possibility, and we will ask what practical responses might then be helpful in such cases for stakeholders and third party conveners as well.

2. Perez can really be expressing deeply held values, but Jones, no fan of these public meetings and always on guard for duplicity and exaggeration, can respond as if Perez is just acting strategically—with the explosive results suggested above. Here an initially difficult situation of value differences escalates and becomes even more difficult.

3. Perez can actually be acting strategically—invoking values or presumed "rights" just as a way to play hardball—but Jones, a bit too ready to acknowledge cultural differences uncritically, thinks that Perez's impassioned pleas really do express deeply held values. Here both parties are likely to do more poorly than they might have, as the costs of posturing and attending to phony concerns distracts their attention from options that really might serve their actual and specific interests.[1]

4. Perez can be appealing to "my values" or "my rights" strategically—and Jones can aptly respond just as if Perez is acting that way. When that happens, we have the familiar dance of wary negotiators. Both parties become vulnerable to the difficulties of positional bargaining and the traps of the "negotiator's dilemma" (Lax and Sebenius 1987). *I'm* afraid that you will exploit me (if disclose my interests truthfully to you), and unsurprisingly *you're* afraid that I'll exploit you (if you disclose your interests truthfully to me). So our righteous "realism" and defensiveness—leading us both to withhold our real concerns—make it difficult for us to explore options to satisfy those real concerns instead of those we have just been willing to trot out. Both afraid of being exploited, we fail to make simple trades, for example, that would make us *both* better off, and so rather than finding ways to "give in order to get" (mutual gain options), we generate only "mutually lousy," lose-lose compromises, if we get past impasse at all.

Payoffs, Dangers, and Respectful Skepticism

So the prospect of facing these four possibilities raises more than strategic concerns. It warns us, as participants in contentious public processes, that we'll do poorly if we don't understand that disputes in which *deep values* seem to be at stake can involve stakeholders' identities as well as their interests. More practically, we'll do poorly if we fail to see how cultural problems come into play here as well: the very rhetoric, the cultural expression, of "fundamental value differences" can blind us, and worse, tempt us into resignation ("It's all relative, what can anyone do?"). Knowing how easily parties or stakeholders can posture, how easily they (we all) can construe preferences, wants, wishes, or interests into basic values, we should be respectfully skeptical when we face others' claims that the lands they must have, the trees they must protect, or the properties they must be able to sell really reflect the manifestation of their deep commitments, their *basic values*.

Knowing that some of our wants are incidental and that some of our values are indeed deeply cherished, virtually part of who we are, we need to listen carefully to others—to respect and not infuriate them—to assess how the *values* they espouse fit into broader patterns and commitments of their lives, patterns that did not just begin yesterday, presumably. We need to know that when others are blind to our basic values, we feel that they are blind to us; failing to respect the cherished quality of the values we espouse, we feel that they fail to respect us.

So, similarly, one lesson of Jones and Perez's four possibilities is that if we are not careful, we can easily be taken to disrespect and offend others, weakening our abilities to work together, to figure out together how to go on—with this project, this property, this environmental concern. We need to understand others' commitments, their histories, the extent to which their previous commitments do or don't hold them hostage, the extent to which the values they espouse define their very identities or happen to have been embraced for the first time last month.

So when we hear claims of deep values potentially at stake, we need to resist two temptations. The first temptation involves a simplistic relativism: "Their beliefs are fundamentally different; they'll never understand us or agree to anything we want." When we find ourselves thinking this way, we end up trapped and blinded by our own presumptions. We have moved, mistakenly, from recognizing a difference in another's supposed beliefs to presuming the character of their identity and possible motivations. Under the guise of "respecting a difference in belief" we easily come to stereotype quite narrowly and restrictively the others' basic tree-hugging or profit-making values, their unwillingness to meet about concerns and explore them with us, and indeed their capacity to teach us about issues and options in ways we may find helpful.

Second, we can face the temptations of an arrogant, economistic "Everything has its price" skepticism—listening to the other's claims about the land, we think (or worse, say!), "Yeah sure, but everybody has their price; what's yours?" Here, of course, we fail to recognize in the first place anything like a deep commitment that can define who a person is as well as what he or she desires. Here we presume that our way of measuring value—be it in terms of dollars or some other measure—can simply replace and transform whatever the other cares about. In so presuming, we not only blind ourselves, but we are likely to throw fuel on the fires of conflict (Gurevitch 1989). We can do much better, though, as we shall see when we consider the track record of accomplished mediators.

Listen now to Canadian mediator Gordon Sloan, who had convened the eighteen-month planning process involving mediated negotiations between fourteen sectors of representatives concerned with formulating a land use plan for Vancouver Island. Sloan had, we have seen, described the parties' presumptions poignantly: "They're each saying exactly the same thing about the other. That's a piece of information that they should know....They discover that there are all kinds of assumptions that one value system makes about the other that have to be debunked" (Forester and Weiser, 1996). As parties in public disputes and participatory processes, we see easily *that* someone is different, but we don't know much about *how* they are different. Seeing difference, we are tempted to presume not only what they think, but what they will (or won't) do as well.

But if we can recognize these temptations of our own, we can also recognize a basic practical truth about dealing with conflicting value claims: we need to learn about the other parties—Danny the environmentalist and Susan the corporate VP—as well as about the issues in front of us. We fall into debilitating negotiation traps if we either take the others' value claims *too seriously* (and so we preempt exploration and search) or if we take those claims *too lightly* (translating them wholly into our terms, we fail to devise solutions that can actually accommodate the other's values). In both cases, we blind ourselves, becoming less able to create options that satisfy our real concerns and respond to the concerns of the other parties as well. Trying to remember that there is a good deal that we don't know, we need to take practical steps to learn about the specific, not stereotypical, history and identity and character of the parties making any claims of basic value differences.

When we listen to mediators reflecting upon their practice, we see that they try to help parties to overcome the presumptions that limit their understanding and invention of new options. Mediators work in part to help vulnerable, uncertain, and often fearful parties to learn about one another's perspectives and values, fears and capacities. Listen once more to Gordon Sloan as he describes the widely shared presumptions held by the Vancouver Island stakeholders early on in their process:

> I couldn't simply say to the parties, "You're going to have to negotiate, period," because that wouldn't mean anything to them. We had to demonstrate, and teach, and do some skills-based training for them to actually practice and role play before they had a sense of what it meant to attempt to solve problems with people whose values were so radically different from theirs—and when I say, "theirs," I mean every group.
>
> Every group shared that impression, that "It's us against them." It's this dichotomy that you run into all the time in mediation, but it's much more serious in multi-party public policy negotiations: "There's no way that the enemy will ever understand me," because "the enemy" is inherently evil, weak, out of touch, all those things. That being the case, "There's no way we'll ever come to terms."
>
> So the way to solve that…is to give people a chance, privately and safely within their own sector, to air their own anxiety, to practice some of this stuff, and to have an experiential bite at seeing that they can do this: they can communicate effectively, they can deal with stupid behavior across the table effectively. Or at least they have a sense of what that would be like. That was very effective.

Getting past the blinding presumptions that all parties can bring to complex and contentious disputes is certainly not easy. Especially when deep value differences may be at stake, careful and sensitive listening becomes more important and perhaps more difficult than ever. With all the best intentions, parties may be more focused on the issues that concern them than on the underlying interests they wish to satisfy. Hardly surprising, this means that mediators, as well as parties, need to probe, to learn, to resist taking anything literally, to search for what really is at stake, to search for the facts that matter. Mediators and parties alike can do that by listening respectfully, skeptically, and critically, asking both "What if…?" and "Why…?" questions, as they try to explore the interests and values that underlie parties' expressed positions and as they work to explore hypothetical trades, packages of options, and resolutions. Focusing here on the clarification of interests, domestic and international mediator Jon Townsend suggests how such critical probing and exploration can work:

> Let's say, I'm dealing with an employee. That employee wants a 10% increase in salary. Well, the proposal that he or she would make would be a 10% increase. The "issue," the agenda item, the "what," is money. But the interest is financial security, and there might be a dozen different ways to help someone meet their financial security, that may never have anything to do with the 10% increase. In fact, there may not even be any money ever given to that person.

Townsend suggests that mediators can learn—and help the parties to complex disputes to learn, too—in a wide variety of ways. Sometimes they make it possible for parties to step back from adversarial conflict to listen to one another's stories and let the richness and the detail of personal and specific stories suggest new concerns, reveal additional interests, and disclose underlying values.[2] Norman Dale (1999: 944) writes of stories, for example, as "so important to navigating long-standing cross-cultural conflict." Noting that the "indigenous cultures of America are noteworthy for having relied on oral rather than written traditions," Dale argues too that, "First Nations people are often preoccupied with the unacknowledged and therefore unfinished business of the past," making, he suggests, "the use of personal and collective stories" particularly important in consensus building contexts (Dale 1999: 944).

In the "Common Ground Dialogue Process on Abortion," Michelle LeBaron and Nike Carstarphen point to the significance of workshop participants' sharing their stories: "participants acknowledged the stereotypes they had harbored. To everyone's surprise, all felt misunderstood, and all wrongly attributed to others stronger views than they actually held" (1999: 1042). In complex public disputes stakeholders who often presume a lot about each other, but actually know less, can learn a good deal in productive and surprising ways by listening carefully to one another's rich and often revealing stories.

Sometimes, too, consensus-building mediators and facilitators can bring in outside consultants respected by all parties to shift the parties' attention from adversarial argument to relevant historical, legal, or technical concerns they share. So, for example, as we saw in the last chapter, in county-tribal government workshops in Skagit County, Washington, Shirley Solomon and colleagues invited local community college staff to cover historical material about the county in the days before and after white settlers came. In Chelsea, Massachusetts, outside consultants were helpful to brief community members on the technical and legal aspects of drafting a new charter for the city (Podziba, 1995).

Sometimes stakeholders facing value differences can come to see the issues before them in new ways because the facilitators or mediators help them to see data in new ways. Referring to a contentious transportation planning case, Lawrence Susskind gives a striking account about the way a slide show about the size of parking garages around the country literally helped the parties to envision the issues of scale and visual and environmental impact in new ways (Forester 1994). In other cases like "search conferences," participants will cover the walls of their meeting rooms with a jointly produced "community history" on butcher-block paper, not just to involve all stakeholders in some more hands-on, "get 'em up out of the seats" way, but to create a joint visual representation of shared concerns. In environmental planning and urban design processes, too, planners may use sketches and visual materials less to represent defined alternatives than to probe issues, interests, and feelings (Forester 1999a, esp. ch. 4). In important ways, the use of visuals—photos, slides, maps, videos and more—can at times allow parties to focus a bit less upon debating one another's claims and a bit more upon exploring fresh sources of ideas, specific concerns, and aspects of issues needing attention.

The drama of mediation, in fact, seems intimately tied to this struggle for discovery, these ongoing attempts of mediators to help parties learn in new ways, to help them understand in fresh and deeper ways what they already are quite convinced they know all about. As Sloan suggested, after orientations and preliminary training in dispute resolution processes, parties come to move beyond their initial skepticisms that "They'll never talk to us!" As Townsend, too, suggests, parties can come to the table initially so focused on the issues at hand that they have not considered more carefully the underlying interests that they themselves really do wish to serve. In these processes of discovery, deliberation, and learning, the parties are losing nothing: they are asked to listen, not to give anything up. They are gaining in self-understanding and in the understanding they have of both the others they have to work with and the issues that practically affect their lives (Benhabib 1995, Forester 1999a).

Probe, Don't Presume

So when we suspect that value differences shape a case at hand, recognizing that we need to "probe, not presume" will be more important than ever—for the parties and the third-party mediators alike. Just because of the blinding power of our cultural presumptions, we need to remember that we need to learn about other parties—enviros or farmers, community organizers or developers, whom we really do not know very well—about values and value systems we "know" from the outside. In contentious disputes, we need especially to make space for a central insight that flows from our recognizing that we are not perfectly rational, all-knowing beings: we always care about more than we can say or can focus our thoughts on at any one time, and so we do ourselves a favor by finding safe ways of learning more about the concerns we do have, the unexpected implications of the actions we are considering, and the deeper motivations of the parties we are facing.

When value differences are at stake, especially when our understanding of those different value systems is not finely developed, we can anticipate that "there's more to work with than meets the eye," more to work with than we have anticipated, certainly more to work with than general public perception would suggest. Not letting our presumptions of deep value differences stop us from listening closely, we may find that hidden or not yet expressed priorities of conflicting parties differ sufficiently so that these parties might yet exploit and *take advantage of their differences* to realize mutual gains. So a developer wishes to maximize numbers of units built and her return on investment; the environmentalist opposition wishes to maximize open space. Both need to ask carefully about options that might cluster units, enabling *both* the developer to build more units *and* the environmental advocates to preserve more open space.

These observations lead to an initial suggestion about both the traps we face and the careful approaches we might adopt in the face of value differences. The shortest version of this suggestion, this lesson for practice, would be "Look and see: probe, don't presume!"

The slightly longer version would be just as simple: *When values conflict, assume the need for all parties to learn:* about each other, about the issues at stake, about the practical options that lie before them. *Recognize that indeed their "value differences" might be irreconcilable* and prevent them from reaching a mutually satisfactory, voluntary agreement about how to go on—*but take that irreconcilability not as a premise, but only as a clearly demonstrated product* of mutual discussions and attempts to learn. In cases involving such ordinarily intractable issues as abortion and sacred lands, LeBaron, Carstarphen, and Dale (1999) show us, too, how facilitated and mediated processes allowed parties with deeply conflicting values not only to listen and learn from each other but to devise practical, collaborative future actions as well.

So despite their temptations to stereotype adversaries who espouse different values, parties in participatory processes can and should commit themselves to learning first, testing their presumptions, even refining the agendas of discussion to enable them to accommodate underlying concerns as they discover them. The verdict of *value irreconcilability* always remains as a real possibility, of course, but it should be the *product* of a fair, inclusive, well-informed learning process, not a self-fulfilling and self-blinding presumption that preempts learning and perpetuates ignorance of other stakeholders instead of understanding them—not a result of name-calling, but one of sensitive, practical recognition.

When parties make claims of "rights," too, similar considerations come into play. Sometimes those claims will be merely strategic, rhetorical ploys as elements of power plays; sometimes those claims will seek to invoke actual legal

Table 4.1 Pitfalls When Our Presumptions and Presentations of Value Differences
          Interact

	Perez Is Expressing Deep Value Commitments	or	Perez Is Posturing: Framing Interests as Deep Values
Jones sees Perez as *expressing deep values*	*Result:* A deep value dispute requiring mutual recognition and practical, collaborative problem-solving		*Result:* An inefficient, short-sighted, hampered negotiation with mutually poor compromises
or			
Jones sees Perez as *posturing: treating preferences as though they were deep values*	*Result:* Anger, escalation, and resentment preempting recognition and problem-solving		*Result:* Positional bargaining

entitlements. Just as no one should give up basic rights—or the ability to consult legal counsel, or other experts—because they join a participatory or mediated process, though, no one should automatically believe or defer to every claim to "rights." Like value claims, rights claims need to be *explored* by parties in light of available evidence, neither dismissed out of hand nor gullibly granted.

Suspecting that our value differences are irreconcilable, we need to look and see, to try to learn more to see if we can discover new opportunities for fruitful negotiation. If we discover those new opportunities, so much the better. If we discover that we can craft no concrete practical moves that we find mutually desirable and acceptable, then we can turn to our alternatives, the courts or other forms of political pressure. The crucial point here is that value irreconcilability can be a real outcome, but it should be an outcome discovered through a real process of searching for alternatives; it should not be a self-fulfilling presumption, tempting as it may be, that threatens to answer questions before they are asked, that threatens to bury desirable options rather than to create them together. Faced with value differences, we may well find, if we look and see, probe more and presume less, that even as we differ deeply on basic beliefs about abortion, for example, we might still come to agree upon specific practical actions—protecting children's well-being, for example—that enable us to address many of the issues that continue to confront us.

Part Three

From Venting and Posturing to Learning and Proposing

CHAPTER FIVE

Practical Consensus Building in the Face of Deep Value Differences: Negotiating HIV/AIDS Prevention

Let's turn now to examine a striking case of bottom-up participation and mediation practice that involved substantial differences of race, religion, sexuality, and politics. How might skillful mediators bring deeply differing parties together and through those confident and self-fulfilling presumptions that *"They'll* never agree to anything that we would agree to!"? We will consider carefully the account of community planner-turned-professional-mediator Mike Hughes, reflecting upon his work of convening discussions to set HIV/AIDS funding priorities in Colorado, discussions involving deeply religious parties and ACT-UP activists in a process they called "Coloradoans Working Together" (Hughes 1999).[1]

Working to formulate and build a broad-based consensus on HIV/AIDS funding priorities for federal monies to come through the state health department in Colorado, Hughes facilitated and mediated a large and diverse group of citizens that included health officials, straight and gay activists, members of quite conservative Christian religious organizations, blacks, Latinos, and whites, employed and unemployed. The discussion involved sixty or more participants—at regular meetings over many months.

After early difficulties recognizing speakers in turn and keeping discussions moving forward with that many people in the room, Hughes and his co-mediator adapted a technique to improve the quality of the group's discussions. He explains,

> What we decided to do was put a little table in the center of the room and put four chairs at that table, and then we made concentric circles of chairs around those four with some aisles so you could get from the back of the room up to the front.
>
> Basically, we said to the group when they walked in… "We heard you. We know the last meeting didn't work very well in terms of this facilitation thing. So here it is. We're going to try something absolutely different. If this doesn't work, we'll try something else. Here's how it goes:

"When we are ready to open discussion on a topic, then I will clearly make the transition as the facilitator, and co-facilitator Derek will do that as well: 'Now it's time for discussion.' We will then get out of the way. If you've got something to say, come sit in a chair. There are four chairs, four of you can talk with one another, loud enough so we can all hear it. When you're done, you get out of the chair. If you see somebody waiting, get out of the chair and make room for them. But *you* are now in charge of the dialogue, and we're not going to facilitate this part. Then when we think that the discussion has wound itself to some sort of conclusion, or we want to ask if you have come to some consensus, or if you've explored it enough or whatever, then we'll interject ourselves as the facilitators to move the process on. But when it's time to talk, it's time to talk and you don't have to be called on, you don't have to look to me to call on you. You don't have to raise your hand. You just have to come talk."

They loved it. They took to it both because it was clear that we were going to be responsive to them and because it was just a much smarter structure. It was a much more effective way for them to dialogue.

By enabling freer and more interactive discussions, including, as we shall see, vivid and moving personal stories too, this technique helped with the discussion of issues—up to a certain point. Then the going got tougher. After generating thirteen clusters of needs, crafted down from 150 or more after many facilitated sessions, one of the issues of very basic value differences arose at the center of the discussions. Hughes tells us,

We're in the discussion. We're at the table. This wonderful participant—he was just brilliant—came into the circle, and he sat down and he said, "Here's a need that is missing. There is a need to shift the discussion of AIDS in Colorado from a *moral issue* to a *public health issue,* and I refuse to participate in moving this plan forward until we wrestle with that."

He went into this eloquent speech about how these moral barriers to effective AIDS education were killing people, and that we were putting in place these moral objections and the effect was that people were dying. The whole room was just captivated. He was really angry.

Other people came to the table. They just ran to the table and started talking with him. The folks from Focus on the Family and from Coloradoans for Family Values came and sat at the table and talked about why for them, this *was* a moral issue and what that meant to them and why they believed that.

The discussion got really intense. It was amazing. As people came to the table to respond to the opening comment, it was clear that people had been moved by the depth of feeling. So people came to the table with a new intensity. So the discussion got very intense, very quickly. Other people came up and they started to tell their story, "From my point of view, here's why I think we have to remove those barriers." Or: "From my point of view, here's why this is a moral issue."

Faced with some parties referring to basic moral beliefs and others adamantly refusing to accept those beliefs, Hughes kept going, and his practice has a great deal to teach us. As he continues, he tells us how important the prior ground rules, precedents, and track record of the group were:

> The thing that was so amazing is that as it got more and more intense, it didn't break any of the ground rules that we'd established. People were speaking to one another respectfully. The language was really appropriate. They were really doing their best to listen to one another. We really didn't have to do very much. Both the work that they had done thus far as a group, and the setting in which they were communicating, worked.
>
> I have to say that the person who had started this had started it in a way that was so captivating and so, it was on such a high level that the discussion stayed pretty much on that level. It was clear that he felt very strongly, and he had framed it in a way that was so clearly aimed at preventing people from being killed by this disease, and it wasn't accusatory. It wasn't blaming. He didn't denigrate the Amendment Two people or folks who really had put those moral barriers in place.

Hughes teaches us here about the importance of respect and recognition, even—or especially!—when deep value differences divide parties. Here the advocate was not accusatory, not blaming, not denigrating, thus not attacking the other parties personally, rather than confronting the problems of life and death at hand. As Hughes goes on, he shows us how the HIV/AIDS conversation focused upon issues and practical options, not personal defensiveness or attacks:

> He simply said, "Amendment Two and the moral barriers are in place and because they're in place, this is the effect." It was depersonalized, in the sense meaning "not accusatory." But it was clearly personal from his own point of view. So it was very much this "I message." This is how "I" see it. It didn't really ascribe any kind of blame or really point any fingers or anything that could have inflamed the discussion. So other people came and just really spoke from their own point of view, just sort of following him, so it really set the right tone.
>
> We hit another issue later on though, where people stood up and said, "All of you people…" It was a racial issue, "You white people all are…" The stereotypes flew out, and the room exploded. But that's what didn't happen on this one: He didn't say, "All you religious bigots…all you Bible thumpers…"
>
> He could have done that. But he didn't. He said, "These barriers are in place." He didn't say who put them there. He didn't point any fingers or make any inflammatory statements. He said, "They exist and here's the effect of their existing." So it didn't slap anyone. He really just spoke from his own beliefs and his own anger and his own pain at seeing people that he cares about die from this thing. It was emotionally very powerful.

Hughes tells us here that the discussion was personal, deeply felt, "emotionally very powerful"—but not personally aggressive, hateful, or verbally violent. The disagreements were fundamental, but the parties were indeed attacking what they took to be the problems at hand; they were not attacking one another personally. Indeed, because they respected their common ground rules—speaking one at a time, respecting each other, using nonincendiary language, avoiding personal attacks—and maintained a safe place in which to disagree, even fundamentally, they were able to move ahead, Hughes shows us, even when moving ahead meant taking exactly opposite views from one another:

> Part of the ensuing discussion was, "Well, those aren't the facts. In fact, why people are dying is because we can't, in our culture, frame these things in moral terms, because we're losing the moral ground underneath us."
>
> So there were people who took exactly the opposite point of view. They said, "No, you don't understand, this must become a moral issue. If it isn't a moral issue, people will continue to behave in ways that put them in danger. It's when you have the moral underpinnings to keep you from behaving in those ways, *that's* when people won't die."
>
> So they took exactly the same moral question and went 180 degrees around and said, "No, no, no—this *has* to be a moral issue. That's the point." But they kept from becoming confrontational.

Hughes then continued with a familiar move of mediators and facilitators, bringing the very lack of consensus to the group for discussion and possible problem solving. Trying to make progress in the face of this deep disagreement led to a mediation within a mediation. Lacking forward movement in the discussion here, Hughes and his co-mediator turned to a mechanism the group had already discussed:

> We had ground rules about conflict resolution. "When we can't resolve an issue within the group, we're going to do something about that." The "something" was a two-party—or maybe slightly more than two-party—mediation. That was their conflict resolution system for the larger group's discussions. That's when we said, "Well, your dispute resolution system says, 'Let's mediate it.'"
>
> So, I said what I would do—between this session and the next: "I will convene a mediation of hopefully two, but maybe a couple more than that, [people] from all points of view on this one, and we will sit down and we will mediate in a different setting and bring back to the group the recommendation."
>
> So I put together a four-person mediation: The person who had presented the issue, a person from Coloradoans for Family Values, and one person to support each of them in their point of view.

It was really interesting. The person from Coloradoans for Family Values said, "I don't want to do it. I don't want to do this with just two parties. I want someone else to come with me, and here's who I want to come."

So then I went back to the person who presented the issue and said, "Looks like it might be more than two, is that okay with you? And if so, who do you want to come?" So it was clear it wasn't going to be two on one. We made it two and two. Luckily, the person from Coloradoans for Family Values selected someone from an organization called "His Heart" (a Christian organization that cares for people with AIDS). The particular person from this organization had entered in the discussion in a very moderate way. The person who presented the issue, from the Colorado AIDS Project, then selected a colleague who also was a very collaborative, very calm presence in the group. They both made the wisest choice for who to get.

Hughes has not helped the group to avoid or suppress the value conflict, but he has worked to help the group face that value conflict more efficiently. Turning to a mediation alongside the larger discussions, Hughes shows us other crucial considerations in handling deep moral disagreements: the importance of selecting spokespeople with commitment, experience, and the ability to work with others, who will have a "calm presence" in a group when emotions run high, when feelings run deep, and of course when time runs short! Hughes teaches us a crucial lesson here: far from being overshadowed by the depth of value disagreements, the personal particulars of negotiators matter a great deal, perhaps all the more as matters of personal integrity, identity, reputation, honor, and sanctity are involved—for these qualities allow parties to distrust less and focus more, to parry less and listen more carefully, learning practically as they go. Hughes goes on, giving away the end of this short story before he explains how he got there:

It was great. Brilliant. So I...got the four of them to agree to sit down together in a room. The five of us went and sat down and did a mediation, and we developed language that the four of them could live with....What I was able to get them to focus on was language for the plan that would say something on this subject that all four of them, and then hopefully the whole group, could agree to. We'd actually modeled this already, because at this stage we'd already worked through the other thirteen needs and had wordsmithed the language together as a group.

So, it was really clear that what we were doing was writing a plan. So if we stayed focused on, "Well then, what words can we use in the plan to say this in a way that everyone can live with?" it would lift it out of, "I have to change your mind about this," and become, "Well, what words can we find together?"

So it was that shift from confrontation to collaboratively developing language that everyone could accept in the plan. That was the shift we had to make. That was the task they were willing to accept....So they did it. We walked out of that mediation after two hours with a message that all four of them agreed to.

Hughes does not suggest that anyone was a pushover here, that anyone gave up any issue of value commitment or any issue of difference in belief. Quite the contrary. The success of the mediation grew from a particular goal: *not to reconcile the parties' beliefs, but to enable the parties' practical agreement on a detailed option.* The mini-mediation here created an agreement on a public statement, a plan, in effect a public promise that would represent the agreement and consent of all the parties.

So this was no matter of mere "words"; they were writing a formal planning document that they expected to shape the policy and resource allocation of the state health department. Bringing together deeply divided parties, Hughes teaches us here about what we can call *the practical wisdom of mediation:* achieving a working agreement not on paradigms, value systems, or belief systems but on practical options to support together. But how did Hughes do this? He continues, showing us crucially the importance once again of ground rules, safety, mutual respect, and recognition despite intense moral disagreement:

We had gone into the room, and basically I took the whole macro process that we were using for the larger group and just compressed it into the two hours. I said, "We're going to begin at the beginning. Let's make sure we all know one another."

We did introductions. And I said, "Okay, let's get the ground rules clear. This two-hour session will work if: You talk one at a time. You respect one another. You use language that's appropriate. You avoid personal attacks..." I just laid out a whole lot of ground rules for how careful we were going to have to be with the way we spoke to each other. So we went through ground rules, and I had laid out a process.

I said, "I'm going to ask each of you to talk about why this wording is important to you, so that you really can become educated with one another about why this issue is so important. And having done that, I'm going to ask you for some options that will meet those needs, and then, we're going to problem-solve, to see if we can't find an option that you all can live with."

Here Hughes lucidly recapitulates a crisp and instructive practical approach. Rather than minimizing any disagreement, he respects it and makes the case for a shared process of discussion that will allow each party to "educate" others about why "this issue is so important." But he does more too. Acknowledging difference and conflict, acknowledging the temptations to engage in personal attacks, stressing "how careful we were going to have to be with the way we spoke to each other," he points a way forward as well. He shapes the parties' expectations: we're here to surface the important values and interests we want to satisfy and to craft options that will do that as best we can—mediation is not "anything goes." He tells the parties that even with their disagreements, moral, religious, and political as they may be—one rejecting another's sexuality as immoral, one arguing for the autonomy and dignity of that sexuality—he will ask them in the mediation process to propose concrete options about the issues at hand.

Hughes makes several subtle and crucial points here. He asks the parties not to change each other's beliefs or commitments; he does not reduce mediation to persuasion. Instead, he asks them to consider options that they find acceptable, within their value systems, for the issue before them. Hughes tells us, as many mediators do, that he had been listening not just to what the parties disagreed about, but to what they both cared about as well, even if they might express those interests in radically different ways. He goes on:

> What I knew to be underneath the wording was a set of concerns and a set of interests that, in fact, all four of them could respect and to some degree hold in common: to stop this disease from spreading. They clearly had that concern in common. So I could remind them that, although they disagreed about the morality, they did agree about the effect that this conflict was having. They really *both* had said, "If we can't get past this, can't figure out how to work this out, more people are going to get sick."
>
> So I had to get them back to that and help them remind each other that they had a lot more in common than perhaps they believed, and that would form the basis for coming up with wording they could live with. I knew that unless they really saw that they ultimately were aiming at the same thing, just aiming at it in absolutely opposite ways, that they were just going to keep aiming in opposite ways, and that they would not find language that the other one would find acceptable. So seeing that they had a mutual interest in getting a plan that each of their constituencies could accept was obviously the key.

Hughes turns once more here to that "practical wisdom of mediation," the recognition that disputes may be settled practically by crafting a working agreement on actual options that nevertheless allows the parties to *continue to honor their differing fundamental values.* The practical wisdom of mediation involves knowing what does *not* need to change, while the process enables participants to climb down from the abstract peaks of value systems and paradigms, general worldviews and recipes, to cook together, to knead the dough together of a collaborative discussion of real options that they can jointly endorse and implement. Hughes tells the story this way:

> Once all four of them had heard from the others that they really did want a plan that worked, a plan that prevented the spread of the illness, then it became a joint task, jointly shared, jointly worked on—and they dropped the pretense of confrontation long enough to find that they could in fact find words for the plan that would work for both sides—*and find that they didn't have to give up their points of view*—so that they could continue to agree to disagree about the things they clearly would never let go of with one another. So that was part of it too, separating out what they weren't going to change, that they weren't going to change the other side, but that they had to write a document that they both could live with. That was much simpler. So I had to focus them on that.
>
> I also have to say that the four of them were just smart, and that was a key— that they were able to be creative and clever with the wording and find things that let them say, "Yeah, I can live with it if you say it like that," while at the same time they clearly were not all that happy to be sitting in a room together...
>
> The first sentence they agreed to was, "There is a need to remove moral objections to HIV prevention and education messages that are appropriate to the target community." Now that's a mushy way of saying what they wanted to say. But then they followed it with, "For communities that include members with a range of moral perspectives, HIV prevention methods need to be appropriate to that range of moral perspectives by presenting multiple prevention messages."
>
> It was messy. But if you really dig under it, what it says is, "Not everybody in any 'community' is going to share every moral perspective." That was pretty obvious to everybody. So if you were going to give people prevention messages, they had to match that range of moral points of view and present multiple options or multiple messages that lined up with those moral perspectives. The only way that we could get the gay rights activists to accept sentences two and three was if sentence number *one* was there, which was, "There is a need to remove moral objections to messages that are appropriate to the target community."
>
> Now, they actually talked about, "Well, in 'real life,' what does that mean?"
>
> Well, it means that you can go into a gay bar and use sexually explicit material to educate people about HIV/AIDS. Why? Because in a gay bar, that's not outside the moral bounds. If you go into an establishment like that, it's not outside the moral parameters in that setting to use sexually explicit material. But if you go into schools, and you've got kids who come from a fundamental Christian point of view and whose parents would be uncomfortable with sexually explicit material, we're going to have to work really hard to present a range of messages that cover the moral perspective and are really appropriate across the spectrum of that community.
>
> So that's the kind of thing they thought would be allowed under this kind of wording. So in two hours they hammered this out: Three sentences.

But the story did not end there, of course. As the mini-mediation wound up, their work was immediately threatened. Hughes describes what happened as humorous, but the event shows us again the importance of bounding discussions, not letting "anything go," maintaining the practical wisdom to focus upon a working agreement and accommodation, instead of debating more abstract and general *beliefs* and *values:*

> It got tough only at the very end, because once I said, "Look, you're all done. The mediation's over: Hurray for you. You get to go back to the group and say, 'We have a draft for you.' Now let's all go home," we stood around and started talking about whether being gay is a lifestyle or not. Then they hit on the word "lifestyle," and they started to have an argument.
>
> It was the funniest thing, and I said, "Excuse me. I really think this is a mistake for you to continue this conversation. This ain't going very well. I think you should get in your cars and go home."
>
> They laughed and shook hands. They said, "You know, you're right. This isn't a helpful conversation for us to have. We did well today. Let's go home."
>
> So it only got tense when the meeting was over....They were not going out for a beer afterwards, I can tell you that. It was really clear that they respected the effort that the other side was making, that they respected that other points of view were possible, and yet they couldn't go much beyond that. But that's awfully far. It certainly is a lot further than the debate about these subjects that I've seen elsewhere in Colorado.

As Hughes argues, that outcome is indeed "awfully far," and we do well to learn from this example. The parties "were not going out for a beer afterwards," so their resulting relationships were anything but harmonious. They had reached a workable and practical result, but they had not compromised their beliefs, values, or commitments. They immediately began to argue once they left the confines of the facilitated conversation, but they recognized themselves that they had made progress and that despite many remaining differences, that progress mattered: "You're right....We did well today. Let's go home."

They respected one another's efforts, and they reached a practical agreement, but they did not change one another's beliefs. They did not change one another's deep values. They did not reconcile belief systems or paradigms or commitments, and they had the wisdom, cultivated by a carefully facilitated and mediated process, to understand that their immediate practical task was done: they had achieved a working accommodation on practical options so that their practice together—their being able to live with the results together rather than turn to violence—that practical agreement, accommodation, or consensus building mattered far more in this circumstance than any more general and abstract doctrinal discussions. Their work was successfully completed, far short of transforming cultures or belief systems, but far beyond personal attacks and destructive sniping, and far beyond impasse in the face of making practical recommendations to the state health department.

Lessons from the HIV/AIDS Priority-Setting Case

Hughes's work in the HIV/AIDS priority setting case illustrates a series of lessons for anyone working in the face of deep value differences. Consider several in turn.

To begin, deep value differences themselves were respected and engaged but neither compromised nor sacrificed in the HIV case. Parties did not hide those differences, and yet they were still able to reach practical agreements without compromising their basic values. This further supports, as perfectly reasonable, the popular distrust of anyone promising to reconcile deep value differences—and change people's identities along the way! Hughes shows strikingly that *even when deep value differences exist* and are *not* negotiable, practical opportunities for mediated participation, collaborative action, and actual joint gains may *still* exist—and so we should be careful not to preempt these real opportunities with our facile presumptions that others "will never agree to anything we'd want."

Like other facilitators, mediators, and community leaders too, Hughes used shared ground rules ("take turns," "no personal attacks," and so on) to protect the autonomy and safety of each party (Kolb and Associates 1994, Forester and Weiser 1996). Even though the parties had deep moral disagreements, they were able to negotiate successfully without coercion.

Notice that the parties brought deep differences, but they were able to leave, to walk away, as well. Their agreement appeared to be fully voluntary—they were not agreeing because they lacked alternatives. Their differences notwithstanding, the parties were able to craft working agreements about concrete priority setting; they were able to *specify* needs rather than to *generalize* about value doctrines!

Hughes also helps us to appreciate the value of stakeholder representation as it helped to formulate well-crafted, locally appropriate options. We hardly know of the relative numbers of constituents; we see instead that the mediation process enabled parties to devise specific agreements that responded to their interests, interests that might well have been more contentiously and divisively articulated by lobbyists, voting publics in referenda, or particularly well-organized constituencies applying pressure to politicians for "results."

This HIV case also suggests that even as complex moral differences can characterize parties' mutual suspicions and distrust, nevertheless those parties can still resolve concrete issues even when no simple economic or monetary trades are possible. Crucially important to creating workable agreements here was a careful process that allowed parties to learn about each other's different sensitivities, their interests, and their limits—a process that enabled parties also to craft options that responded substantively to the diverse interests represented in the process, even if weakly organized outside of that process.

Hughes shows us, too, the importance of personal style and lack of posturing, on both the parts of the mediators and the parties, in the HIV/AIDS negotiation. He teaches us that the success and failure of a mediated process will depend on very much more than the simple existence of deep value differences, moral or otherwise. Hughes makes clear that his parties were not pushovers; they did not compromise; they did not cave; they did not sell out their constituencies or betray the faith of those constituencies. But they did not posture unduly either, taking positions for the sake of taking them, rather than trying to reach the ends they cared about. Value differences certainly do matter, Hughes suggests, and he shows how parties can both respect and handle those differences as they abide by ground rules, listen carefully, think creatively, and articulate and work to satisfy their own interests effectively too.[2]

Not least of all, Hughes helps us recognize the wisdom of not being blinded by our self-fulfilling presumptions of others. Given deep differences, parties on all sides might be tempted to think, "They'll never talk to us," but they may well be wrong, and the job of the mediator, community leader, planner, or manager is surely to provide the context, occasion, and safe process in which parties can actually meet and break bread and speak to one another, listen and learn from and invent options with one another.

Perhaps most importantly, Mike Hughes's story illustrates this "moral" about the practical wisdom of mediation in the face of "fundamental value differences": we should *not* expect parties to reconcile their *general* value systems—but we should instead explore how the same parties might still effectively resolve practical disputes by crafting very *specific*, implementable options. Hughes's story suggests that we need to anticipate and avoid falling into *traps of our own misplaced abstraction:* we jump too quickly to misleading conclusions—we think that because we can't agree about religious doctrine, we won't be able to agree to lower a local speed limit, or to increase nurses' salaries, or to lower student-teacher ratios or to locate stop signs here, and so on. To avoid these traps, we need to focus far less on debating abstract values and their rationalizations, focus less on belief systems and more on practical interests, counteract self-fulfilling stereotypes and labels—and we need to help parties actually to meet, listen, learn, and decide together where they can and where they cannot make progress.

Can Practical Wisdom Be Practical in the Face of Deep Value Differences?

Hughes's example is deceptively simple. It suggests that participatory processes that involve deep value disagreements would do well to incorporate elements of more ordinary mediation practice. Skillful mediation can help disputing parties with deep differences to live together peacefully, even if not harmoniously, Hughes shows us. What more might community leaders, public administrators, planners, and others learn here about facing disputes that involve such value disagreements?

As mediators assess a conflict, they assess parties' willingness to meet and explore issues with practical ground rules in place, for without early agreements on ground rules that provide a newly created "safe space" for conversation, deliberation, and negotiation, parties who tell their stories may only humiliate and antagonize one another further. But with these agreed upon ground rules—as Hughes suggests, for example, "Take turns talking," "No personal attacks," "Listen to one another respectfully," and so on—parties with deep value conflicts can begin to recognize one another's history and concerns and start to explore new options for going on together. Convening discussions and maintaining such "safe conversational spaces"—in which conflicting parties can listen to and probe each other's stories without fears of being attacked—remains an essential part of facilitators,' mediators,' and community leaders' jobs, especially when deep value conflicts are at stake.

So parties can find themselves surprised and learning too as they listen to one another's stories. Even though participants begin by presuming a great deal about issues and other parties, too, they often find much that they did not know before. They often learn, for example, about new issues, environmental and political changes, new uncertainties and opportunities—and that other parties may not be as simple, thick-headed, and intransigent as they might have seemed.

In plenary and small group discussions, through formal fact-finding and informal meals, perhaps less through direct questions than indirect explorations, too, facilitators, mediators, and community leaders can create rich and varied opportunities for parties to learn (Forester 1999a). Many forms of media and representation—poetry and song, film and slide presentations, dramatic enactments and field trips, expert judgment and stories within other stories—can help parties teach each other here. In participatory and mediated negotiation processes, apparently innocuous stories reveal a great deal, and parties who do not listen well risk missing the action—and the satisfaction of seizing opportunities. Barely glimpsing in the beginning what they still need to know, parties in effective mediations come to learn about the specifics rather than the generalities of the issues at hand. They learn about *detail, not doctrine*—about practical proposals, not public propaganda. When they begin to do that, the parties can explore specific options together: they can build working agreements about practical steps forward—instead of pursuing far more vague statements of allegiance to abstract principles or worldviews.

When parties learn about the *specific, detailed concerns* of the other parties, they learn that some of those concerns are much easier to satisfy than others. They learn, crucially, that what's most important for another party may be far less important for them—and vice versa. With that understood, they learn that they can make offers that cost themselves little even as they benefit others significantly. They learn, as Lawrence Susskind has so often stressed, that they can devise options that create mutual gains. Instead of settling for equally devastating compromises, they can create packages of *trades* that actually satisfy the concerns and interests that they have brought to the table. By getting to specifics—realizing the practical wisdom of mediation by *avoiding the fallacy of misplaced abstraction*—parties in contentious participatory processes can produce not poor compromises but significant gains that satisfy their differing interests, even in the face of broader, deep, and significant differences.

When parties tell stories, they can say a good deal about themselves, too, their social relationships and histories, their cares and fears. Telling pointed stories, they are not entertaining, not just relating events that matter, but disclosing their own identities too, and with those identities, they reveal the senses of what they honor, what they owe to their constituents or elderly or ancestors, what they find incidental and what they find sacred. In the storytelling of parties, we can risk ignoring and dismissing their senses of historical identity or we can recognize and learn from them. So critically attentive parties listen to the person speaking as well as to their words, to the silences, cadences, and tone of what's said and done, and to whatever's said most emphatically and dramatically (Forester 1989).

As a result, productive participatory processes may be impossible unless the person-to-person, party-to-party work of acknowledging one another's concerns precedes the work of problem solving. As long as you're calling me a stupid jerk, I'm going to find it very hard to sit down with you to solve a problem about which you feel strongly. Once mediators make it possible for parties to agree to disagree as they come together to learn about each others' concerns, though, once parties begin to recognize that they both inherit complex histories, that they both have real problems that worry them, then and only then can they begin to work together to solve their own problems effectively. When the loudly declared values of the participants differ significantly, the facilitators, mediators, or third party helpers need to work to create opportunities for the parties' mutual listening and recognition. In this work of learning about issues and one another, parties will distinguish between peripheral and central concerns. They will be more able to put aside what need not be settled in favor of focusing on practical strategies now. Recognizing their different histories of commitment, struggle, and often loss, parties can together come to honor the past *and* actually explore how to create their futures too.

Lastly, then, after assessment, and the mutual recognition that convening parties together makes possible, comes exploration, listening, learning, invention, proposals, and creative work: not compromise, not betrayal of commitments, not giving up, but *crafting practical options that work for both parties*. The developer singing the virtues of private property may still cluster units to protect revenues, even as deeply committed open-space advocates press to protect environmental quality—all because clustering of the units might provide a practical option that works to satisfy both parties. The rule here is simple but powerful: stress learning, not solution. Probe practical options; don't presume shabby outcomes. Learn about what each party wishes initially to do, given what *they presume* now about their options, and then use a safe, protected, mediated process to create and explore new strategies and new options.

With skilled facilitation and mediation—essentially a form of wise public management, the wisdom to focus on the specifics of practice rather than on the abstractions of worldviews—participatory governance and outcome-oriented deliberations in the face of deep value conflicts can empower parties to act together rather than resign them to impasse or business as usual. How to do it? In a nutshell:

Don't promise the "resolution of value conflicts" in the case at hand because this will, quite rightly, sound like one part fantasy, one part snake oil to much of the concerned public. Instead, *do* promise joint learning, better information, exploration of solutions, analysis of options, the testing of future working relationships, and possible provisions for renegotiation in the future. *Do* remember that the practical wisdom of mediation can produce mutually beneficial agreements about how to go on together, not a compromised deal betraying deep values but a real, workable, and mutually productive agreement on practical strategies to implement now.

CHAPTER SIX

Planning and Mediation, Participation and Posturing: What's a Facilitative Leader to Do?

Now, what about the theatrics of participation in community conflicts? Stakeholders posture and bluff, exaggerate and overdramatize demands, and often withhold and hide valuable information. Everyone sees high stakes—our land, my house, the environment, our health—and many don't hesitate to say so. If community leaders, public officials, or planners try to encourage more inclusive participatory processes, they will likely find these kinds of rhetorical games "in their faces," bewildering if not expected, and hardly just a game. How can those hoping to foster inclusion and participation respond when many of those in contentious public meetings seem mainly committed to announcing and defending their party line?

The community planning and public policy literature provides little help here. If we can expect not just random political rhetoric and name-calling in contentious situations, but regular patterns of misrepresentation or exaggeration of what people really care about, we should certainly explore politically and ethically realistic strategies of response.

So let's try to learn from those facing these problems all the time, from facilitators and mediators of public disputes who work in between diverse and conflicting, often suspicious and impatient stakeholders—old residents, new residents, developers, environmental groups, industrial interests, agency representatives, and still others, for example. Like some planners and public managers, too, these facilitators and mediators, these *facilitative leaders*, seek viable, practical working agreements to satisfy stakeholders' interests and provide the basis for sound plans and even public policies.[1]

Working in the face of long-standing public conflicts to try to resolve specific disputes, though, these mediators can say the strangest things. They suggest, in several different ways, that often intensely passionate parties somehow have not really thought thoroughly about their own interests. They say that even calling mediation, "mediation" might sometimes hurt and not help participatory, dispute-resolving processes. They say that faced with bitterly opposed parties, they might begin discussions not directly with the concerns at hand, but quite indirectly—even, for example, with the stories of everyone's names.

Introduction: Difference, Distrust, and Posturing over Interests

Nevertheless, there's a method—or at least a set of strategies—to this madness, and the practice of public dispute mediators can provide us with rich lessons of practical judgment, practical wisdom, and hope for governance and planning in the face of expectable posturing and gamesmanship—in disputes over land uses, design, or environmental quality, for example. In politicized, emotional, and painful public conflicts, how can community leaders and planners learn to respond wisely and effectively? Let's begin with the kinds of problems that experienced mediators tell us they can face, and then we can consider their improvised responses.

Listen first to Jon Townsend, a mediator who's worked in the United States, Eastern Europe, and Central America:

> A mediator needs to think like a negotiator because that's what the parties are. The parties are negotiating, or their negotiation-communications have broken down. But they are negotiators nonetheless.
>
> I mean, they may be poor negotiators, i.e., poor communicators: they may not know their best interests. They may not know what their interests are—most people don't, because most people are positionally-based, right?
>
> Be it in formal negotiations, or, if you go to mediation, you usually take a position if you're a party. You usually don't think about what your interests are. (Forester and Weiser, 1996)

What can he mean? Surely parties in conflict have thought about their interests more than anyone. Townsend gives us a short lesson about *positional bargaining*— and the ways it blinds us. He explains,

> It's helpful for me to know what the difference is between an "interest" and an "issue."...In most cases, in my experience, be it negotiation or mediation, most people come to the table with their issues, but they really have not thought a lot about what their interests are.
>
> In my experience [he stresses the point] people don't negotiate on their interests. They hardly know their interests. They haven't thought about their interests. As a people, generally speaking, we don't think in terms of interests.

Perhaps an employee raises the issue of an increase in salary, Townsend had suggested, but he or she's really interested in having cash on hand soon, or in assuring greater financial security, or in gaining recognition for work well done. So Townsend goes on to stress the kind of listening, searching, and probing he must do:

> Because in my own experience people usually don't come to the table with their interests known,...I need to listen for that. So, I make assumptions, I guess, in the vast majority of cases when people say...that this is what they're fighting about—they sure are, but that's not the real reason. There's something else:...and we can work for issue resolution through interest satisfaction.
>
> We'll satisfy people's interests in order to get the issues resolved. So people still have to address those issues, because they're the surface things. That's what people aren't comfortable with, and that's what they're there for.
>
> But the end result may be—and probably and usually is—about something a little bit deeper, about their interests...

Townsend tells us a great deal here: not only can "issues" distract attention from and obscure "interests," and not only does he work to resolve issues—to address the concern with money or salary, for example—by seeking proposals to satisfy the deeper, underlying interests (in financial security, here), but at the same time he's warning us that if we're distracted by the literal rhetoric of issues and positions so that we fail to address underlying interests, we risk solving the wrong problems, jumping to conclusions about what needs to be done without assessing what parties really hope to satisfy.

So Townsend expects, he says, to hear a great deal about issues that bother people, but *he knows that people often mean and care about more than they say*—so that he will have to dig, to probe, to listen—to recognize what's at stake. But telling us to expect hidden interests is one thing; telling us what to do about such hidden or obscure interests is something else again. To make matters worse, this is the easy part—Townsend hasn't even mentioned that often in situations of conflict, distrusting, angry, and annoyed parties have reasons to be deliberately obscure about their interests and even to posture about those interests.

We can consider this problem in three parts. First, we'll listen closely to mediators who can teach us about the gamesmanship and posturing that community leaders, planners, and public managers ("facilitative leaders" more generally) can often expect to face. Second, we'll consider a way to map these problems of learning about parties' interests: is there any expectable political structure or logic, we'll ask, to make sense of how these challenges arise? Third, we'll listen once again to the accounts of the mediators: how do they handle these kinds of problems? All along the way, we will ask, "What lessons can we learn not only about these problems of posturing and exaggeration, but about our real possibilities of public governance, inclusive participation, and deliberation?"

Sources of Posturing and Gamesmanship that Limit Learning about Interests

Racial Conflict Fueling Presumptions

Listen first to a planning consultant who worked with a small California city's Hate Crimes Task Force to refocus its efforts. Trained at MIT, Karen Umemoto had done extensive geographic information systems (GIS) analysis of the distribution of race-bias hate crimes in the larger metropolitan region. In the face of gang violence and racially motivated murders, the city council—quite unsure itself about how to respond—appointed a task force, then renamed the "human relations commission," that turned out to be internally divided as well.

As she assisted the commission not only with data analysis but also with holding a retreat to reformulate its work, Umemoto faced challenges that community planners will find familiar. Racial tension and the prospects of racial conflict—which surfaced past pain and stirred up present fears—hardly helped to clarify parties' actual interests.

Umemoto tells us what she was getting into (Forester and Love, 2004: 10–11):

Anything can happen in these kinds of situations. After I read the results from the surveys of the Commission members, I realized that there were some deep differences—in terms of whether or not some people even think there's a problem of racial tensions and what the sources of those are. This was a microcosm of the nation in terms of the differences in ideology, in racial attitudes, and in backgrounds.

She goes on,

Half of this small city is flat, and half of it's on the mountain. You have million dollar homes on the mountain, and you have barrios, poor, very low income, highly dense neighborhoods and apartments down below—in certain neighborhoods below, not all of them. You have some people who just don't think race is a problem, that there isn't racism—even in the face of the murders and everything else—even on the Commission....

[P]eople have such different lived experiences and perceptions of the problem—and whether or not there even is a problem or not—that it's hard to get people into the same room face to face, confronting each other's beliefs and attitudes.

Umemoto tells us that her work in this city was hardly an exception to the rule. She'd spent years studying community development, and here, she says, was a "microcosm of the nation," in background, ideology, and attitude, and very practically in their differing "perceptions of the problem and whether or not there even is a problem," "even on the Commission"!

But Umemoto tells us more, too, about the conversation she expected at the retreat, and this discussion was unlikely to take the form of any sober, interest-based negotiation. She put it this way,

> In a situation where there's so much pain because people have experienced racism or the deaths of friends or family, it's a highly emotionally charged environment. People are so sensitive to the touch.
>
> And you could have the same type of polarized debates—some are saying, "The problem is that we have single mothers that don't watch over their kids, and that's why we have this problem," and, on the other hand, people will say, "It's poverty that's causing this, not single parent families."
>
> I was anticipating all of this from within the Commission itself—and all that was likely to come together at the retreat, through divergent views, experiences, attitudes, and points of view—converging in one room around an issue that was so highly sensitive.

So Umemoto tells us that she expected the commission members to raise lots of "issues" from their different points of view. Not only that, she expected a certain form of discussion that she would have to work with: what she called "polarized debates"—not exactly a culture of joint problem solving or collaborative planning.

Why'd she expect that? Our emotions matter, she reminds us, in case we needed the reminder: "In a situation where people have experienced racism or the deaths of friends or family, it's a highly emotionally charged environment. People are so sensitive..."

So Umemoto was walking into a situation that confronts community leaders, public officials, and public-serving professionals all over the country: the humiliations of racism haunt some of us just as they seem invisible to others of us, and the pain and polarization, the debates and the "emotionally charged environment" present everyday challenges to countless community members as well as to organizers and planners, officials, and many others who would like to see that practical community strategies and policy measures actually do address the real needs and interests of our cities' residents, residents of all colors and communities. We will have no real inclusion or participation, empowerment or learning about one another until we learn much more about race and ethnicity, racially and spatially shaped identities, and more.

Getting Stuck in "Problem Wars"

Listen now to planner-mediator Carl Moore, who has assisted cities and nonprofits alike with work ranging from dispute resolution to visioning and strategic planning.

Moore warns us of the "problem wars" that stakeholders can fall into. He also suggests a strategy of response, to which we'll return—but first, consider the challenges that he adds to Umemoto's. He tells us of his early work with a Midwestern municipality:

> One of the things I learned...was that to be grounded in people's problems was really risky when you're seeking change, because people like their problems more than they'll fess up to, and they'll stay connected to those problems. If you really want to get people to open up about how to change, you're far better off enlarging the shadow of the future than you are being traditionally analytic—in the Western civilization sense of that word—saying, "What's your problem? What are the causes? What are possible solutions?" So that was the start in my path of learning how to shift the focus to the future and enlarge that shadow.

I pressed the point and asked him, "What do you mean, 'People "like" their problems'?" and he smiled and replied,

> Well, they do. They stay attached to their problems and, moreover, often they're going to go on and on about their problems. They know how to talk about their problems so they get some kind of acceptance, some kind of social reward, because they've talked about their problems.
>
> Moving them off the problem, then, is really hard because there's the felt belief by parties...that "*If* I let your version of the problem be the basis for continuing the conversation, it's going to go in the direction *you* need for it to go, rather than the direction *I* need for it to go"—so people really can get into problem wars: "My problem is worse than your problem," or "My problem is the one we need to spend time on," or "My problem is the real reason we're here."

"What's the risk here?" I asked. He explained,

> The risk here is that you don't move off the problem. You don't get to some sense of what people can collectively do. Now, if you had limitless time, it's okay to go there. But if you don't have limitless time, and your goal is to make progress with the group, beginning with the problem can really stall you.

Moore doesn't refer here to situations as emotionally charged as Umemoto's, but he tells us, too, that when he meets with diverse stakeholders, he doesn't expect initially to find a peaceful kingdom of collaborators, a trusting and cooperative culture of citizens eager to have a heart-to-heart dialogue. Instead, he tells us that when time is short and resources are limited, feelings of vulnerability and "need" will pull in different directions.

Stakeholders may well worry, he suggests, "If I let *your* version of the problem be the basis for continuing the conversation, it's going to go in the direction *you need* for it to go rather than the direction *I need* for it to go." Here we see a politics of problem framing, a competition for the scarce good of attention, a competition for power in the form of agenda setting: the ways we set the "basis for continuing the conversation" and the "direction" it needs to go (and not to go).

Moore tells us much more here too. If convenors of participatory processes jump prematurely to a rational-analytic problem-solving approach, they may simply *go too fast* and miss the action: in their hurry to get answers they may forget that before problem solving comes problem framing. This after all is Planning 101 (and for engineering or science students, "Problem Set 101"): before we can ever solve a problem, we first have to figure out what the problem really is. What do we have here to work with? What's hidden—because of fear, distrust, or other strategic reasons? What's really important enough here to pay attention to?[2]

Moore adds an interactive politics to the complexity of the situation: problem statements, the rhetoric of problem stating, he warns us, will be partial, contested, and, too often, backward looking rather than future oriented. Like Umemoto, he says that emotions matter too: people often "stay attached to"—and may "go on and on about"—their problems, even if, in a participatory setting, this might not help a group to explore new steps, to make plans together, to act in new ways, to change. So Moore makes no argument against problem solving, but he's asking us to slow down, to pace ourselves, to worry more about problem framing, about listening critically beyond posturing or sound bites—if we're interested in planning for change, if we really do want not only to talk but to take programmatic or policy steps to resolve the problems we face.

Solution Wars: Drive-By, Hit-and-Run Solution Seeking

Listen now to a third dispute resolution practitioner, Peter Adler, involved with land use planning issues and conflicting rights to land. Having worked in the United States and a good deal in Southeast Asia, Adler reminds us that in contested settings, patience can be in short supply. As he tells us just a bit of what he hopes to accomplish, Adler warns us of political "instincts" that he (and we, too) can be up against. He puts it this way:

> I'm hoping...that people will move through a process in which they're acquiring new understandings and information about each other, about their views and their positions—that they will be able to stay pretty tolerant, for a while—as opposed to acting on the instincts which are to do drive-by solution seeking: Hit and run.
>
> It's drive-by: hit-and-run—"We're all busy people." "We've got to get it done." "There's a big political issue." "What's your solution? Ah, this is never going to work."

Adler then explained this group dynamic another way:

> Everyone comes in with their own predilections about what's the issue, what's the question, and what the answer's going to be....They all come in with answers. My assumption is that they come to a public issue like this land use case with a lot of answers—but we don't know the questions all the time.
>
> We don't know what question your answer is trying to answer exactly. It's a little bit like Jeopardy.
>
> So: you've got your answer. But what's the question that that's designed to answer?

He gives us an example: a case of conflict over indigenous Hawaiians' access rights to private lands—rights they claimed legally so they could continue to practice their traditional customs. He tells us,

> The banker says to me in our initial interviews, "I'm trying to figure out how to create stability in the mortgage documents that lenders give out...I want to figure out how to clear title from land and transfer titles, and I can't do it if there are these access rights encumberments and so on." So he comes in to the meetings with his answer to that.
>
> But, if I'm a native here, I might not even know what the banker's question is—all I hear is his answer.
>
> And similarly, all the banker's hearing is, "I want to come onto your property. I want to come onto any private property, any time I want."

So if Moore has warned us about "problem wars," Adler is warning us about solution wars. "We're all busy people," he hears, "We've got to get it done."

Here, too, we see limited time, limited framing of "the problems" at hand, and a temptation to do "drive-by," "hit and run" solution seeking. "They all come in with answers," he tells us, "with a lot of answers, but we don't know the questions all the time."

So as he faces parties' "predilections" about the issues, the questions, and the answers, Adler suggests, he can lose just those "new understandings and information about each other, about their views and their positions"—that he's trying to encourage so that the parties might together work to craft planning and policy measures that actually satisfy their interests.

Obstacles of Training and Meeting Design

So far, we have listened to practicing mediators and planners talk about "the parties"—whose fears and emotions, political struggles over agenda setting, and hit-and-run solution promoting seem to threaten participatory processes. But surely the planners and public officials might make a mess of things too—from the ways they talk to the ways they have traditionally structured public meetings.

Listen first to a community development planning consultant, Wendy Sarkissian, who's quite critical of her profession, then once more to Carl Moore, who extends her point. Sarkissian (Forester, 2004b) says,

> I think manipulation and humiliation and embarrassment are the stock and trade of many of my planning colleagues...Planning processes often get into those problems. They're elite and formal, and people speak in a secret language.
>
> The suits are on the stage. It's a cold drafty hall. The people are sitting in rows on the floor. You can't hear properly. There's no roving microphone.
>
> You feel like you're being toyed with, even when the planners are trying to get information to, or sell something to, people in a so-called "participatory process."
>
> So the planners can get in their own way. Sometimes, it's just plain ineptitude. I don't even think it's bad intentions often.

So much for ordinary "participation," Sarkissian suggests! Even with good intentions, she finds planners structuring processes in ways that lead to "manipulation, humiliation and embarrassment," to "elite and formal processes" with professionals who may appear to "speak in a secret language."

Moore adds to her observations:

Citizens…have been "civically dulled." There's a way in which representative democracy has invented ways for citizen participation that are antithetical to that participation. They turn people off, they make it so "peanuts" for people to engage in civic life that most people won't do it because they think it's going to be a meeting like those meetings that they once participated in and hated.

You can go to public hearings, or go participate in some kind of referendum that the city council is sponsoring, in order to see where an issue is. You'll see, you get people who come out only because they feel like they've got something to lose on that issue, and they feel strongly about it, and they're not polite to each other, and it's usually just not a very good experience for anyone. So consequently, most people don't want to engage—so they don't or won't.

Here Sarkissian and Moore tell us that participation means much more than having access, and much more, too, than having "voice," if "voice" simply means the ability to get up for three minutes in a public hearing and say what's on your mind—before the next person, to whom you won't be able to respond, takes his or her turn. They both point to political irony, if not tragedy and farce. Here are processes that promise to promote democratic participation and yet they seem, all too often, in the form of public hearings, to do just the opposite. They create settings in which citizens feel they have little, just "peanuts," to gain, in which they can wonder if they need to know another language, in which they wonder if they'll be "polite to each other," treated with respect, or instead be attacked by other "participants."

No wonder, Sarkissian and Moore both imply, many affected citizens "don't or won't" want to engage in participatory planning processes. How could these kinds of discouraging processes, after all, help them really to learn about anyone else's interests or actually help anyone else to learn about their interests? If participation too often means noise, aggression, and humiliation, anyone caring about the possibilities of democratic politics has a lot of work to do.

But these difficulties present us with practical challenges. Historically and institutionally shaped, they confront us not with metaphysical inevitabilities but with political tasks. So community leaders and organizers, mediators and planners alike must address these issues. As we shall see, Umemoto and Moore, Adler and Sarkissian bring a repertoire of approaches and strategies, of skills and insights, to anticipate and respond to these challenges.

Assessing Interests—Existing or Emergent—Masked by Posturing

These challenges pose practical *and* theoretical questions. Because we often judge planning and policy proposals by how well they might satisfy community members' real interests, we need to worry about the obstacles we face to learning about which interests can actually, and not only rhetorically, be at stake. If mutual posturing in a public negotiation results in agreements that satisfy the rhetorical games that the parties have played, but squander opportunities to meet real but still hidden interests, we have lose-lose agreements, lousy compromises, and only a greater burden on public resources. Gamesmanship and strategic posturing here lead neither to justice nor to community well-being, just to pathologies of strategic negotiations, negotiations gone bad. If our theories of governance, politics, or ethics don't help us out of these traps that quite expectable posturing can create in participatory processes, we need far better theories of governance or community planning as well as better practice (Hillier 2002, cf. Flyvbjerg 1998).

But mediators work to address just these problems of multistakeholder participation and negotiation—and because community activists and leaders, planners and public managers of many kinds face such interest-hiding posturing and gamesmanship all the time, those community leaders and planners can learn a good deal from probing accounts of mediators' real work. So turn now, first, to a mapping of these problems and then, second, to initial lessons that Umemoto and Moore, Adler and Sarkissian offer us here.

The Logic of Misrepresenting Stakeholders' Interests

We can array the difficulties of learning about parties' interests that we've considered so far in table 6.1. Consider the problems you face as a negotiator listening to other parties. You have your own interests and worries, and you have a sense of your priorities. You may not know the other parties terribly well, and even if you do, you may have reasons to wonder about how forthright they'll be in your negotiations. They're often worried about losing any more than they need to lose, and so are you.

This creates a familiar but perverse "negotiator's dilemma" (Lax and Sebenius 1987). If you play it safe by hiding information and posturing, and they do much the same, you can *both* do far more poorly than you otherwise might. But if you don't posture, you worry that you might be exploited. They have just the same worry. So you both posture, and you both do more poorly than you could have done. Such lose-lose outcomes seem all too easy to reach. This dilemma, of course, provides one compelling rationale for all those in community, state, and larger governance negotiations to look for mediators'

Table 6.1 Obstacles to Learning about Other Parties' Interests

	Parties Can Have Interests in		
	Relationships (between the parties)	or	Substance (negotiated by parties)
Parties deliberately and strategically misrepresent interests	Public hearings encourage posturing Humiliation silences weaker parties ("Secret language"; Sarkissian, Moore)		Exaggerating to extract gain or to avoid loss Problem wars to control agendas ("My problem is worse"; Moore)
Interests can be undisclosed because:	[Quadrant IV]		[Quadrant I]
parties define interests presumptively, contingently	[Quadrant III] Past fears frame hopes Parties presume identities Racism colors problem framing ("hard to get people into the same room face to face"; Umemoto)		[Quadrant II] "Predilections" regarding solutions Presuming answers Presuming joint inquiry is not possible ("drive-by solution seeking"; Adler)

assistance to avoid these problems. Here we can try to clarify the several obstacles we face as stakeholders trying to learn about others' actual interests.

As a stakeholder, you realize that the other party might have interests, not just in the substance of what you're negotiating (the budget or land use or new policy), but also in your ongoing relationship (they'd like you to be less threatening or to grandstand less in public, for example), and they can be more or less forthright about each of those kinds of interests (we'll call them "substantive" and "relationship-oriented"). For example, another stakeholder might exaggerate an interest in price or quantity or time in hopes of giving up less of some other "substantive" interest they care about. Or they might strike a pose of confidence or assurance in hopes of not appearing as vulnerable to you as they feel—and so they don't appear to be very interested in really working this out with you. So you, as a negotiator, can wonder what really to believe about their valuing of *either* their relationship with you or the substance of what you're after, or both.

These simple examples of exaggeration should remind us, too, of strategic bluffing—strategic actions designed to seek gains. We don't know what the other's interests are, in part because the other can act deliberately and strategically to misrepresent those interests, because they're afraid that if they tell us the truth, we'll exploit them. (Similarly, of course, we might have exactly the same fear about them—so we might misrepresent our own interests to them, and to others listening!)

To make matters worse, we can face still other obstacles to learning about their interests. We might find it difficult, for example, to explore possible cooperative arrangements not because they wouldn't be interested, but because they've presumed (from the tough way we've acted in past meetings, for example) that we would never even consider it—and so, of course, they haven't ever mentioned it in their public demands! Or we might find it difficult to learn about their interest in a piece of property—because the technology to assure its safety has not (yet) been made available. In these kinds of cases, we have trouble learning about their interests, not because they have *strategically* wished to misrepresent them, but because they act with historically informed *presumptions*—contingent, even tentative presumptions—about what's possible in the first place. Washington DC–based mediator Don Edwards captured the power of such presumption wonderfully once when he remarked to students, "If you don't think something's possible, you don't go looking for it!"

We have seen these distinct possibilities in table 6.1. Table 6.2, in contrast, portrays these difficulties of learning about interests as a list of obstacles, either strategic or presumptive, in four categories that correspond to table 6.1's quadrants.

These tables map regular, systematic obstacles that we can expect to arise in participatory settings. Because we can *expect* these obstacles, we should consider how we can *respond* practically to them—so we do better both in our day-to-day meetings and in the ways we design them in the first place!

Lines of Mediators' Responses: Practical Wisdom, Practical Judgment, and Hope

So let us turn now, having posed these diverse problems of participatory posturing—democratic dissembling, exaggerating, presuming, assuming, scheming, and worse—to provide at least an initial sense of how practicing mediators can face these problems. Again, because community leaders and pub-

Table 6.2 Obstacles to Learning about (Our Own or Others') Interests

I. Strategic Misrepresentation of Substantive Interests [NE Quadrant I]

1. We posture, misrepresent, and exaggerate some interests, and minimize others (the "problem wars" of "My problem is worse than yours").
2. We hide and suppress interests for fear of appearing weak or mistaken ("If I let *your* version of the problem be the basis for continuing the conversation," I'll suffer).
3. Our fears define our interests.
4. We try to win yesterday's war; a blame game defines our focus.

II. Presumptions of "Substance" Involving Complexity [SE Quadrant II]

5. We focus on positions and obscure interests ("predilections" about solutions).
6. We lump interests and don't tease them apart (answers presuming questions).
7. We follow conventions and let others speak/imagine for us (principal-agent).
8. We are unclear about our own priorities (perhaps due to fluid context).

III. Presumptions of Relationships Involving Contingencies [SW Quadrant III]

9. Expectations of safety or risk in discussions influence what we might consider (fear).
10. Past relationships foreclose options; evolving relationships allow new considerations (refuting the suspicion, "They'll never talk to us").
11. Evolving self: their or our interests can change (aging, maturing, losing others).
12. Changing technology makes new outcomes and interests possible; for example, better mobility.

IV. Strategic Misrepresentation of Relationship Interests [Quadrant IV]

13. In adversarial processes, as we interact defensively we fail to invent options to satisfy broader interests (zero-sum traps; public hearings).
14. In moderated but not mediated processes, we refute claims without probing ambiguity and specifying interests (formal procedures, secret languages, etc.).
15. In argumentative processes (without joint fact finding), exploring interests is difficult.
16. We can play to the audience, get locked in (having taken a position, e.g.).

lic officials, planners and managers can also confront just these problems of parties obscurely representing their interests (strategically or presumptively, or both), these community leaders and planners might listen carefully to mediators' reflections about ways to deal with these difficulties. In participatory settings, then, how can we think smarter about not being waylaid by posturing: what might we do?

Responding to the Strategic Structuring of Relationships

Let's begin with Peter Adler to see how he can work with parties when he knows that the framing and strategic structuring of participatory processes—the practical setting out, the "institutional design," of procedures and structuring of relationships—can produce just "those meetings that people have hated."

In the case he was discussing, working on access rights to private lands, he'd decided to frame the process not as "a mediation" at all but as "a study group." Adler says,

> I suggested...that we not call it anything to do with "mediation"—we do not call it anything about "facilitation"; that we not call it a "round table," which are all words I've used in many other settings...I said, "Let's have a study group."...
>
> If I called it "mediation," it sounds like there are deals to be made, and my sense after my initial interviews was, "We don't want to talk about deals. We want to try to think this thing through, and better understand the needs, the interests, the drivers, if you will, and the politics of this particular issue."

So what happened? Adler explained:

> One of the things that happens—as the conversation develops—is that a group like this gets on a learning curve together. It's "a study group."
>
> So, they're asking questions, and they're trying to frame questions together, which is nice because it means that we may get to some common answers downstream.
>
> It also gets them actively engaged in the information or data gathering...it helps them circle around a problem as a group.

So here, he says, his assessment interviews led him to convene the conflicting parties very deliberately as "a study group." Adler suggests how he tried to frame and design the process to shape the character of the conversation—let's not "talk about deals," "Let's better understand the needs, the interests...the politics of this particular issue." Let's frame the questions together "so we may get to some common answers downstream."

Responding to Presumptions about Substance

Now, remember, Adler had warned us that many parties enter discussions with strong presumptions about the problems at hand: "Everyone comes in with their own predilections about what's the issue, what's the question, and what the answer is going to be."

He then continued, "What I'm trying to do is defer that answer for a while and see if there are joint questions to which they can seek a joint answer, and set the stage for that over a period of time, over a period of meetings." So here Adler suggests that overconfidence in what he'd called "drive-by" solution seeking can give way to new questions, shared doubt about common uncertainties or vulnerabilities—What might the courts do next?—and then to joint inquiry to inform recommendations, or as he says, "joint answers." In the same interview he kept returning to a central question he'd put repeatedly to the group, "What information do we need to collect to address our issues?" What do we need to find out more about—what do we still need to know—to know how to act well? We will return to this crucial question below.

Responding to Presumptions about Relationships

But how can these mediators—or community leaders and others—work with, and then overcome, parties' strong initial presumptions about each other and what "they" really (or only) care about? Both Karen Umemoto and Peter Adler point here to the power of personal narratives to displace stereotypes and expectations. Listen, once more, first to Umemoto as she describes the results of a powerful exercise she used to elicit personal stories from members of the renamed hate crimes task force. She tells us,

> There was an African-American young man who was working for a church…and doing a lot of youth outreach, and some people had suspected that he was part of the problem, that he was fanning the animosities. He told a very moving story that showed that he was concerned in a very deep way about this issue and had something to offer in terms of solutions.
>
> Another person, who people thought was a bigot, who didn't care, shared their history which was apparently very different from what people thought that person's history was…
>
> One of the Latino women said, "I'm here because I don't believe in color and my boyfriend is black, and we go around everywhere in the city scared that something is going to happen to him or something is going to happen to me…"

Umemoto goes on,

> So people shared things about their history that helped them connect across the color lines….People were talking to each other. There was so much buzz after the exercise ended that people were shaking each other's hand and walking across the room to approach each other and thanking them for sharing their stories. People were feeling like they were included in this process.
>
> People who were formerly asked to sit in the chairs in the back were feeling that they were part of the process now, and others were feeling like, "Yeah, we should include these people in this process." So I was trusting that my decision to include them had been the right decision.

Adler echoes Umemoto's approach in a general yet practical way too. He says,

> In addition to getting them to loosen up, to slow down from the "drive-by" syndrome, I want them to have both a set of intellectual understandings and emotional understandings.
>
> Actually, it starts with the emotional side and then goes to the intellectual side—because that's part of having people talk about how this issue touches them personally, and kind of staying patient with that.
>
> Someone says, "You know my family goes up into the mountains and we gather...leaves for this particular customary ceremony."
>
> Or someone else says, "I'm a lawyer here, but you know what, I grew up in this community and it pains me that Native people hate me because I'm not a native."
>
> So stories start where people are personally, but I also don't want it to turn into personal therapy—I don't want to stay there, so really that's a jumping off place....I'm hoping that people will understand that this is not a just a theoretical problem, that it's a problem that touches them, touches people personally. The only way that you can get at that is by asking the question as innocently as you can and letting them talk...about how this issue comes into their life.

Even as he's warned us about turning storytelling into personal therapy, he says,

> I can say I found you can't go wrong by asking [how the problem touches them personally]. I mean, I've asked that all the time. "How's this issue come into your life?" and I can't remember a time when somebody's run away from that, done something wrong or bad...I just haven't had that experience. Usually it becomes revealing of things and humanizes discussion.

So Umemoto and Adler suggest several ways to help impatient and distrusting parties to move beyond their stereotypes of each other, to recognize much more clearly one another's concerns and fears, to build new respect and shared ownership in working groups—and so to learn together.

Responding to Posturing over Substance

But what now about those "problem wars," the parties' inclinations to get stuck in their own sound bites about their problems? Carl Moore had mentioned working to "enlarge the shadow of the future" as parties listened to one another, to move in part from a discussion of the past, as he put it, "to shift the focus to the future."

He goes on now, beginning with what he calls "the very definition" of his job, and then suggesting what he tries to do:

> When I work with a group, I want it to be a real productive experience for them...I have to decide how to frame the meeting—so that they feel safe enough to say what's on their mind—that's my primary goal—I mean it's the very definition of what my job is. So that usually means that I'll give a lot of thought to how people get into groups that are small enough for them to participate.

So, what does this mean practically? He has a lot to say:

> That means I might count them off into the groups so that they're not in the same group as their husband or wife, who's sitting next to them and causes them to behave in a formal, rather than spontaneous, way.
> It means having enough facilitators. It might mean having trained local people to be the facilitators, so that it's neighbors helping them participate.
> It means giving them time to think before asking them to speak, which is a cardinal tenet of most of the tools that I use. It means collecting ideas in some kind of serial turn-taking fashion usually, rather than letting those people who are clever about how to participate in groups just be clever.
> It means focusing, usually, on making sure you're clear about their ideas—rather than encouraging their argument over those ideas.

Moore's comment about "focusing, usually, on making sure you're clear about their ideas—rather than encouraging their argument over those ideas" bears special emphasis—for it stresses once more the difference between *moderating* a debate that encourages adversarial argument and mediating an interaction or meeting to solicit concerns and ideas for action, clarifying interests so that the parties themselves can then craft proposals, to "shift the focus to the future," to actually satisfy those interests. Moore put it this way:

> So, if I'm working with a group, and an idea comes up and I say to the group, "So what do you think of that idea?" I'm going to appeal to a very natural instinct that most of us have which is to be very quick to assess, but if I can hold off that quick assessment, I'm much more likely to get out ideas that would not have come out—because the assessment would have turned off some people from contributing their ideas....So,...I'll ask them, not "What do you think of that idea?," but "What does the idea mean?"

Conclusion

So we see that parties can often have trouble learning about one another's actual interests for at least four good reasons. Not only may parties strategically misrepresent their own or too quickly presume one another's interests, they may also focus narrowly on either *substance* or *relationships*—or do several of these in combination.

To respond to these difficulties, though, we now have four approaches to consider: (1) framing what we do to produce joint inquiry rather than "deals," (2) evoking stories to break down initial presumptions, (3) assessing uncertainties and information needs to clarify questions that move parties beyond their initial "hit-and-run" answers, and (4) structuring "time to think" to enlarge the shadow of the future rather than fueling debate. These approaches provide not recipes and easy answers but avenues for work in the face of what we might call the real democratic "messiness," if not the predictable democratic pathologies, of posturing, bluffing, and misrepresenting stakeholders' real interests.

In participatory settings, suspicion and fear, passionate presumptions and strategic posturing can all set the stage. But experienced mediators of public disputes face these problems all the time, and if we probe both their accounts of these problems, as well as their practical responses, we might learn how they have wrestled with these challenges, learning about interests beyond problem wars, beyond drive-by solution seeking, beyond public hearing gamesmanship, learning about interests even beyond racial stereotyping and fear. We might then come away with more than a glimpse of their practical wisdom, their practical judgments, and so with a better view of our own real possibilities too.[3]

Part Four

From Arguing to Inventing, from Presuming to Enabling Action

CHAPTER SEVEN

Making Public Participation in Governance Work: Distinguishing and Integrating Dialogue, Debate, and Negotiation

Dealing with differences in public life means facing many of the challenges of "public participation." But even if many applaud and only a few voice deep objections to public participation in governance, fewer still seem to know how to carry it out successfully in practice. So this chapter will examine a contentious environmental case in California to show how a skillfully mediated participatory process can provide instructive lessons to help us do better than we have.

In the face of long-standing, bitter conflict, even at the state level, we will see, mediated participation might enable conflicting parties to learn from one another, rechannel their deep suspicion into joint inquiry, and build relationships enabling them to explore practical options rather than simply to continue escalating demands and threats. Not least of all, we will see how in the face of conflict the work of *facilitating dialogue* differs radically from that of *moderating debate*—and, even more important, we can then see how *mediating negotiations* can move substantially beyond both dialogue and debate to produce public-serving outcomes that can accommodate diverse interests and reflect practical multistakeholder agreements too.

Beyond Mere Talk: Actual Participation Requires Astute Negotiation

Involving the public in processes of governance, planning, and public management seems as easy to preach as it is difficult to practice. Such "public participation," we shall see, calls for sensitivity and technique, imagination and guts. Community leaders, planners, and public managers must have not only skill and thick skin, but the abilities to listen astutely, to probe practically, and to know how to "enlarge the shadow of the future"—how to sharpen diverse stakeholders' views of both their vulnerabilities and their practical opportunities. The practical artistry in question here interweaves challenges of learning and deliberation, negotiation and politics too.

In any real case, for example, neighborhood residents will be suspicious of planners' good intentions. Real estate developers will be just as wary. Planners and community leaders can easily feel caught in the middle: wishing to work with all those affected, they find themselves feared or distrusted, not welcomed, as residents, developers, and others fear any official agency's real motives and agendas. So public involvement and participation often pose uphill battles for planners and public officials, in part because in these processes citizens want not just to talk, talk, talk, but really to deal with deeply felt differences and to defend diverse interests—promoting affordable housing, protecting their neighborhoods, providing parks and open spaces, developing the local economy, and more. The politics of governance and planning, as a result, involves not simply "Who gets what?" or "better communication," but an imaginative and creative "art of the possible": planners and stakeholders work with and in between affected parties to create new options that few thought possible and to organize together then to make those new possibilities real.[1]

But public participation often threatens to be messy, unpredictable, and uncertain, and planners who espouse participatory ideals have reasons to worry. Inequalities of power, income, and information threaten participatory processes. Multiple and diverse stakeholders—agency representatives, private developers, neighborhood residents, or spokespeople—posture, hide information, stereotype one another, and presume strictly zero-sum, winner-takes-all outcomes, to say nothing of exaggerating, manipulating, or misrepresenting "data."

In many public meetings, speakers who have little time often "decide, announce, and defend" their positions, shoot first and ask questions later, and bring an almost visceral skepticism that anything collaborative or cooperative "with them"—be they bureaucrats, blacks, whites, aboriginals, developers, or environmentalists—will be possible at all. Officials and professionals, too, at times have acted in just these ways: posturing, simplifying, hiding real interests, presuming zero-sum outcomes, being impatient with process, and being quite skeptical about cooperating "with them" at all.

As a result, planners know that today's claims of good intentions hardly erase citizens' long histories of distrust of public authorities and those who work for public agencies. So planners and public managers in many fields face broader challenges here too: from facilitating a one-time community meeting to designing and staffing multiyear participatory task force processes to make recommendations to legislative bodies—challenges of fostering the voice, participation, and influence of affected parties on issues of their and the broader public's concern.[2] As we shall see, though, skillful practitioners and carefully designed processes *can* respond to these real problems and challenges in surprisingly successful ways—ways that are inclusive, responsive, efficient, expertly informed, and even community building too.[3]

Learning from Mediators of Environmental and Land Use Disputes

At the risk of making land use planning disputes seem deeply intractable before we clarify real opportunities, listen first to an experienced Canadian mediator who's been concerned with intermunicipal planning disputes such as those involving land annexations or road realignments. Bill Diepeveen recognizes the difficulties mentioned above, but he suggests that collaborative processes might still offer promise.[4]

When I'd asked what gave him a sense of possibility as he faced contentious public disputes, he replied, in part, this way:

> It never ceases to amaze me that people, when push comes to shove, haven't taken the time to really understand where the other is coming from and what's really driving them. It's still "your grand-pappy did it to my grand-pappy"—and they're so fixated on that. They identify themselves so much in the history and the bad situation, the bad relationships, that they can't see beyond it—and that's the challenge that I see that really gets me re-invigorated—that there is a way beyond it.

Here Diepeveen raises not only the problems of who's "taken the time to really understand" and the difficulty of understanding "where the other is coming from," but he points as well to the "blame game" that parties can all too easily play. Still, he says, his challenge is to show skeptical parties mired in such a history of "bad relationships" that "there *is* a way beyond it," that mediated processes do actually offer practical promise. But why do experienced municipal politicians listen to him?

He continues,

> They listen because they recognize that the traditional process has not been satisfactory. Administrative tribunals are costly, and they're antagonistic. They do

absolutely nothing for inter-municipal relations. They basically create "win-lose" outcomes. It's a very, very distributive kind of process and it does nothing to address what—I think they realize at the end of the day—is their ultimate desire, which is to improve inter-municipal cooperation and to work better with their neighbors.

They're seeing that the traditional processes aren't working. But in some ways it's hard for them to give it up, because that's all they know.

So Diepeveen reminds us that we're guilty of one hand clapping if we simply recite the many difficulties of "participation" or "mediation" without asking if and when politics as usual, or the courts, have done better. Here he seconds Lawrence Susskind's abiding argument that planning strategies must vary as cases do: if we're going to wonder about the prospects of mediated-participation or consensus-building processes, let's ask, very practically, "Compared to what?"

Our ordinary administrative and legal processes raise significant problems themselves, Diepeveen suggests: they are costly, adversarial, and may often, as he says, "do absolutely nothing" for ongoing relationships. But of course just suggesting a better way doesn't yet get us there.

So let's examine in detail just what a messy and difficult case of mediated participation can involve. When the parties are angry and impatient, besieged and distrusting, fighting each other in the political process, in the media, and perhaps in the courts too, what might a skillful mediator really do? Although an emerging literature now begins to address this question, this chapter presents a fresh approach that not only complements that literature but explores participatory practices "from the inside" via oral histories of challenging practice.[5]

To learn about the practical possibilities here, we look through the window of a skilled mediator's striking account of her practice in a long-standing, bitter multistakeholder dispute over the environmental and land use regulation of off-highway vehicle users. We hope not to generalize any simple recipe or single participatory planning model, but instead to reveal the kinds of practical judgments and moves that many planners trying to improve participatory processes in contentious situations might effectively make, learning as they can from the insights and wisdom of skillful mediators.

So we turn now to examine closely a striking—and perhaps even disturbingly familiar—account of an environmental planning dispute in California. As we hear echoes from other fields of planning, echoes of conflicting interests and feelings of deep distrust, anger, and even revenge, we can infer practical lessons and note more general insights.

Inheriting Years of Contentiousness and Trying to Make Participation Work

Here's what an experienced mediator, Lisa Beutler, faced after a State of California Department of Parks and Recreation deputy director asked her to work with an off-highway vehicle stakeholders' roundtable on hard-fought issues of regulating and managing off-highway vehicle use.[6] These issues involved access and sound, state and federal land uses, and the stakeholders included environmentalists, private property owners, local communities, off-highway vehicle enthusiasts, as well as equestrians and mountain bikers, businesses, and multiple public agencies.[7]

In the Beginning

Lisa begins this way:

> The Deputy Director had a vision—that instead of the ongoing contention—that had been classic and well known and well-described for years, and years and years, perhaps they could all come to the table together and begin to think in a more collaborative way—and talk about the best way to manage this program—and that would be a much more preferable approach than having the usual thing that happens, which is that the land managers, the planners in this case, go do something and get yelled at by everybody."

Here we have again the sense—echoing Diepeveen and Susskind, from inside government as well as outside—that the existing regulatory processes are not doing so well. Lisa mentions "years and years" of "well-known and well-described" contention—that apparently state government had been able to do all too little to resolve. But the agency had not called her first.

She says,

> What had happened was they had called a person who typically provides facilitations for the Department, and they had two meetings—at which point, according to the stakeholders, if you were to interview them, they would say that they nearly ran the first facilitator out of town on a rail. I took a look at what the first facilitator did—it was a disaster.

Now, we might think this experience surely to be atypical, but history often provides us with less than a clean slate or a fresh beginning. Planners take new jobs and inherit the gifts and the mistakes of their predecessors, and they find as they try to build new relationships with community members that the shadows of those who have come before them can still linger. What community planner has not found his or her good intentions met with suspicion by community members who, as they quickly say, "have heard it all before"?

So just what did Lisa face? She explains:

> What had happened in the first two meetings was that the previous facilitator—and this was part of my assessment of what was going on—had come into the process with a classic problem solving model....a complete step-by-step process, and so he was just going to go through the seven steps of problem solving....
>
> Well, here, though, you had this really high level of contention in the room, and I had people who weren't even speaking to each other. So asking them to begin to define the problem just immediately put them into saying, "The problem is, the other guy is a jerk!"
>
> That was going nowhere very fast. Plus, you've got 55 people. Plus, you've got a guy that was used to working with maybe six to twelve people. It was a complete mis-match."

So Lisa's job was to try to get the process back on track. We need now to learn not just what she accomplished, but *how* she midwifed whatever she did as well. From that story, the practical drama of her own work to overcome this history of anger, contentiousness, and the failed efforts that preceded her, we can learn from practice, not so much about general principle, but a good deal about mediated participation, public management, and participatory planning, about responding to community contentiousness, and about sensitive and skillful practices of community building too.[8]

The Practical Outcome—"Dramatic Agreement"—to Explain

I asked Lisa early on about what she and the stakeholders had been able to achieve in this case, if they had reached any practical agreements at all. She responded this way:

> Probably the most dramatic agreement was...to lower the "point-of-use" sound standard to 96 decibels from what was formerly 101 decibels.
>
> That was a huge agreement. It's the strictest standard except for one other state in the United States. We also had side agreements associated with sound—for continuing study, manufacturing standards, and that sort of thing. The "point of use" standard is so dramatic that the U.S. Forest Service and the Bureau of Land Management are both looking at adopting the standard, so it could end up having national implications.

Here already she tell us not just that they produced several agreements, one central and others more peripheral, but much more—that the central agreement was quite "dramatic," no routine compromise, and more too, that it was "huge," that two major federal agencies were considering adopting the standard as well.

So we might well want to know, now, how Lisa took fifty-five angry stakeholders from the disaster of their earlier experience with the facilitated land use discussion—as well as their preceding "years and years" of difficulty—to an agreement "so dramatic" that it could have national policy implications. Here's how she explained the heart of the central agreement:

> What was key about this particular agreement was that it was a "point of use" standard rather than a manufacturing standard....Up until now, no other agreement had been able to achieve this, because the sound is emitted from a vehicle. Only the U.S. Environmental Protection Agency can set manufacturing standards for vehicles, and that is a federal requirement, and the state does not have the ability to preempt the federal law. However, the state does have a right to determine how land is used—so, this is a "point of use," a land-use, standard, not a manufacturing standard....and that was the key to this negotiation.

And how, more than perhaps a dozen meetings into the process, did the group come to this "point of use" breakthrough? Lisa recapped it this way:

> We realized that the State has a right to say you cannot use alcohol on State property. It's not illegal to have alcohol...if you're a certain age...But the State has a right to impose that restriction. So somehow that came into the mix, and so the next question was, "Could the State impose a similar type of a standard for other uses?"
>
> ...So, we investigated that question, and the answer came back, "Yes, you can."
>
> Ok, if you can, you've got room to move forward—so then what would have to be the piece of this that we can move forward on? So, then we actually got to talking about numbers,...a strict, straight-up negotiation about numbers: what could we physically do?

So the stakeholders reframed their problem from one about which they could do nothing (changing federal regulations, the vehicle-focused manufacturing standards) to one that they could influence (recommending changes in state land use regulations about acceptable noise). This crucial reframing grew, we shall see, not from parties arguing or bargaining with each other, but from a process Lisa crafted so that the parties could together identify key issues, learn about them, and only then later negotiate real agreements with spatial implications.

How Did They Do It?

Their beginning did not seem at all promising. Recalling this group's early contentiousness, I asked Lisa if the parties had foreseen their ultimate, "huge" agreement about the point of use standard. I asked, "Did they know they might achieve that at the beginning?" She replied quickly, "Oh, no. They didn't know what the agreements would be. They had no idea. They didn't even have a single topic to discuss. One of the first things I had to do was assess what could even be negotiated. I mean, I didn't even know—no one even knew—what could potentially be discussed."

Here Lisa can teach us a good deal. She facilitated a state-level process that produced an agreement of national significance, and she had done that with a group of stakeholders who were so mutually suspicious and adversarial that they had no agreements even upon a basic agenda for discussion, a basic sense of the issues that they needed to discuss. Hardly mincing words, Lisa says of the stakeholders' group at the beginning: "They didn't know what the agreements would be. They had no idea."

They had no idea, she says, but Lisa mentions her early work to move them in that direction (even if *she* had no idea of that agreement either!): "One of the first things I had to do," she says, "was assess what could even be negotiated." She's saying here not just that the stakeholders did not *by themselves* formulate an agenda for discussion and negotiation—that she needed to work with them to do that, to move beyond those "years and years" of contentiousness—but that the stakeholders began with little real *hope* of such a dramatic outcome at all. Many planners and community leaders will find this situation familiar: working with an open space task force here, or an economic development working group there, public officials, planners, and organizers find that differences of history, knowledge, and interests create not only broader perspectives, but also, often, problems of internal suspicion and antagonism, polarizing rhetoric, and hot-button issues (Lowry et al. 1997).

The Initial View from the Outside

Lisa put the initial situation this way:

> This program had continuously, for every single State administration, been a complete thorn in their side and a source of all sorts of chaos and problems, and typically it was a source of bad press—and litigation—and a million other things. The Program Director and the Governor both had said to the Deputy Director, "You get that friggin' thing under control: it's a nightmare for us."

And what about the deputy director who hired her? She said, "I think what the Deputy Director who set this up was really looking for was some way to get people in the room and change the quality of the discussion to go to a more civil dialogue." What Lisa seemed to accomplish with these stakeholders went far beyond creating "a more civil dialogue," but even that original expectation suggests just how poor were the working relationships between the stakeholders, how much distrust they felt for one another.

So how, we should ask, did a woman whom almost none of the stakeholders even knew have the insight and skill, first, not to be discouraged or dissuaded by angry and skeptical stakeholders with little idea of possible agreements, and second, to actually find a way to innovative agreements having such potential significance for national land use regulation? What kind of understanding of conflict resolution and inclusive participation, what kind of abiding practical vision, did Lisa bring to these warring stakeholders so that they could produce such dramatically unexpected results? What was she thinking—and what kind of imagination does this suggest that planners and community leaders might have as well?

Reframing the Issue by Acknowledging Mutual Vulnerability

Lisa knew that parties might often focus more on self-protection—on what they don't want their opponents to do, or on mitigating the damage they were already doing—than on the interests they really hoped to satisfy. What might an "optimum" state program that would really serve their interests actually involve?[9] So she continued this way:

> What we had to do there was start with a classic reframing. We sat down and we said, "We're not here first to do problem-solving work. We're here because it's in everyone's interest for this program to operate at an optimum level. Can we agree, in principle, on that?
>
> So we spent the first two meetings in that conversation—to reach the agreement that it was in everyone's interest to find an optimum approach to physically managing this program.

She gave an example to illustrate what she meant:

> The environmental community…realizes that the potential for environmental harm with an unregulated use is far greater, because you can mitigate for a regulated use. So this was an important piece of the conversation, to say, "Ok, we're

going to stipulate that you don't like off-highway vehicles—we'll stipulate to that. But that being the case, are you willing to agree that an optimum management of this program is in your interests?"

Notice the initial reframing from individual interests to shared needs and vulnerabilities: let's back up from what you want, let's back up from solving the problem your way, and let's see if we can agree that it's in *all* of your stakeholder interests to have an optimally targeted and administered program, however differently you may now think about what *optimally* means. Notice that Lisa does *not* ask anyone to give up anything, but quite the contrary: she broadens stakeholders' attention from *their* particular views of the issues to a problem that they all share—they all *share a vulnerability* to a poorly designed and poorly administered program of state regulation. To paraphrase Bill Diepeveen, quoted above, "the traditional processes weren't working"; their history of state regulation had produced, it seemed, a chaos of "bad press" and "litigation" hardly serving them well—so, was it in their real interests, she asked, at least in principle, to have a better, *optimal* program?

Mediators might teach planners here not to help parties to compromise, but help them to do better than stick with a poor status quo—help them to do better than resign themselves to lose-lose outcomes—and work to find new ways of satisfying their many underlying interests, as our last chapters have argued.

"Mind Mapping" to Define Common Challenges

But Lisa only began there:

> So from there, what we did was a "mind-map"—to say, "If we were going to write a book about this program and what the elements of this program are, what would be the chapters of the book? What would have to be in the book—in a conversation about an optimal program?" And so we spent a meeting building this book: It was like a sun-burst: in the middle, we had "optimum program" and shooting out from there—there would need to be a chapter on funding,...a chapter on mitigation for X,...a chapter on soil,...a chapter on sound....
>
> So we drew the picture—and we took a whole wall, and we drew what would need to be in the book, and then I had the group prioritize what they had energy to work on in writing the chapters of the book—so they multi-voted and picked through these.

Notice again what Lisa has and has *not* done here. She has *not* asked one party what his or her dispute is with another party. She has *not* asked what criticism of the existing state program the nonstate stakeholders may have. She has *not* asked these parties to make any compromises. She has instead asked the group as a whole a common question, "If we were going to write a book...what would have to be in the book, in a conversation about an optimum program?"

She has put a common question to the group and asked them to do work together to respond. They were now facing the wall and trying to figure out the domain of relevant issues, and they were not, to begin with, talking about one another's failings. Echoing the work of other mediators, this *reframing* shifted attention not only from personal antagonism to substantive issues, *but also* from past failures to future possibilities.

Lisa summed a bit of this up as follows: "What the mind-map does is help you describe the universe. What is the universe of issues I'm working with here?...And then from there, understanding this universe of issues, we asked, 'Where is your energy? Where do you have an interest in paying attention and doing some work?' Or, to follow the book metaphor, Which chapter would you want to work on?"

Multivoting: Choosing What We Can Work On

In the multi-voting system, Lisa explained, each constituency had voted with a particular color of dot to select the topics they wished to address:

> So I was looking for a space where there was energy to work collaboratively, where the colors were mixed and there were a lot of them, which meant that they would be willing to make a commitment to spend some time investigating that.
>
> Well, once we had some priorities set, then I could move into a lot more of the classic things, like doing "issue and interest statements...."

She reminded us, though, "I was dealing with an open universe, you know—there was no topic even defined. We were just in the process of trying to begin a conversation with parties that wouldn't even speak to each other, hardly."

Framing the Conversation in a Less Adversarial Way

Here in our interview I wanted to press the point: many planners might be skeptical, if not quite discouraged, at the prospects of facilitating a practical conversation between parties who were hardly speaking to one another. Little in planners' training prepares them to work with strong emotions. So I wondered, how did the mind map help here? Lisa put it this way:

The mind-map did a couple of things that were helpful with the contentiousness of the process. The energy was directed to the wall, not at each other. So, by having people focus as if we were writing a book—what would the chapters be—it was content-based and all the attention was on the wall...

When I'm writing a book on a program, one of the chapter headings is not, "Joe is a jerk!" But if I ask you what your issues are, one of your issues might be that "Joe is a jerk!"

So it's a way of framing the conversation.... it's less adversarial.

We can learn a great deal here. As many planners and community leaders do too, Lisa knows very well, of course, how easily Susan might point a finger and say, "The problem here in getting the State to act is that Joe's a jerk"—and not only that, Lisa knows, too, that Joe wouldn't waste much time to respond, telling the group just what he thinks of Susan and her environmentalist groupies... and from there, Lisa knows that the conversation heads over the edge into antagonism, recrimination, escalation, and very little productive being accomplished.

Experienced mediators know that all this chaos can follow from a question to the group that seems as innocently simple—and as *apparently* respectful—as, "Well, what are your issues?" So Lisa suggests to us, instructively, that before she can even begin to explore disputed issues, she must first "frame the conversation," as she put it, to make it possible for stakeholders to speak together without attacking each other or, as she says, to speak in a "less adversarial" way.

Lisa has told us about the "energy" in the room and the role of the mind map to focus that energy "not at each other," but at the wall, on the substantive questions that the group together would need to address. So Lisa, remarkably enough, does not find herself put off or threatened by the hostility in the room, for she seems confident that she can redirect the attention of the stakeholders to the substance in which they're all interested, to that optimal program *whose current absence* makes them all vulnerable, all potential losers, as the shadow of the future looms. If she can work with the group to define substantively those elements of an optimal program, as if they were chapters in a book, and if she can work with them to define their *stakes* in future regulations, she could then turn to a series of practical, future-oriented tasks. She put it this way, summing up the process so far:

So, the first thing was, "Can we get an optimum program?"

"Yes, we can."

So, we came up with about five or six things that we thought might be useful to talk about, and once we had defined those things..., then we moved into an "education phase," where we began, based on the topics that had been identified, to learn what was involved, to learn what the parameters were.

Education

She explained that education phase this way:

> We did one meeting for each of the topics. We actually set up the meetings around them. In the beginning, we met monthly. It was pretty intense…So, for example, when we got to "Sound," we'd called the U.S. Environmental Protection Agency, and we had their "sound expert" come, and he spoke to the group and explained what the federal laws were.

So notice now the transitions, and the transformations, that Lisa marks here. She has enacted a process—and seems not nearly to have talked *about* it so much as practically performed it: doing the mind map, for example, and doing the multivoting priority ranking to focus the future efforts of the group.

Beginning with the fifty-five stakeholders in a stall or, worse, mired in a history of recrimination and hostility, Lisa tried to move them through issue identification to assessing priorities for exploration (where stakeholders had the energy to work) and to go further, too, to a process of joint education so that the assembled stakeholders could learn from outside experts about questions posed by the group. All that work, striking as it was, was nevertheless still essential preparation for the mediated negotiations to come: crafting practical agreements about actual regulations. So let's see how these contentious stakeholders turned that corner.

Listening for More than the Words: Practical Interest Analysis

After *education*, Lisa tells us,

> To get the issues and interests statements, I gave them a set of questions to work on: "The areas where my constituency…has deep concerns are…; if we were to think about how to make this program work correctly, the way we would describe that…would be such and such—and the reason that I think that this will really solve the problem is…"—and that, of course, is a real interest, when they explain why it is that they think that this is the optimum solution.

She goes on to stress this point:

> It's not what they actually present as how to make the program work correctly, it's their reasoning that provides what their interest is, but you can't get them there directly. So, you have to walk them through it.
>
> So once they had done that, we actually presented those to the others, so each of the caucuses shared with the others their perspective. So, I took away the solution and only talked about their reasoning…

So Lisa helped "each of the caucuses" to learn about one another's underlying concerns. Here she follows familiar mediation practice as she tries to look beyond *positions* to *interests,* beyond initial bets about solutions to less clearly articulated, but no less important, wishes and needs, aspirations and concerns, obligations and fears that might be driving any adamantly proposed solutions. But why, I wondered, would she have to do this *indirectly?* She explained it this way, "When you ask people, people typically think in terms of a proposed solution, not the underlying assumptions or premises that led them to a solution. I think...that in our society people are actually trained to be solution-proposing....I know the solution to this problem; the solution is X."

So Lisa knows to expect—and she tells us to expect—*solution proposing,* and she knows, crucially, as well, that she must listen for far more than those proposed solutions. She has to listen carefully to the reasons why those solutions seem desirable—for those "reasons why" disclose underlying, motivating interests. We might call this "the classic mediator's response":

> So you...hit a "pause button," and you say, "OK, you've proposed a solution, but you have reasoning behind that. What are you thinking about when you propose that solution?"—because typically, what people are reacting to is not one another's interest, it's their proposed solution. That's what they're typically reacting to.

These comments offer a distinct and practical lesson. When stakeholders can very quickly argue against each other's favored solutions, Lisa echoes the work of other mediators as she tells us that we need to listen not only carefully to what the stakeholders are saying, but just as carefully to what they're not saying, to their interest-based reasoning as well.

Was the process all smooth sailing? Hardly. As Deborah Chavez and Robert Fitzhenry (2005: 31) wrote about the obstacles Lisa faced, "It was extremely difficult to get stakeholders to appreciate that they were living in two worlds—they served as representatives for their group, yet at the same time they were part of the Roundtable's collaborative effort."

Lisa's story suggests that indirect strategies can help in such situations, especially when parties will otherwise waste no time explaining the inadequacies of each other's proposed solutions. Other mediators, too, suggest that facilitators often need to slow processes of argument, to step back from parties' positions or temptations to focus upon this solution or that one, to resist the urge to debate options, and instead to work early on to learn about multiple and diverse and often underlying motivating concerns, the interests that the interconnected, interdependent stakeholders are really trying to satisfy (Adler 2005, Umemoto 2005, Forester 1999a, 2008b).

Mediated Participation: Not Moderating a Debate, but Mediating Negotiations

So, Lisa warns us, too, planners who hope to plan collaboratively with diverse stakeholders must be keenly aware of their own temptation to moderate a debate between stakeholders' positions instead of working carefully to mediate a negotiation to serve their practical interests. Moderating turns argument toward counterargument, and so it surfaces (and risks escalating) debate; mediating turns parties toward their multiple and diverse interests, and so it *surfaces practical proposals from the parties* to negotiate. Moderating helps parties to sharpen conflicting arguments and terms of disagreement; mediating helps parties instead to respond to one another's concerns to craft workable, mutual gain accommodations and agreements.

Lawrence Susskind has put this very succinctly:

> The essence of the process here is acknowledging the other's needs as well as your own, and making proposals that respond to both. Arguing that you don't like what the others want, and you want something else instead (which is the old model of bargaining), doesn't produce agreement. Remember, we're trying to get an agreement. We're not done until we get agreement. (Forester 1994: 343)

Like Lisa, he stresses the crucial difference between having a *debate*, arguing that you don't like what they want and that you want something else instead, and conducting a *negotiation*, developing proposals to enable agreements, ways now to act together to address the real concerns of *both* (or all) parties.[10] Like Lisa, too, and like Bill Diepeveen before her, Susskind also stresses the importance of creating a less adversarial mode of conversation ("acknowledging the other's needs as well as your own"), and he, too, contrasts "the old model of bargaining" to the challenge of mediating participation as a more constructive process, enabling parties to make proposals that try to meet *both* the other's needs as well as their own.

Notice the immediately practical lesson that this implies: recognizing one another's *multiple and diverse* motivating interests can provide opportunities for parties—who can then collaborate, form practical coalitions, and effectively respond to each other precisely because their real *priorities* are often *not* the same!

So these mediators show us that in processes of dealing with differences we ought to cultivate not an argumentative, even if "healthy," debate but something else altogether: a robust capacity of parties to listen carefully to one another—not just to *hear* bargaining positions but really to identify one another's multiple and diverse underlying concerns. And why? *So that, in turn, those parties can craft options and accommodations together that meet those concerns*, practical options, and accommodations for real mutual gain and even mutual aid.

But we learn more here too. To work well, mediators struggle to improve both *process* and *outcomes*. Mediators often reach far beyond "process people" for they seek outcomes that satisfy not only the parties and the interests they represent, but also basic considerations of justice and fairness, efficiency and joint gains, timeliness and durability.[11]

Furthermore, the work of joint inquiry and education as discussed above introduces substantive threats, dangers, and opportunities into stakeholders' discussions and considerations of proposals, options, and workable agreements. Mediating a participatory planning process well, these chapters have argued, requires building upon planning expertise—certainly not substituting empty process for substantive knowledge! Working carefully to identify and satisfy diverse stakeholders' interests also protects against the dangers of "good process, but bad outcome," for the stakeholders together focus precisely on the *outcomes* that they can achieve—compared to their best default alternatives—given the best available information they together can obtain.[12]

Working with Anger: Harnessing the Energy in Acrimony

I have explored Lisa's reflections and her practical judgments at such length not only because she can help us to understand the challenges of participatory land use planning processes—and mediated participation more generally—but because her ways of dealing practically with so much acrimony and contentiousness can teach us about much broader community planning as well. How *was* it possible, after all, that Lisa saw real opportunities as she walked into a room of fifty-five stakeholders hardly speaking to each other—when so many planners in her same position might have thought that nothing but even more heated argument could now result?

I asked her just that question. I said,

> Some planners will feel that when there's so much bad feeling going around, they'd prefer to turn around and walk. But you came to that room, you saw all that

contentiousness, and you nevertheless thought, "Well, there's a set of things that might be possible here." So, the question to ask for community planning students is, "What do we need to be thinking in the face of such contention?"

I pressed the point: "So when you're in that room and you feel that energy, and people might wish to be beating up on each other, how is it that you're still hopeful, you're thinking, 'Yeah, they're angry, but we can get something done'?" She answered simply, and then she explained herself in a quite instructive way:

> Whenever there's conflict in the room, it means there's energy to work on some-thing—conflict is always better than apathy: so that's where I start….
>
> As a party, if I'm angry, I'm angry about something—and I'm angry because I don't think something is working right, and I want things to work right.

I tried to explore this insight further, to learn what else she might see here. "But maybe, as a party, you're angry," I said, "that they're a jerk, and they lied to you at the last meeting, and their boss lied to your boss." She replied, "All that's true—that's the Hatfields and the McCoys. There was a piece of that here too, but you have to differentiate the Hatfields and the McCoys, which is about, 'Your brother shot my brother,' from 'I have a fundamental public policy concern with the way business is being conducted.'" But after Lisa distinguished these two, she immediately interwove them:

> Often times, both things are true, because I might have started out with my fun-damental disagreement—"I shot your brother," or "You shot mine"—so then my job is to say, "We're going to stipulate to the fact that you shot at each other. Now, we can go on all night and day about that, but that doesn't fix the fact that you are very unhappy with the way that this is working."
>
> So I'll say, "I'm walking into the room today and there isn't a single thing that I can do about the fact that people messed around and got shot. The only thing that I can work with today is the reality of today, and the reality of today is that this situation isn't working for you, period, for all of you. If you're sitting in front of this room and thought that this situation was working for you, you wouldn't be in this room. So, your big question—that you have to pick up your mirror and ask yourself about—is: 'Am I willing to not be in this situation anymore?…Am I willing to take the risk to be in a conversation?'"

Here again, we hear an echo of an earlier theme, recognition of past grievances as a step *toward*, not as any substitute for, future action: "to not be in this situa-tion anymore." But notice, too, that Lisa makes no claim to preempt the justice system—she wants instead to press a community *planning* question to each party: are you willing to be in a conversation about rebuilding the community? As she put it,

> We can say it right now—we can put it up on the wall—we can do whatever you need to do to say, "In the past, I've been shot," or "In the past, you've been shot." That's not a secret!
>
> This is true, and so I ask, "Do you choose to continue suffering—do you choose to be shot at in the future, and choose to shoot at someone in the future? Is that your choice?"

She says this quite deliberately: "I will say that to them twenty times. You have to say it constantly—because that's really what it's about: is it worthy of your time to cease your suffering?"

Her abiding insight here challenges the all-too-common misunderstanding that mediation in planning settings seeks to erase differences of worldview, values, or identity. On the contrary, we see that what fuels effectively mediated participation—and mediated negotiation more generally—may well be far more the desire to diminish suffering than the desire to achieve any lofty ideal or ideological meeting of minds. Throughout her story, Lisa asks us to consider collaboration, dealing with difference, and mediated participation not as vague and abstract ideals but as specific, manageable processes, not as romantic aspirations but instead as realistic hopes: actually practical strategies of acting together that can serve all parties wanting to do much better than the status quo, wanting really to improve on the often inadequate business as usual of traditional community planning processes. She wants us, too, to be able in deed to ask, as we work with others, "Is it worthy of your time to cease your suffering? Are you willing to take the risk to be in a conversation to that end?"

Conclusion: Mediated Participation to Diminish Suffering and Organize Action

We have here no gimmicks or recipes that promise to make multistakeholder collaboration and mediated participation foolproof, but we can identify important lessons for participatory planning and for public management much more broadly.

Community planners and leaders should expect to inherit, recognize, and work proactively to move beyond their constituents' all-too-reasonable dissatisfactions with past government efforts. History and memory, experience and sense of identity matter, and because these histories can be quite painful, echoing for years and years, planners can hardly ask residents to check these parts of their identities at the door. These histories can involve legacies of power and politics, promises made but never fulfilled, cultural and racial bigotry, outright neglect, or, of course, as in Lisa's case, botched attempts at addressing community problems.

So when stakeholders seem all too ready to highlight each other's faults, indirect strategies to explore issues, to sidestep escalation, and to build relationships can be essential. So Lisa's mind-mapping exercise shifted attention away from positions, away from debates over whose solution was better or whose problem was bigger, and it prompted proposals addressing a common task: mapping the necessary elements of a potentially optimal program. Face-to-face meetings, we see, do not have to be head-to-head arguments, head-to-head confrontations. Indirect strategies can involve field trips and tours, role-switching and role-playing exercises, small group meetings complementing plenary sessions, informal times and spaces complementing more formally programmed ones, and most commonly of all, no doubt, occasions for food and drink: all these can provide the settings, rituals, and institutional spaces for planning stakeholders to argue less and to listen more, to dig in on positions less and to inquire about broader interests more, to stereotype and presume a bit less about "them" and to actually learn more about what we can now really do.

Mediated participation processes do not happen by themselves. Because parties often bring their fears, suspicions, uncertainties, and vulnerabilities to community planning encounters, these processes of dealing with real differences require trained facilitators or mediators: these must be skillful and imaginative, not just well-intentioned community members, facilitative leaders, or planners. They must be keenly aware that the most productive way to learn about the parties' views of issues may very well *not* be to ask each party, when everyone's together, "Well, what are your issues?" Just because these processes are not self-organizing, just because they require skillful and imaginative design and guidance, schools of planning, public administration and public policy, and applied fields more generally (social work, public health, education, among others) must address these competences in their curricula.

In the face of complex public disputes, we must be wary of technical fixes, of labeling too quickly. We should study mediation and facilitation, collaborative problem-solving and consensus-building processes as first cousins, participatory practices closely related to one another, at times overlapping and at times distinct. Rather than reduce a striking case like Lisa's to one narrow and inevitably ambiguous category (was it *collaborative problem solving? activist mediation? facilitation?* all of these in combination?), we will do better if we appreciate and cultivate the broad repertoire of skills and strategies she has practiced, all of which might improve our capacities to bring parties together to plan and act for mutual benefit—in the face of conflict.

Mediated participation enables us to act carefully both to recognize the past *and* to address real future possibilities too: to acknowledge past suffering—perhaps to recognize and even reframe anger as a resource for change—and to generate concrete proposals for mutually beneficial negotiated agreements as well. Few have put this better than Lawrence Susskind, as our bibliography makes clear. Drawing upon decades of practice and writing all along the way as well, Susskind argues that when stakeholders in public disputes are interdependent, when no party can get what it wants unilaterally, not only can stakeholders often steer clear of the traps of setting each other off, the traps of mutual escalation and gamesmanship, that so easily produce lose-lose, mutually lousy outcomes, but they can, via mediated negotiations and facilitative leadership, find workable agreements that provide joint gains to all parties—satisfying real interests, significantly, of weaker parties who thus are pleased to agree as well.

Experienced mediators like Bill Diepeveen and Lisa Beutler illustrate Susskind's argument in their practices as well—as has the work we have examined in earlier chapters. These mediators' work also suggests that existing processes of governance—most notoriously seen in versions of *public hearings*—too often polarize community members rather than help them to listen and deliberate together, too often erode rather than enhance their abilities to act together, too often encourage stakeholders' posturing and mutual fears but do very little to help them craft practical steps to address their real interests, to help them practically to build stronger communities and reduce today's real suffering.

Now we might see more clearly that because mediating participation enables parties to craft mutually beneficial agreements to act, community leaders and planners need to distinguish carefully and at times integrate the practical work of (a) fostering dialogue, (b) moderating debate, and (c) mediating negotiation. *Fostering dialogue* can promote understanding and mutual recognition between parties, fostering trust and respect, beginning the work of relationship building—even as skeptics may always voice suspicions of this as "just talk." *Moderating debate* can sharpen arguments, identify crucial or missing information, and clarify critical differences between parties—even as such sharp argument always risks escalating antagonisms and undermining relationships between the parties. *Mediating negotiation*, in contrast, crafts agreements to act—signed commitments to give in order to get, to act together to satisfy the represented stakeholders' interests—even as further, deeper structural issues require ongoing organizing (Chesler 1991, Reardon 1993). So planners and community leaders must be clear, with themselves and community members alike, in any given meeting: are we here to foster a dialogue, to moderate a debate between perspectives, or are we here to act, to agree together upon a plan of action (or, of course, do we want to combine these processes in some ways to serve our ends)?

So we need to learn more about the ways that planners and community leaders in diverse fields respond to disputes and conflicting arguments among the stakeholders with whom they work. In the face of heated differences and impassioned argument, how frequently do planners and officials, for example, fall back on the apparent protection that either technical or narrowly procedural, semiformal *moderating* roles appear to provide? How often do community planners' choices to <u>moderate</u> debates lead to the practical consequence that these planners become all the less engaged in recruiting representative stakeholders, less sensitive to inequalities and less able to provide training and information to all parties (in part to "level the playing field"), and far less able to probe interests and alternatives en route to crafting creative, practical proposals?

This chapter leads to important questions for further research too: how can mediators and planners contribute to legitimate governance processes by recruiting "representative" stakeholders? How can mediators and planners foster participatory processes that minimize exclusion and deal making, that maximize both learning and mutual gains in agreements that will be practical, stable, and fair?

I have tried here to examine central challenges of dealing with differences and thus of participatory planning too—challenges whose relevance I hope readers will find it difficult to avoid considering carefully: *How* will you walk into rooms of stakeholders dissatisfied with existing programs and try to help them fashion innovative and powerful agreements? How will you deal with histories of suspicion and acrimony that threaten to cripple working groups? How will you try to identify issues and interests without making participants vulnerable and without opening the door not only to, "My issue? It's simple: Joe's a jerk!" but to Joe's hot response as well? How will you work to acknowledge past pain but help diverse and distrusting stakeholders to learn about issues, to learn in part about their differing interests, and to propose mutually beneficial, mutually agreeable options not for compromise but for joint action and real joint gains? Lisa Beutler's work—taken with the other mediators' accounts considered in earlier chapters—gives us a running start at these questions.

CHAPTER EIGHT

Envisioning Possibilities: How Humor and Irony Recognize Dignity and Build Power

When dealing with differences gets tough, it turns out, irony and humor can help, *not* by being funny but by conveying respect and humility, appreciation and solidarity, shared vulnerability and an abiding sense of possibility too. So this chapter explores the practical micropolitics of *having a sense of humor*—that deceptively simple capacity that community leaders and managers, mediators and planners can bring to bear at dicey times in negotiations or participatory settings. In particular, we wish to learn how irony and humor can help in those critical moments in processes of community planning, governance, and public policy negotiations when the conversation between parties threatens to fall apart, to escalate or degenerate, or to turn toward such mutual suspicion or recrimination that all hope of mutual agreement appears lost (Wheeler and Morris 2001, Wheeler 2002).

When we call a process *inclusive, participatory,* or *democratic,* we imply that diverse and affected stakeholders have something substantial to say to one another. At the same time, we also imply that those stakeholders have *different* things to say—they don't all agree—and so, this book has argued, the practical drama of democratic participation and democratic politics involves the challenging work of reconciling differences, building relationships, finding ways together to craft new possibilities of going on rather than finding ways of destroying one another.

A wry and responsive sense of humor and irony in the face of conflict can have complex practical and political effects. Both irony and humor, at once imaginative, creative, and serious too, can play important roles of simultaneously recognizing past suspicions and hurts, disrupting the conventional political expectations of parties and encouraging new actions and social relationships. As we shall see, recognizing felt experience, disrupting practical expectations, and actually creating new possibilities all at once is no small accomplishment.

Our "having a sense of humor" involves the ability to show another person several angles of vision all at once. But it does that—and often very much more—without being heavy handed, even in situations of great stress, pain, or anger. At critical moments in governance or negotiation processes, having a sense of humor has very little to do with being funny, but very much to do with responding to others with understanding and imagination. This capacity calls not particularly for expert knowledge, nor for substantive ideas or concepts—though being well informed and prepared rarely hurt—but for practically responsive and critically improvised wit, "ironic performance," even though we hardly seem to understand the true complexity of such quick thinking on one's feet, such practical action.

In situations of negotiation and conflict, having a sense of humor requires the ability to respond to others in the moment, being sensitive to others' experiences while recognizing a group's larger sense of hope and danger, frustration and possibility. Having a sense of humor, as we will explore it here, then, has almost nothing to do with canned, prepackaged jokes and everything to do with perceptively getting the spirit of the moment in the heat and flow of work: with words that acknowledge and honor, reframe and change worlds, with perspectives that help us to look at a situation in new and different ways, seeing what's right in front of us—as we have never seen it before—and perhaps laughing with some relief as we do.

In some cases to be sure, though, having a sense of humor in a meeting might backfire. So Laura Bachle recalls being told by mediation trainers never to use humor in her mediating practice; apparently the trainers worried that the harm possibly done by novice mediators would far outweigh the benefits they might achieve.[1] One or more parties might feel left out, for example, or, worse still, singled out, or feel perplexed, wondering if they have understood what's been said or what's really been meant. Yet care and sensitivity (the "street smarts" of good judgment) can protect us from these dangers and risks, and we would do well to appreciate the organizational and practical, ethical and political contributions that having a well-developed sense of humor can make as we work to deal with differences.

Listen first to an experienced public policy mediator, Susan Podziba, who suggested broadly the difference that her sense of humor has made at critical moments in the flow of negotiations, moments at which she sought to transform real uncertainty and difficulty into new opportunity: "I've been in meetings where things have gotten to an incredibly tense moment—and a well-delivered, humorous statement was like a wave that cleansed the room of the tension, and delivered a fresh, tension-free space to continue discussions."[2]

In the following sections we explore critical moments in governance and negotiation processes through the experiences and accounts of third parties—who, of course, have critical moments of their own to navigate. These examples will provide us with windows onto the world of practice, and they will help us to see more clearly what's involved when a sense of humor can shift the course of a conversation, change expectations and relationships, and even turn suspicion and pain toward hope and practical action.

Exposing Our Imperfect Expectations—and Our Need to Learn

Consider a land use planner's handling of a developer's team who treated him with suspicion and wariness. A senior city planner with substantial experience, Nathan Edelson tells us of his efforts to put others at ease:

> Having a sense of humor can make it possible to talk to each other, but it depends on what it is. If it's disrespectful, then it doesn't work—but if it's something about the absurdity of the situation that we're in, or if it's something where one person has said something that you would have expected from the other side, that can help.[3]

Humor, here, Nathan argues, must be respectful: it must not make fun of others, dismiss their concerns, or make light of what they take to be serious matters. Disrespect will make the work of talking to each other far, far more difficult, rather than less. This much is not surprising, but it helps us to understand that humor need not be dismissive or disrespectful in high-stakes situations.

Notice that Nathan has given us two examples of what can help: "If it's something about the absurdity of the situation" or "if it's something where one person has said something that you would have expected from the other side," either of those moves can help, he suggests, but we should ask, "Why?" or better still, "How?"

What do these two examples share? Both "the absurdity of the situation" and what someone's said "that you would have expected from the other side" lie beyond the frame of the parties' reasonable, considered, and well-informed judgments. They're both surprising; they're unexpected. They're out of our control. They're in our face. But moreover, they give us pause. They ask us to step back and think again, to relax our absolute certainty about what's going on. Paradoxically, both of Nathan's examples suggest instances that show us that when we don't know everything we need to know, when we recognize that we were caught unaware, we can come to *realize that we need to learn.*

Together with other parties in this "absurd situation," we all need to learn: we have been surprised together. A sense of humor can give us the gift—even if we rarely see it coming—of recognizing that something links and connects us as adversaries in the room. We now see something that we mutually share: uncertainty and a need to learn to understand this situation in which we actually find ourselves now interdependently connected. So that gift of humor can then contribute in a small but perhaps still important way to creating a *we* of nevertheless distrusting and skeptical parties who need not just to compete, but now also to talk to one another—both to review and reframe what we see and to learn more than we now know too.

Recognizing Vulnerability and Building Community

A sense of humor can connect us too, and laughter can express not just release but also mutual acknowledgment: "Yes, we thought we fully understood the situation, but clearly there are crazy things happening here that we cannot fully control, or anticipate. Who knows what this unpredictable governor's going to throw in our lap this time?"

Humor provides us with gentle lessons of surprise. Even our grudging laughter—at the out-of-control absurdity of a situation we're in—can enable each of us as stakeholders, for example, to see that it's not just one or another of us individually that faces this unpredictable situation, with its contingencies and pressures that we can't control, for we can see that all of us, as disputing parties, face a situation that *none of us* can fully control or anticipate. So we might then acknowledge that we are all vulnerable. We are all at risk. All of a sudden, a sense of humor has helped each of us to see that we nevertheless share concerns, and even such interests as getting better information, that we had seen less clearly before.

When a sense of humor makes it possible for us to laugh together, we *hear*—and so recognize not just conceptually but intimately, aurally, even prereflectively— that we do share something even as we distrust each other. Yes, the situation's absurd in part because we can't predict what the city council, if not the governor, will do. Or, yes, Jones just said what we expected her greatest critic instead to say—and in hearing one another's laughter at this surprise, we recognize not just our own fallible expectations, but our own fallibility together, and we begin to suspect that we each realize this.

Further, as we realize that we individually are not quite as all-knowing as we thought, we see that our shared, spontaneous laughter can humble us together. We appreciate that we're both laughing at the absurd situation we share—and so now suddenly, even as adversaries, we may be closer together than we were, seeing now that we are more alike in our limits, and even in our needs, than we thought.[4]

So in situations of suspicion, complexity, and heavy expectations, Nathan teaches us that having a sense of humor can be respectful and instructive, and more too. Being able to laugh together as we recognize some absurdity of our situation, we find it now more possible *to talk to each other.* We discover not just absurdity, but *shared dependency and vulnerability,* shared fallibility and lack of control, and mutual recognition of our limits too: we're both, after all, laughing at a shared situation.

Challenging Presumptions of Power and Powerlessness

A sense of humor can challenge political expectations too. Normajean McLaren, a community-planning consultant with extensive experience involving issues of racial, ethnic, and cultural conflict, explains:

> For example, in a development situation (where people are often hiding things they want), you have people come in, and they're feeling very strongly that you're there as part of the bureaucracy and there are all of these hoops that they have to jump through. So you're about to sit down at the table, and they're already good and grumpy because they've been through this fifteen times, and you're the sixteenth person they have had to talk to.
>
> Everybody's looking at you impatiently, and someone says, "Well, where are you going to sit?"
>
> And you might say, "Well, according to the by-laws, subsection such and such, I actually have to sit right here!" which makes it as stupid as it really is. You're not making fun of them—you're really making fun of exactly what you're doing, which immediately says, "I don't take myself this seriously."[5]

Notice the pains Normajean takes to stress that the humor must be respectful. Her humor is directed toward herself; it's not about her "personally" but about her "officially" as *the planner* or *the bureaucrat* they're expecting to meet or encounter, who, they worry, will soon make them jump through more costly hoops.

Normajean acknowledges their uneasy anticipation of her political role. She tries not just to have a sense of humor but to share it as well. In part, she wants to say, "Relax! Lighten up!" But she can do that only if she shows them that she will go first. Instead of demanding something from them, she will make the first offer: she will *lighten up* first and so make it easier and less risky for them to follow suit.

Her humor actually begins with respect: she acknowledges in effect that she knows that "they're already good and grumpy because they've been through this fifteen times," but she conveys even more than that recognition. She acknowledges that they are all together in a situation deeply entangled in political and legal structures, with all the accompanying mandates, regulations, and bylaws. She acknowledges that they all have to take those mandates and regulations into account, but she also recognizes their limits and the ways they can be taken to absurd lengths ("subsection such and such"!). Her example of "having to sit right here" announces that she has no intention of subjecting them to such a rule-mongering use of her authority. In a few words, she both acknowledges the importance of the development and planning regulations and recognizes their indeterminacy, their openness to interpretation too. She wants to be taken seriously—she's there, indeed, in an official and authoritative capacity as a planner with an important role in the development process—but, at the same time, she wants everyone to be able to talk about the important issues at hand, so she also wants them to know, "I don't take myself too seriously."

So her humor here does the political work of conveying several perspectives all at once. Her sense of humor recognizes power and authority, and its playfulness creates a space for conversation and innovative negotiation that might enable the parties to craft creatively improvised outcomes not already pre-scripted and predetermined by *the bureaucracy*.[6] As we shall now see, other practitioners show us how to do what Normajean does as well.

One of the Greatest Jobs in the World: Being Phil Donahue, Bob Barker, and Jerry Springer

Another regional planner, David Boyd, stressed how his sense of humor allowed him, in quite adversarial and contentious meetings, to present the complexities of his own role and to suggest a way of moving forward that would be respectful rather than vindictive, open rather than rigidly proscribed, light rather than morose and somber—all at once![7] He tells us,

> I use humor quite consistently throughout my work. Sometimes it's sort of wry, sometimes it's sarcastic, sometimes it's just dumb. For instance, I facilitated a series of town hall meetings—often on very controversial subjects, such as planning or

inter-municipal collaboration. The panelists were often adversaries, and the audience occasionally was downright hostile.

I always started the evening with an introduction to the series, and then would say, "I have one of the greatest jobs in the world—I get to be one part Phil Donahue, one part Bob Barker, and one part Jerry Springer."[8] This usually got some sort of smart aleck response from a panelist or an audience member, "Hopefully there'll be no chair throwing," and the place cracked up.

Its purpose was two-fold: to serve as an icebreaker, but also to set a norm—to say, "It's OK to dig in hard, to discuss and debate—but there will be some fun and entertainment to it as well."

There wasn't a facilitation or a mediation that went by that I didn't do something similar...

Like Normajean, David takes an ironic and humorous view of his own power and authority as he refers to three very different television hosts to indicate the challenges of his official role. Like Phil Donahue, he will try to ask good questions and explore the parties' points of view in front of a live audience; like Bob Barker, he will moderate the parties' turn-taking as they keep their eyes on the prizes and hope to take home the goods; and like Jerry Springer, he will not be surprised if the parties give vent to histories of broken promises and distrust, anger and fear, strong feeling and suspicions—and so he acknowledges all that even as he asks everyone present to "dig in hard, to discuss and debate," but to have some fun doing it too.

Like Nathan and Normajean above, David also emphasizes, "I always poked fun at myself, and never at the participants." He recognizes and conveys powerfully in the moment the ambiguities of his role as an authority figure. Though to his audience his role may at first seem directive and prescriptive, his sense of humor nevertheless suggests both to us and to that audience how he really hopes to perform his duties—with seriousness *and* humor—and so how he hopes to work, to improvise practically and creatively in the scene at hand. Notice how very different his practice would be if, instead, David announced to his audience, "I will try to improvise with seriousness and with humor"—a statement that, although true, might well be quite a bit more flat-footed and very much less effective than his ironic and playful reference to performing as the three talk-show hosts.

Acknowledging Painful History and Easing Conversation

Normajean's and David's stories resonate with an example given to us by Frank Blechman, political consultant turned public policy mediator.[9] Echoing now and adding to these points, Frank argues that humor can be a double-edged sword. He tells us,

> Seeing the irony, ridiculousness, or downright improbability of a situation keeps us humble. However, expressing that perception may not be appreciated (or may not be appreciated equally) by others present.
>
> Let me give you an example. I grew up in the South under segregation and went through a totally segregated educational system, through college. There is still a lot of garbage rattling around in my head.
>
> When I am working with very diverse groups, I often introduce myself as a "short, fat, white guy." This usually gets a laugh, but it also serves several facilitative purposes:
>
> It acknowledges the importance of identity, including race, and other physical classifications. It licenses others to talk about their identity and what that means to them.
>
> It legitimates different perspectives. Mine may be silly, but it is still mine, and just because it is silly and mine—not correct and yours—doesn't make it irrelevant or dismissible.
>
> When I add my history, it allows me to talk about how, out of ignorance—not out of malice, I may offend. I actively request that people let me know if I have offended so that the offense can be corrected. I ask folks to give me the benefit of the doubt that I did not offend intentionally, to disrespect or disempower someone. Having raised the issue proactively, I almost always get that benefit of the doubt, and it almost always helps the group interact more easily and honestly.

Frank's self-parody as "a short, fat, white guy" says and does several things at once. He acknowledges race as germane not just to felt identity but to a powerful way that he and those in the room, too, can be seen by some and, as importantly, *not seen* by yet others. But his parody calls into question whether race, or bulk of build, or height is really going to be germane to the issues at hand. Furthermore, his naming rather than hiding racial identity helps to make difficult and painful issues that face very diverse groups more discussable, by putting them on the table—in naming his whiteness—for the parties to engage rather than to skirt.

Frank does more too: he shows others that he sees how others can see him, and so he suggests that others, too, might recognize that they can all see and be seen in several ways. In effect, he says, we will all bring multiple perspectives to bear here, and we need to consider all of our points of view.

Frank's quip about himself allows him to recognize—to suggest to the group at hand—that slights of identity can be subtle and unintentional, that parties may offend each other at times without knowing they have done so, and so he asks the group as a whole to collaborate, to help each other to recognize and repair disrespect, to work to build trust as they go on. That request, he tells us, "almost always helps the group interact more easily and honestly." He explains: "Good humor in such meetings is almost always a balance between the serious and the ridiculous. Once we have acknowledged that much of life can be both, then taking enjoyment is not seen as disrespect, and unmitigated seriousness is not mistaken for respect."

Having a responsive sense of humor in contentious settings, he suggests, weaves together laughing matters and deeply serious ones too. But Frank warns us as well: we should not mistake "unmitigated seriousness" for respect—a neglected theme to which we will return—for a respectful sense of humor, in contrast, can be both responsive and enlightening all at once.

Other practitioners corroborate and extend Frank's insights. Puanani Burgess, a mediator/facilitator who's done substantial work on racial and cultural issues observed:

> Humor and my ability to express it—without people thinking they are being made fun of—are really important. I think humor is a way of showing that you can see deeply.
>
> Humor is pretty serious stuff. Most of the stories that I tell have humor in them, and I use these stories to set up the process and to relate two important things to people: i) some of the principles by which I will facilitate; and ii) my values—so they can relate to me and trust me...So humor and stories are the most critical parts of my practice. They allow people to go into deep water without being so scared.[10]

Puanani stresses that in contentious situations, not just any humor will do. Our sense of humor, she says, can reveal a great deal about who we are: what we're capable of seeing, how we're likely to treat people, elements of our style, our character, and a bit of our values too.

She suggests that sharing one's sense of humor is a way of "showing that you can see deeply," showing that you can see beyond the superficial, beyond surface distractions to the more important matters below. Showing that expresses her willingness and ability to listen, to respect, and to take people seriously. So, she says, when she has begun to build trust, her stories with humor allow people to risk taking on deeper issues—issues of value that matter—because they now feel more safe than they have.

Here again, we see the suggestion that a sense of humor might simultaneously be serious—recognizing the "deep water" and providing a sense of safety, trust, and reassurance—and yet, as humor, be light too. But how can this really work?

To explore these issues of trust and safety, our ways of deliberately and deliberatively together exploring "deep water," we turn now to Normajean McLaren's reflections about the challenges of community development and governance in diverse, multicultural settings (Sandercock 2003b).

Safety, Release, and New Collaborative Relationships

Hoping to learn about deliberative practices in multiethnic settings through a series of oral histories, I had asked Normajean about her practice involving First Nations peoples, Caucasian inhabitants, and recent Asian immigrants (Forester 2004a). She'd mentioned that having a sense of humor was essential in her work. "How so?" I wondered, and so I asked, with a bit of mock skepticism, "What would you lose if you didn't use humor here? Would anybody care?"[11]

Normajean explained that humor provided safety and connection, and much more:

> I couldn't survive without it. This work is too hard without humor. It's too bloody hard. Without our humor, we have no salvation.
>
> Humor is such a connector. It's such a leveller, and it's such a release—because tension will build in a room when you're doing community development work, and you're dealing directly with issues that are so much in people's faces.
>
> It's important of course that you're not making fun of their issues—ever. But the tension gets so high that humor's like a safety valve that you open up, and if it's at my expense for the first little while in the room, that's fine.
>
> So it's a salvation and a release. It starts as a connector between me and them, and then that says it's safe to be with me, because I won't hurt you: I'm not going to bring you out here, stand you up, and say, "Here's a victim of racism, and she's going to tell you her story and bleed all over you."
>
> It's safe because I'm not putting myself above you as someone who can't be poked fun at. So humor's a leveller and it's a release when the tension gets so high.

We should unravel several of the closely interwoven themes in this powerful passage. First, Normajean asks us to recognize that community development work very often involves histories of difficulty and pain. Second, she emphasizes the matter of respect: what humor ought *not* to do, she suggests, is convey disrespect or dismissiveness. Third, she argues that in practice her humor is not about having a good time, not about being funny, but rather about creating a space for release and recognition, "a safety valve" that can enable work on very hard issues to move ahead. In the ability of parties together to survive and emerge connected after such difficult conversations, humor can engender a sense of "salvation" too.

Here again, we learn about the politics of such humor through the reassurances it can provide. This facilitator hopes to say to a group wary of her power, "I'm not going to try to use my authority to bring you out in front of others here. I'm not going to use my power to objectify you and separate you from others and from me. I'm not going to talk about you without your consent, in ways that would humiliate you in front of others. We will, instead, work together..."[12]

As many of us work with community residents on issues of services or jobs, for example, Normajean suggests that those residents will want very quickly to check out how we think about *ourselves*, because that will also suggest how we are likely to think about and treat them in turn. So our ability to make light of ourselves or what we have done signals a political openness to the group: a willingness not to be single-minded, not to be rigid or authoritarian. In so doing, we offer a gesture of our own vulnerability to the group, an expression of "We're here *with* you," rather than "above you," to provide a measure of release and safety for all those present.

We might now appreciate the political as well as the psychological character of this sense of *release*. Normajean's self-directed humor can suggest to the group that they need to worry a bit less than they have about this potential authority, about this facilitator who enters with an ambiguously authoritative and interventionist role. "If she takes herself with a sense of humor," community members may in effect feel, "perhaps we can be less anxious about her being self-righteous toward us."[13]

Normajean speaks as well to a theme touched upon by the planners and mediators whose reflections we have considered earlier: in tough and conflict-ridden situations, her sense of humor works to build new collaborative relationships based on mutual respect rather than humiliation, collaborative relationships based on humility rather than professional presumption or arrogance.

But how does a facilitator or manager's taking *herself less seriously* make others' practical action more possible? A sense of humor does *not* put a happy face on a bad situation. Reducing barriers, it can help build working relationships with others who have been wary, distrusting, or uncertain of what they're about to face.

Humor and Hope: Closing Down or Opening Up Possibilities

So consider now how a sense of humor can encourage not just recognition but a sense of community, not just momentary release but a sense of capacity, not just safety but a glimpse of possibility too. Recall once again that the practical point of humor here has nothing to do with telling canned jokes and even less to do with making fun of anyone.

Normajean shows us how our "having a sense of humor" can help us not to avoid or dismiss, but actually to recognize serious problems without being so very serious that we're immobilized. Speaking of her work on community and neighborhood issues, for example, she continues,

> Having a sense of humor's hugely important, and it's a dance. It's a dance, because we're dealing with such heavy-duty painful subjects. You're dealing with people who have been kicked out of restaurants or not served, who have been called "dirty squaw" as they're walking down the street.
>
> We're dealing with pain—and that has to be dealt with seriously. I do not make light of that kind of stuff—I may tell a story that is about exactly that kind of thing—but, on the other hand, you've got to let it go, it's got to move…They can't stay there otherwise.

Normajean moves us here from a general claim, that having a sense of humor in difficult situations is "hugely important," to a practical one: that dealing with "such heavy-duty painful subjects" calls for much more than using some pre-programmed response. So she says, in these cases, "It's a dance," implying that dealing with such painful situations requires her to be light- not heavy-handed, flexible rather than rigid, responsive and attentive in the moment to those she works with rather than responding to them with some preprogrammed moves, or with some pat or facile clichés.

Normajean stresses, too, that in these same situations she's "dealing with pain—and that has to be dealt with seriously." But then she moves to action, to the need to go on, not to ignore or dismiss the pain but to act upon it. So she tells us of the need for distance, "but, on the other hand, you've got to let it go, it's got to move…They can't stay there otherwise."

We need limits, she goes on to argue, to our own seriousness even—or especially—in the face of pain, precisely because we will often try not just to recognize another's hurt and distress, and try not just to treat others as victims, but to do more. So Normajean goes on,

> "What's the risk of being too serious? If you're too serious dealing with these subjects—and I've been in groups that have done it—it's literally a cycle down, like a reverse tornado or something. The *seriousness* cycles the room down. It gets heavier, and heavier, and heavier—and I don't believe that hope is built on heaviness."

Hope, she suggests, can be held hostage to a seriousness and heaviness that substitutes earnestness and even commiseration for the encouragement of action and change. So she continues,

> I don't believe that when I'm at my most, "Oh my God, this is terrible…This is awful…" that I'm thinking at the same time, "Oh goody! I can go out and change this."
>
> Personally, I don't work that way. Change is possible when somebody says to me, "If we can make it, here, in this little bubble, then we can take this piece of it with us out there."
>
> I ask them, "You don't have to change the world—can you do that little piece?"
> "Yeah, I can do that little bit."
> "I thought so."
> But in order for me to feel that way, I have to have a sense that it is manageable—which doesn't come from cycling heavier and heavier and heavier and heavier, because then it's a mass, it all becomes a lump. It's all the racism in the world. It's every war we're ever going to fight. It's the Israelis and the Palestinians. It's all the armaments; it's everything all at once.
>
> I've been in groups where we've gone through all that.

Here we begin to see the connection between humor and hope, between not taking oneself too seriously and suggesting, instead, that we together might act. We can't act on everything at once, on all the racism in the world, on all the poverty, but we *can* move to act on particular pieces.

But maybe we can do that little bit only if we can imagine for ourselves what we *can* do—and that might mean that community leaders and planners, activists and facilitators would do well at times to lighten up, too, and heed Frank Blechman's warning—even or especially in the face of racism—not to mistake *unmitigated seriousness* for respect. Instead, having a sense of imagination and humor can, in critical moments, open up their own roles, as well as those of others, for improvisation, new action, and change.

Leveling Power to Encourage and Build Power

Normajean argues that her sense of humor helps to empower others just as it undercuts the presumptions of her own power:

> So using humor sometimes says, "I don't take myself so seriously." That's a big part of it. That shows up in various ways in the community development context. If

I come there as the enlightened teacher with the serious answer, I'm telling them two things: "You don't know what you're doing," and "I do, and I've come here to tell you."

When I do that, I don't make *their* actions possible.

With these observations, Normajean suggests again how her sense of humor can help her to unravel and then reconstruct her audience's political expectations of her role. But now she tells us more—not just about their sense of release, but about their own possible empowerment too.

By taking herself *less* seriously than the esteemed outside expert that she could otherwise claim to be, or be taken to be, she can convey that she and the assembled community residents, too, need to take everyone present *more* seriously. So she recognizes how her claims to power can *disempower* just those residents whose actions she wishes to encourage. She explains:

> Part of what the humor does is pull me out of the power,...out of the power place of saying, "I'm the one that knows and I'm bringing you the wisdom from the mountain."
>
> Part of it is saying things just like that: "Guess what? I didn't bring the wisdom from the mountain. You've got all the wisdom from the mountain in this room, and our whole week is going to be just figuring out how wise you are. If you didn't come in wise, you'll be leaving wise—isn't that good news?"

Normajean connects her humor about others' expectations or worries about her own role to credit them, to suggest a vision for them: with your experience of other outsiders, you're right to worry, but you've got all the wisdom from the mountain in this room, and coming—together—to understand what that can mean is our mission.

Now saying that much, of course, still implies that she knows something that the community members don't; she doesn't claim ignorance—but she suggests a collaborative role instead of an authoritarian one: "So when instead I make fun of myself, for example, and become a player in the room, I enter into the room as another person there. I enter into the community, and first of all I'm saying to them, 'Thank you for letting me come into the circle with you.'"

In these passages Normajean has been suggesting powerfully how all those in facilitating, planning, or managing roles, even those in the helping professions, can disempower or alternatively empower those with whom they work. She has told us, "When I come there as the enlightened teacher with the serious answer...I don't make their actions possible." Lacking a sense of humor, she could well disempower rather than empower a group of concerned citizens. She makes the point lucidly:

> In the first years that I worked as a community developer and facilitator, I came in and showed them all these brilliant and wonderful things that I'd done and could do. I did it so well that when I left, they were all convinced that they couldn't do it.
>
> Now, they did want me back again, which is good as a consultant. But that's not the point.
>
> In the past four years, at the end of these long training sessions that I do, the group goes around and says what changed, what's been the most powerful experience for them. In the old days they'd say, "Normajean, you are the most incredible facilitator, I've never met anyone like you. You are just—I can't even imagine doing what you're doing."
>
> And that was the kicker line, "I can't imagine myself doing what you're doing." I just failed. I may have felt grand, but I just failed.
>
> Now what I hear is different, and I'll tell you exactly what came out of Prince George, the community I'm going back to this week. At the end of it, we went around the circle, and they said, "This is the most powerful group of people. I can't believe we're together. This is amazing! Oh, Normajean, you were great, too."
>
> *That* is success.

This striking reflection about power and empowerment teaches us about far more than this practitioner's own evolving strategies and measures of success. Her sense of humor, she has suggested, becomes deeply political here in several practical ways: leveling roles and providing safety, encouraging conversation and enabling discovery, building confidence and power too.

Politics, Surprise, and Sources of Change

So this appeal to having a sense of humor is political through and through. The humor works to flatten hierarchies between outside experts and less-esteemed community members—and to connect people and build relationships. Normajean's humor responds to political presumptions of experts' power and community perceptions of powerlessness too—and it challenges and counteracts them both.

Her sense of humor also offers collaboration: she's here not to bring word from on high, but to explore together what's possible to do. Her humor does not just express, but it also enacts—it brings into the world—a new, politically practical collaboration. Her sense of humor does not announce but instead creates in deed a socially deliberative space in which to consider just that *what to do* question. Opening up that question for real discussion moves away from the community members' dependency upon experts and toward exercising their capacities and deliberative abilities to craft their own strategies of action.

Normajean put this vividly:

> When I can say with a sense of humor that I don't take myself so seriously, it conveys that things are possible—that possibility comes through the whole band of human interaction. It comes through the pain, it comes through the laughter, it comes through our tears, it comes through grieving together, and it comes through eating together. It comes through dancing. Through that whole band of human interaction we find solution, we find possibility. We find soul mates, we find teachers.

All that is possible though, she suggests, only if we can maintain a certain breadth of vision:

> But when we take just one heavy piece out to work on, we don't function very well—when we say, essentially, "We're only going to look at the pain, and nobody's allowed to talk about anything but pain here this afternoon. I'm sorry, that's all we're dealing with—so if you didn't come with your pain, you get to come and we'll give you some: you'll hear my pain, and then you'll feel so shitty by the end of the day that I can assure you, you'll be in pain then!" (laughs)

These passages present as moving and lucid a criticism of narrow professionalized roles—in the context of community development work in the face of challenges of racial and cultural differences—as we are likely to find. We see here what we might call "the commiseration trap," attending so much to pain and suffering and victimhood that possibilities for change go ignored or unconsidered at all.

We learn instead here that possibilities of change come in many forms: through the sharing of pain and the sharing of laughter together too; through the solidarity and support we might feel in crying together; through the strength we develop in witnessing, appreciating, and grieving for our losses together; through the relationships and civic friendships we develop in sharing meals together; and through the beauty and rhythm we can share in dancing together. In all these ways, we may begin to appreciate the subtle but practical gestures and acts that can weave together humor, not taking ourselves too seriously, recognition, and hope.

For our own parts, we should not lose Normajean's point behind the poetry of her language. In messy and conflict-ridden community settings, professionals bring their own blinders, and they may not see how community members can learn together and come to act in many ways. So through sharing both pain and joy, through making music and meals, community members can connect with, can strengthen and empower, one another—can discuss their issues and histories, options and strategies—and draw, of course, upon professional advice, too, as they work together to find "solutions."

In exploring issues together, deliberating together rather than depending on outside advice alone, we find out who we can turn to, vent, cry or laugh with, learn from, act with—and we may not only find ways to approach immediate problems, but ways to discover other possibilities as well. In probing issues and concerns together, we discover relationships that have meaning as well as payoff, depth as well as utility; we may find "soul mates," Normajean observes, as well as "solutions." Having a sense of humor, our not taking ourselves "so seriously" might help us to recognize more clearly what we do *not* yet know, what we need to learn—and so we may come to "find teachers" too.

Prescriptive Lessons, Advice, and a Few Hypotheses

So what lessons about dealing with differences might these practitioners' reflections suggest for our own future practice? Consider just a few:

If we don't have a practical sense of irony, a responsive sense of humor in practice, then we'll be more likely to reinforce others' prior suspicions and expectations of our roles (as insiders or outsiders), and consequently, we will find it *more difficult* to build trust, connect collaboratively with parties, look together at shared problems, and improvise within shared norms or guidelines. We will find it more difficult to resist passivity, dependency, or passive-aggressive behavior; more difficult to encourage the autonomy and creativity that prior expectations of our expert-authoritative role can undermine.

If we don't *show* that we have a sense of humor in practice, we're more likely to get stuck when negative comments about outsiders begin to escalate, when acknowledgment of pain and hurt threatens to become a *sink* evoking more of the same, and when parties express pessimism about action. Hardly least of all, our having a sense of humor in practice will enable others to see that we appreciate multiple perspectives at any given time and that we recognize that rules and guidelines are ambiguous—so we can invoke and implement them in several ways. Bringing a responsive sense of humor to our work will encourage a space for fresh exploration and discussion, and it may help others give us the benefit of the doubt when we err.

Conclusion

In situations full of inequality and distrust, complexity and bureaucratic entanglements, racism and histories of humiliation, having a keen sense of irony and a responsive sense of humor can help. In practice, we have seen that a sensitive and respectful sense of humor can do quite responsive, politically astute work—not by telling jokes but by pointing to shared perplexities, uncertainties, and vulnerabilities, by encouraging engagement rather than resignation, by welcoming rather than punishing multiple points of vision on painful topics and difficult issues at hand.

A potentially powerful form of ironic practice, humor shapes attention deliberately but indirectly, intentionally but nonargumentatively. What's actually said matters, not to argue claims but to show a new way of acting together—and to recognize real complexity and the legitimacy of multiple perspectives. So the very ridiculousness of saying, "Well, according to the bylaws, I'm supposed to sit right here," conveys far more than any descriptive truth of the matter. The self-parody of introducing oneself as "a short, fat, white guy" can be both funny and serious at once, a source of relief and insight too, a refreshing and encouraging source of recognition of tough issues, revelation of the manager's openness, and hope for candid and useful discussion as well.

So when participatory settings get tough, it turns out, having "a sense of humor" has very little to do with being funny. Enacting rather than claiming, performing rather than arguing, mediators and facilitators find that their irony and humor reveal multiple meanings and uncertainties, multiple perspectives and their limits, and parties' needs and opportunities to learn. Their humor can go wrong, of course, and these practitioners stress a sine qua non: humor must be respectful, never used at the expense of a negotiating party.

At critical moments in dealing with differences, facilitative leaders' irony and humor can be sensitively responsive to others, improvised with respect to tone, timing, affect, dignity, and more. That irony and humor can deconstruct and reconstruct parties' presumptions of others' authority, recognize vulnerability, create moments of intimacy and suggest possible community, acknowledge painful histories and enable difficult conversations, and provide safety and release and new collaborative openings. In all these ways facilitative leaders can signal possibility and hope and, not least of all, level power to encourage autonomy and build capacity—so creating deliberative space and encouraging deliberative practice as well.

In all these ways, too, these facilitative leaders show and teach us how we might achieve important ends: acknowledging others, defusing expectations and providing relief, signaling one's depth of understanding, probing the ambiguity of obligations, recognizing the unpredictability of broader contexts, displaying personal style and character, acknowledging pain and enabling response, interweaving multiple perspectives that might be apt and practical in the moment, and, not least of all, empowering others and encouraging collaborative action together as well.

CHAPTER NINE

Conclusion: Transforming Participatory Processes

Integrating and Transcending Dialogue, Debate, and Negotiation

So mediators don't make agreements any more than midwives make babies. But when disputes and participation get contentious, well-trained mediators with skill and good judgment can help. If that's the good news, the bad news we already know: *public participation* has a notorious history, and *negotiation* often seems to threaten still worse. So-called participatory processes can simply raise hopes but accomplish little, and when mutually distrustful negotiators get together, even less prevents them from reaching outcomes that suffer from their mutual gamesmanship and deception—if skilled mediators, planners, or other facilitative leaders do not help.

No wonder, then, that processes of dealing with differences often remain as frustrating and risky as intriguing and promising. We see great potential often squandered. We see stunning examples of success—Ken Reardon's work with the East St. Louis Action Research Project, for example—and these keep hope alive, even as more often we see traditional public hearings produce public resentment and cynicism (Arnstein 1967, Reardon 1993).

Perplexing Elements of Participatory Processes

Throughout this book we have explored what facilitative leaders and public dispute mediators might teach us about dealing with differences, about public disputes and conflicts—about handling both public participation and practical negotiations as well more fruitfully (Schön 1983, Forester 1999a). These practitioners have made intriguing observations about the challenges of working in participatory settings:

1. Typical public hearing procedures and strategies of moderating meetings so often encourage "decide, announce, defend" exaggeration and posturing, as well as public cynicism and resentment, instead of fostering mutual respect, listening, and learning (Susskind et al. 1999, Susskind and Field 1996).

2. Passionate parties to public disputes haven't always thought very thoroughly about the full range and ambiguities of *their own* interests. How's that possible? As community development mediator from Washington, DC, Don Edwards explained to my students, "If you don't think something's possible, you don't go looking for it" (2006). As today's knowledge shapes our expectations, so those expectations shape our imaginations of our possible futures, how we might live, separately and together.

3. Parties can *"like" or become attached to* their problems or causes, possibly saving or gaining face, being appreciated or respected, or gaining prestige from others by being intimately identified with their missions—protecting habitat, saving buildings, or developing new housing, for example.

4. Mutually suspicious parties can say of each other, "Sure, we'll talk to them, any time; but *they'll* never sit and talk and listen to us!"—even as they then express surprise to learn that their adversaries have righteously professed just the same skepticism about *them*.

5. No matter how parties might initially frame problems, there's always more going on: in public disputes, mediators know, there's a great deal to learn, and they know well that it can often help to ask, not so much, "What's the problem?" but instead, "What's the story?" and not so much, "What do you *think about* that?" but, "How have you *handled or responded to* that?" (Forester 1999a, 2006b).

6. Parties reaching agreements in contentious disputes can express surprise at their own achievement of creative, satisfactory agreements—as they say, for example, "It's magic what happened!" Mediators teach us that behind that surprise lies not magic, no mysterious rocket science, but hard work—hard work to pay careful attention to what *can* happen, not just to what *cannot*, to how initial skepticism and cynicism can transform through joint inquiry and mediated discussions into well-informed judgment and creative, collaborative work together.

7. Not least of all, careful *process design*—going slower initially sometimes to go faster later—can not only prevent the costs of long delays, prevent relation-

ships from being further damaged, but can improve the quality of planning decisions and stakeholders' ownership of those decisions (Susskind, McKearnan, and Thomas-Larmer 1999).

Finding Possibilities When Apparent Impossibility Looms

We need to remember that disputes—over resources or regulations, for example—signal the *absence* of agreement, not its impossibility. So we have explored here especially how experienced mediators can teach us about finding or *creating possible agreements* when initially, of course, the distrusting, contentious parties themselves—including planners, governmental officials, and community activists—may well have seen few cooperative possibilities at all. These chapters have suggested how mediators can at times create processes that generate real opportunities when residents, developers, local officials, environmentalists, farmers, and others have initially seen only intractable conflict.

Mediators of environmental, community, or broader governance disputes, for example, have enabled possibilities when the parties in traditional planning processes have missed opportunities to build relationships, to explore options, and to find mutually satisfying agreements—rather than settling for the poorer lose-lose agreements that parties so often reach as they very deliberately game, bluff, exaggerate, withhold information, and more. We can draw together now what mediators have learned to see and do—being sensitive to relations of power and being realistically pragmatic too—that the rest of us often do not, and we can do that in three steps.

First, by recognizing just how limited our knowledge of the future can be when we need to deal with differences, we can recognize, too, how much we need to learn, to engage in joint inquiries. Second, we can see how we might *integrate* processes of *participation* with those of effective *negotiations*. And third, we can return to a series of practical insights offered by the mediators on whose shoulders we have tried to stand throughout this book.

Recognizing Our Need to Learn about Our Interdependence

So, first, if we admit that none of us, as parties in participatory processes, can truly be the economists' perfectly rational actors—can be so perfectly informed about the world beyond us, about our myriad networks and relationships or even our own complex values and interests—then we come to the underwhelming but humbling conclusion that in cases of any social or political complexity, we all typically need to learn about our vulnerabilities to political change, about our interconnectedness, and about our needs to manage such interdependence. Not being omniscient, we might still learn about information and options, intentions and interests that can really inform what we can do to serve our ends and interests—*far better than we might have seen initially*. The greater the complexity and contentiousness, the greater our need to network, listen, probe, and learn.

Individual stakeholders will have their own internally conflicting priorities of interests and values; they, too, can feel stuck in relations with others; they, too, can doubt that others will act less selfishly than they have before; and yet they can admit, too, that they have no crystal ball to foretell the future, that there's information they need, that they need to learn (Schön 1983, Forester 1989). This much might sound like old news, for we have thought about participatory processes as modes of social learning for many years, dating not just from the systems literature of the 1960s and 1970s, but from work like John Dewey's wonderful and prescient *The Public and Its Problems* another 40 years earlier (Churchman 1968, Dewey 1927)!

Integrating Processes of Negotiation with Participation

Second, students of participation in many disciplines, though, seem not to recognize multiparty negotiations as actual learning processes—if they have thought at all about how practical negotiations fit into processes of participatory governance. Here we come to an area of practice in which the insights and judgments of experienced mediators can teach us a great deal, for these mediators, because of the very nature of their jobs, have had to worry not just about stakeholder representation, and not just about stakeholder learning in the abstract, but about how diverse stakeholders can actually speak together and interact, so that *they* can then reach practical agreements together that serve their ends, agreements that they, as engaged, public- *and* private-regarding stakeholders value—that they autonomously and consensually legitimate—as elements of their own democratic self-governance.

Washington-based consultant Frank Blechman illustrates this work vividly when he says that as a mediator first assessing a public dispute, one of his questions to every stakeholder goes roughly like this: "Are you having fun yet?" If the answer's "Yes," he says, then he has little as a mediator to offer. A party who feels happy enough as things are may have very little incentive to deal with others to try to do better: if the status quo's fine for me, why should I change it? But when parties are not, in Blechman's words, "having fun yet," when they're angry that they don't have more access or services or jobs or land, sooner, better, freer, *then* the mediator can be helpful, then the stakeholders have incentives to talk, to listen, to try to learn, and to work to come up with options (and thus to negotiate) so that they can actually implement agreements to serve their own private and public ends and concerns, hopes and interests (Blechman 2005).

How might this work? Consider the practical task presented in table 9.1, which maps out the challenge of *integrating processes of voice* and forms of public participation *with processes of practical, outcome-oriented negotiations.* This table arrays higher and lower voice/participation from left to right across the top and more effective and less effective negotiations from top to bottom. This array produces an overly simple but still instructive two-by-two mapping. We can move quickly through several of the resulting combinations, but we should pay careful attention to the challenge presented by the upper-left-hand combination of "high voice/participation, effective negotiations"—because this whole book has addressed, in effect, how to integrate just such inclusive voice with fair and efficiently interest-satisfying negotiations.

In the lower-left quadrant we have lots of "voice" with very little being negotiated. Here we might think, for example, of the common pathologies of public hearings. Perhaps many speak, but they negotiate nothing, agree upon less, and leave public hearings still more upset, less trusting, and often more resentful of public governance processes than when they came in, supposedly to participate. These all-too-common hearings give public participation a bad name, and we can only hope that Lawrence Susskind's recently published *Breaking Robert's Rules* might help public officials in many settings to do better than they have in convening contentious multiparty public meetings (Susskind and Cruickshank 2006).

In the upper-right-hand quadrant we have the combination of "low voice/participation, effective negotiations": here we find varieties of deal making by "the old boys," the insiders or the elites. Those with access and muscle cut the deals; the many affected, if not necessarily organized or represented, participate hardly at all. Negotiation triumphs here, participation suffers.

Table 9.1 Integrating Participation with Negotiation

	High Voice/Participation	Low Voice/Participation
Effective negotiations	Dealing with Differences via mediated negotiations and facilitative leadership	Deal making
Weak negotiations	Public hearing	Bureaucratic procedure

In the lower-right-hand quadrant we find those governance processes in which little participation or negotiation takes place. Here we might think of "bureaucracy as usual." Experts and official agency staff study problems and make recommendations. Planners and analysts present options for officials to consider. The city council (or legislative body) will make decisions, but that process might well have involved little participation (once the council's elected) and, most likely, not much stakeholder negotiation before the staff's recommendations land on the city council's or another decision maker's desk.

These three combinations leave one or the other of effective participation and negotiation out. So we come to the fourth set of possibilities in the upper-left-hand quadrant and to the practical challenge that this book has primarily addressed. With skill and careful design, we have seen, we can organize complex and networked governance processes that integrate high voice and diverse stakeholder participation with efficient and practically pitched negotiations—to produce not poor compromises but implementable, interest-satisfying agreements with lasting results. Experienced facilitative leaders and mediators of public disputes have insights and lessons to share here because they have often faced this challenge: they have encouraged inclusion and representation of affected stakeholders *and* they have sought efficient, well-informed, stable, and consent-based agreements that go far, far beyond saying, "Let's just make a deal and get out of here."

So what have we learned from these practitioners? Integrating inclusive participation and effective negotiation takes skill and preparation, thoughtfulness and a sense of humor, commitments to fairness and joint gains, and more, we have seen—but not rocket science. We can summarize a series of tips or suggestions that inform the typical phases of a mediated participation or public dispute resolution process: (1) assessing a dispute, then (2) convening the affected stakeholders, then (3) enabling learning and joint inquiry, all before (4) managing negotiations about options to implement (Susskind and Thomas-Larmer 1999).

These mediators' insights hardly capture all of what these chapters have taught us, and they provide no recipes or quick fixes, but each might help us to do better work that integrates inclusive voice and practical negotiations. We can offer the following summary lessons for planners and citizen leaders, for public managers and administrators, and for facilitative leaders more generally.

On Assessing Multistakeholder Disputes and Interdependence:
Lessons from the Field

I. Mediators teach us that if curiosity kills cats, *presumptions* about what *can't* be kills negotiators—and they know that many negotiating parties are likely to come to participatory processes with at least as much so-called realism and narrow presumption as cats come to electric wires with curiosity. Here again, we see the wisdom and challenges of Don Edwards's observation quoted earlier: "If you don't think something's possible"—if you presume it isn't—"you don't go looking for it." So public managers and citizen leaders must work carefully to expand and probe the horizons of the possible long before they turn to managing any negotiation about those options.

2. Mediators know very well, too, how many self-fulfilling reasons parties can find as justifications *not to talk* to those they see as adversaries, not to talk to those they see as repugnantly treating nature or finances or values differently from themselves. Even as mediators know, of course, that many disputes can be irreconcilable, they nevertheless teach us that far, far more can be possible than many passionately involved, but understandably distrusting and skeptical parties can believe. Our limited vision and knowledge, mediators know, mean that we have much to learn—that we have much we might do together that we can't jointly see or invent if we don't meet together in carefully structured processes—even as progressives deeply distrust the fundamentalists (and vice versa), even as the greens think developers repugnant (and vice versa), as distrust and skepticism, overconfident "realism" and posturing have kept parties from productive conversation and negotiation (http://www.publicconversations.org/pcp/index.php, Forester 1999b, Umemoto 2001).

3. So mediators teach us to *probe possibilities* rather than to *presume outcomes*, and they urge us as a result to be neither presumptuous cynics nor naive optimists. In cases of increasingly common interdependence, when interconnected stakeholders—recreationists and environmentalists, residents and developers—can make each other miserable by taking a toll of time, money, natural resources, and opportunities lost, mediators see opportunities to bring parties together in pragmatic, forward-looking ways to ask new questions, to build new relationships, to generate new options, and to solve problems together in new ways.

We can summarize the challenges of assessing disputes and practical interdependence as follows (see also Appendix I):

Assessing Interdependence or Disputes: Questions to Explore with Stakeholders

> Ask potential parties the following:
> Blechman's question: "Are you having fun yet?" (What do you wish to change? Whose cooperation does your welfare depend upon?)
> What do you see as your best options, with what likelihood of success and costs?
> What's your best practical alternative to a multistakeholder negotiation?
> Would you *explore* issues and options together—if you could leave at any time and use your options in the courts, political process, or streets?

Who's affected? Who should have their say?
Under what conditions would you meet to explore issues and options with others,
    even if you have little trust in them and lower expectations of them?
Who'd represent you well?
If other key actors were to meet, would you want to be there, at least to listen?
What would a safe meeting space require in your view?
What do you see as the main issues, and which matter more and less to you?
What information would help you better assess your options over the next years?

On Convening Parties: Lessons from the Field

I. Experienced mediators teach us that parties often enter participatory set-tings after they have hammered out an emerging sense of priorities and concerns that have reflected discussions with their own constituencies—*and* these media-tors tell us that those priorities and concerns may very well *shift over time*—that we shouldn't take them as definitive last words, that a great deal remains to explore

2. Mediators have learned and teach us, too, that parties' accumulated anger may not only threaten but can also *fuel* efforts for change. California media-tor Lisa Beutler put this powerfully, we have seen, this way: "Whenever there is conflict in the room, it means there's energy to work on something—conflict is always better than apathy...So, now, if [as a party] I'm angry, I'm angry about *something*, and I'm angry because I don't think something is working right—and I *want* things to work right." Moving against the grain of those who might be *conflict avoiders*, she argues that anger and contentiousness can provide energy *for* change, if mediators, public managers, and facilitative leaders do their work well (Forester 2006c).

3. Experienced mediators know, too, of course, that words matter and that names and frames matter. So mediators can be reluctant even to call their pro-cesses *mediation* because that might too narrowly frame parties' subsequent discus-sions. In a striking case exploring native gathering rights in Hawaii, we saw, Peter Adler quite deliberately convened a multiparty process, at the request of the state legislature—a process involving native Hawaiian cultural practitioners, bankers, and real estate agents—and he worked to call it not a *facilitation*, not a *mediation*, but a *study group*—to focus first on investigating the issues and only then to turn to designing policy alternatives (Forester 2005).

So consider the following summary of the challenges of convening parties (see also Appendix II):

Convening Affected Stakeholders' Representatives: Elements to Consider

Naming the process will insinuate goals and possibilities—for example, "study group" versus "negotiation" may signal (safer) *learning* versus (more adversarial) *conflict.*

Creating nonargumentative spaces (meals, site visits, etc.) may enable relationship building, beginnings of trust, and mutual recognition.

Cogenerating norms of meeting, *ground rules,* can build shared process expectations of mutual consideration, time, and space to speak.

Expecting posturing, exaggeration, and passion motivates listening for detail and priorities, for broader interests and fears.

Recognizing anger amongst parties as potential "energy to fuel change" can help, taking that anger not only as divisive, escalating arguments, and weakening relationships.

Respecting parties' abilities to learn and gain new insights can enable parties together not to be locked in to initial positions, first words, or opinions.

Taking a stance of nonpartisanship, not neutrality, can enable facilitative leaders to help every party express views, listen, learn, propose, and decide *as they wish.*

Creating the space for each party to actually tell their story can enable not just information sharing but mutual *diplomatic recognition,* seeds of respect.

Identifying representatives who can press for their constituents' interests while listening and learning as new information arises can help all parties gain.

On Enabling Learning and Joint Inquiry: Lessons from the Field

1. The mediators whose work we've explored remind us that none of the parties in participatory processes are likely to be omniscient, that all of the parties can learn, and what's more, that the parties can *all* in some ways feel *vulnerable* and so recognize their need to learn—potentially then turning their attention a bit from fighting each other to figuring out how better to achieve their goals and satisfy their interests (Laws and Forester 2007b, Sandercock 2003b).

2. These mediators know very well too, and can teach us as well, that directing a group's attention to a shared challenge or vulnerability mapped on the wall can subtly bring participants' focus *away* from attacking one another *to* facing issues and uncertainties and further questions that many in the room may wish to explore. This lesson can be as stunning in its simplicity as in its practicality: map the issue on the wall.

3. Mediators also teach us that pictures tell thousands of words—that visual materials will often open up participants' commentaries and stories far more

than pages and pages of text will, and so photographs and slides, family albums and photos of neighborhood "goods" and "bads," assets and deficits, can all help transform the vociferous parties' claims from generalities about transportation conditions to quite specific instances of particular intersections—in turn enabling parties to learn *from* each other rather than lecturing *at* each other.

4. So mediators know that processes of dialogue differ from processes of debate. In moments of *dialogue*, we seek understanding of meaning and sentiment, understanding of perspective and "where they're coming from," and we need skillfully attentive and probing *facilitators* to help us clarify meaning rather than have hot-button words lead us astray. To foster *debate*, in contrast, we encourage parties to sharpen their arguments, and we need skillful work not so much of facilitating but of *moderating* an adversarial series of claims and refutations, counterclaims and counterrefutations (Forester 2006c, Corburn 2005).

The following list summarizes the challenges of enabling learning and joint inquiry by parties (see also Appendix III):

Enabling Learning: Elements to Consider

> Identifying "information needed" by parties can address shared uncertainties and vulnerabilities to contextual change—creating processes of joint inquiry.
> Employing joint fact finding rather than the warring experts of adversarial science can enable mutual learning, problem redefinition, and focus on new options.
> Using best available knowledge of issues and contextual changes can enable parties to reassess their own vulnerabilities, opportunities, priorities, and even values.
> Taking the ambiguity of values and interests as an invitation to inquiry, not as a barrier, can enable creative exploration of proposed options and stakes.
> Remembering that stakeholders *can* differ fundamentally about what their deities require while they *can* still produce practical agreements about "where the stop signs go" can help all parties deal together with deep value differences.
> Using visual information to complement text can enable rich, multimedia learning via evocative, instructive photos, sketches, actual site visits, and more.
> Anticipating parties' impatience or overconfident solution seeking enables respect for initial proposals as well as for learning about mutual vulnerabilities.
> Using hands-on model building, participatory mapping, or other tactile design exercises can enable nonverbal, nonargumentative exploration of options.

On Negotiating Agreements about What to Do: Lessons from the Field

1. Mediators often note the importance of *working indirectly*, the importance of *not just trying to sit the parties down to cut a deal.* Americans can be notorious for a vulgar

pragmatism, even as others might take prenegotiation rituals to great lengths. The wisdom of indirection helps us to acknowledge that any, even apparently straightforward, negotiation involves not only the *substance* being negotiated by those present, but the complex relationships involved and the legacies of their histories, in addition to a changing *and uncertain* environment that can subtly put both relationships and substance, vulnerabilities and opportunities, all in new light over time. The most commonplace strategies of indirection, of course, include making time and space for the rituals of sharing food and storytelling, the time and spaces enabling parties to acknowledge and learn new things about one another at the same time (Forester 1999a, LeBaron 2002, Sclavi 2006a, 2006b).

2. Mediators know and teach us how critical the turn *from* escalating "blame games" *to* generating proposals can be. Blaming quickly becomes personal, fueling defensiveness, justification, and counterargument; asking for proposals opens up possibilities of crafting agreements. So mediators know the risks of accusatory "you" language, and they try to create space for participants to ask and explore variants of the essential "What if ...?" questions: "What if we do this? What if we try to do that?" (Kolb 1994, Kolb and Williams 2000, 2003).

3. Mediators know, too, crucially though, that both *dialogue* and *debate* can differ from *negotiation*, and that *each of these requires different forms of assistance. Facilitating* a dialogue calls for different sensitivities, skills, and goals than does *moderating* a debate. Likewise, both facilitating and moderating differ as practical strategies from *mediating* a negotiation. Dialogue can seek understanding (not necessarily agreement); debate can seek to sharpen arguments (even at the cost of further antagonizing relationships); negotiation, in contrast, seeks agreements upon practical action—so we can answer the question, "What are we going to *do?*"

So mediators—integrating multistakeholder participation with practical negotiations—will be very careful *to do even more than what facilitators and moderators do;* building *upon* both of these related strategies, mediators will work to evoke practical proposals, to probe possibilities of joint action and agreement, to explore how parties might go forward together (Forester 2006c).

The following list summarizes the challenges of "negotiating agreements about what to do" by parties (see also Appendix IV):

Negotiating Agreements: Elements to Consider

> Explore stakeholders' differences so they can *trade*, each gaining on their priorities because their priorities *differ* (so *don't* focus only on *common ground*).
> Preempt solution seeking with *options analysis* by exploring "what we could do if ...," generating and widening before narrowing and discarding options.

Help parties reduce gamesmanship by providing means to broaden what they
know, reframing needs to learn, and generating options without commitment.

Encourage not "blaming them" but "proposing what we could do."

Balance any shuttle diplomacy with face-to-face meeting, listening, learning, and
making small offers to test the ground for larger working agreements.

Work to achieve each of the four criteria of good agreements: (1) fairness via
inclusion; (2) efficiency via maximizing joint gains/trades; (3) intelligence via
best available information; and (4) stability via structured opportunities for
possible renegotiation.

Address two-table negotiation issues by ensuring that parties remain accountable
to their constituencies.

Recognize that agreements can often improve; ask *every* party how they might help
the others at low cost—so all might gain.

Remember that no agreement upon action, "agreement to disagree," may be a
"good outcome" in itself, with many parties learning, better informed, and
pursuing the strategies they desire.

So when we need to work practically through networks to bring into play
diverse experience and expertise and judgment, we need to deal creatively and
pragmatically with differences—differences in priorities, interests, and values, in
worldviews and perspectives, in class position, political standing, cultural identity, and more. When we want or need to act not unilaterally or autocratically
but responsively to affected stakeholders, we need to deal with a similar range of
differences.

When we need to work in public meetings to build confidence and ownership
rather than skepticism and cynicism, we need to deal with these differences. When
we hope to work collaboratively on public problems through multistakeholder
task forces or by bringing together specially formed working groups or committees or other participatory bodies, we need to deal with such differences—and
we can build upon and extend the insights and lessons of experienced mediators,
public managers, and facilitative leaders.

We have argued that "dealing with differences" does not abolish differences
or deny them so much as honor and build upon them. Dealing well with our differences tells us much more about what we can do together than about who, if
anybody, is right or wrong. Dealing with our differences means not assuming or
presuming impossibilities where skillful mediators might still show us real and
practical opportunities for serving our own and broader public interests as well
(Forester 2006d). Dealing with our differences means, then, to *recognize* power
differences but *not to resign* ourselves to them, so we can come to see difference as
ineradicable and yet not paralyzing.

We need no longer believe that *participation* means just "talk, talk, talk" and likely chaos. We need no longer believe that *negotiation* means making poor compromises and betraying values we cherish. We can instead improve many governance processes by integrating inclusive voice and representative participation with efficient and well-informed, practically oriented negotiations.

We can understand better now where we began: how it may indeed be more difficult to hurt each other once we know one another's stories. We can now understand better, as well, the practical depth of J. P. Lederach's insight with which we began: "Advocacy chooses to stand by one side for justice's sake. Mediation chooses to stand in connection to all sides for justice's sake."

If we build upon the practice stories we have considered throughout this book, we can come to be less gullible and more inquisitive. We can respect naysayers but not so readily simply agree with them. We can honor deep value differences and still act together practically. We can refuse to reduce *participation* to the pathologies of public hearings. We can encourage diverse and practical forms of deliberations that distinguish carefully, integrate, and even transcend processes of talk in dialogue, of argument in debate, and of acting together in inclusive negotiations. In so doing, we can come closer than we have before to realizing the democratic promise of empowering transformative public participation and honoring and building upon our many deep and abiding differences as well.

Appendix I

Assessing Interdependence or Disputes: Questions to Explore with Stakeholders

Blechman's question: "Are you having fun yet?" (What do you wish to change? Whose cooperation does your welfare depend upon?)

What do you see as your best options, with what likelihood of success and costs?

What's your best practical alternative to a multi-stakeholder negotiation?

Would you *explore* issues and options together if you could leave at any time and use your options in the courts, political process, or streets?

Who's affected? Who should have their say?

Under what conditions would you meet to explore issues and options with others, even if you have little trust in them and lower expectations of them?

Who'd represent you well?

If other key actors were to meet, would you want to be there, at least to listen?

What would a safe meeting space require in your view?

What do you see as the main issues, and which matter more and less to you?

What information would help you better assess your options over the next years?

Appendix II

Convening Affected Stakeholders' Representatives: Elements to Consider

Naming the process will insinuate goals and possibilities—for example, "study group" versus "negotiation" may signal (safer) "learning" versus (more adversarial) "conflict."

Creating nonargumentative spaces (meals, site visits, etc.) may enable relationship building, beginnings of trust, mutual recognition.

Cogenerating norms of meeting, ground rules, can build shared process expectations of mutual consideration, time, and space to speak.

Expecting posturing, exaggeration, and passion motivates listening for detail and priorities, for broader interests and fears.

Recognizing anger amongst parties as potential "energy to fuel change" can help, taking that anger not only as divisive, escalating arguments, and weakening relationships.

Respecting parties' abilities to learn and gain new insights can enable parties together not to be locked in to initial positions, first words, or opinions.

Taking a stance of nonpartisanship, not neutrality, can enable facilitative leaders to help every party express views, listen, learn, propose, and decide *as they wish.*

Creating the space for each party to actually tell their story can enable not just information sharing but mutual diplomatic recognition, seeds of respect.

Identifying representatives who can press for their constituents' interests while listening and learning as new information arises can help all parties gain.

Appendix III

Enabling Learning: Elements to Consider

Identifying "information needed" by parties can address shared uncertainties and vulnerabilities to contextual change—creating processes of joint inquiry.

Employing joint fact finding rather than the warring experts of adversarial science can enable mutual learning, problem redefinition, and focus on new options.

Using best available knowledge of issues and contextual changes can enable parties to reassess their own vulnerabilities, opportunities, priorities, and even values.

Taking the ambiguity of values and interests as an invitation to inquiry, not as a barrier, can enable creative exploration of proposed options and stakes.

Remembering that stakeholders can differ fundamentally about what their deities require while they can still produce practical agreements about "where the stop signs go" can help all parties deal together with deep value differences.

Using visual information to complement text can enable rich, multimedia learning via evocative, instructive photos, sketches, actual site visits, and more.

Anticipating parties' impatience or overconfident solution seeking enables respect for initial proposals as well as for learning about mutual vulnerabilities.

Using hands-on model building, participatory mapping, or other tactile design exercises can enable nonverbal, nonargumentative exploration of options.

Appendix IV

Negotiating Agreements: Elements to Consider

Explore stakeholders' differences so they can trade, each gaining on their priorities because they differ (so don't focus only on common ground).

Preempt solution seeking with *options analysis* by exploring "what we could do if ...," generating and widening before narrowing and discarding options.

Help parties reduce gamesmanship by providing means to broaden what they know, reframing needs to learn, and generating options without commitment.

Encourage not "blaming them" but "proposing what we could do."

Balance any shuttle diplomacy with face-to-face meeting, listening, learning, and making small offers to test the ground for larger working agreements.

Work to achieve each of the four criteria of good agreements: (1) fairness via inclusion; (2) efficiency via maximizing joint gains/trades; (3) intelligence via best available information; and (4) stability via structured opportunities for possible renegotiation.

Address two-table negotiation issues by ensuring that parties remain accountable to their constituencies.

Recognize that agreements can often improve; ask *every* party how they might help the others at low cost—so all might gain.

Remember that no agreement upon action, "agreement to disagree," may be a "good outcome" in itself, with many parties learning, better informed, and pursuing the strategies they desire.

NOTES

Introduction

1. Though these chapters often refer to the variety of roles that include community leadership, public officials, public administrators, planners, and community organizers, throughout we explore the challenges of decision-making and consultative processes seeking to foster inclusive participation of diverse and affected stakeholders whose interdependence in fact requires their interaction if not explicit negotiation. As we shall see, Susskind and Cruickshank have usefully characterized this quasi-mediating role in between diverse parties as "facilitative leadership" (2006). I have written about the micropolitics of this work in Forester (1989), especially on "listening" as the social policy of everyday life and on planners playing "in between" roles among multiple and conflicting stakeholders, and then more concretely and experientially in Forester (1999a) especially in regard to the moral significance of storytelling, interpretation, participatory infrastructures or rituals, and problems of inherited pain and traumatic memory demanding recognition in participatory processes. Cf. note 8.

2. The more I have worked on this book, the more I have recognized the inadequacy of our language to describe the practical skills and wisdom that these practitioners employ in the face of conflict and particular disputes. They *do more* than facilitate or mediate; they do more than organize or manage—they do much of what these terms imply and still more. I will refer to their work as *mediation* but I insist on using that term (and *facilitative leadership*) broadly—because the work we will assess has vast implications for community leaders and organizers no less than for public administrators and public and private managers as well. I will take my chances, then, with reviewers who, failing to read endnotes (or often much at all), will discover earnestly that the work this book describes reaches far beyond "mediation" as conventionally and narrowly understood in ordinary discourse. Cf. note I in Chapter I.

3. Cf. note II in Chapter I. For relevant literature that provides the broader background to this claim, see, for example, on the politics of negotiation and deliberation, Arnstein (1969), Baum (1997), Forester (1999a), Hoch (1994), Innes and Booher (1999), Schön (1983), Susskind and Cruickshank (2006), and Susskind et al. (1999). On participation, power and inequality, and diverse interests, see Sandercock

(2003b), Hillier (2002), Marris and Rein (1973), Hoch (1994), Flyvbjerg (1998), and Yiftachel (1998). On the disorganization of hope, see Forester (1989), Baum (1997), and Sandercock (2003a). On deliberative possibilities, see Reich (1988), Fung (2004), Forester (2006a, 2008b), Laws and Forester (2007a), Sandercock (2003b), Innes and Booher (1999), Healey (1997), Susskind and Cruickshank (1987, 2006), Susskind et al. (1999), Lewicki, Gray and Elliott (2003), and Fung and Wright (2003); and on public management, cf. M. Moore (1995). On distrust of public authorities, see, e.g., Corburn (2005), Flyvbjerg (1998), Forester (1989), and Needleman and Needleman (1974); and on the inadequacies of traditional processes, see, e.g., Diepeveen (2005), Innes and Booher (1999), Sandercock (2003), and Susskind et al. (1999). On community build-ing, see, e.g., Forester (1999) and Sandercock (2003a). On the relationship of medi-ated participation to alternatives, see, e.g., Arnstein (1969), Susskind and Cruickshank (1987), Susskind et al. (1999), and Fisher and Ury (1991), and on the emerging plan-ning literature, see also Susskind and Field (1996), Shmueli et al (2008), Innes (2004), and Innes and Booher (2003). On joint inquiry or fact finding, cf. Adler et al. (2000), Andrews (2002), Laws and Forester (2007b), McCreary et al. (2001), and Ehrmann and Stinson (1999). On largely ignored issues of history and memory in governance pro-cesses, cf. Baum (1996, 1997), Forester (1999a), Marris (1975), Sandercock (2003b), and Susskind and Field (1996). On facilitative leadership, see Susskind and Cruickshank (2006). On shared vulnerability, cf. Axelrod (1985) and Moore (2002); on mind map-ping and related techniques, cf. Weisbord et al. (1992) and Dukes et al. (2000); and on the broader denial of relevant emotional life in planning and governance, cf. Baum (1996), Hoch (2006), and Susskind and Field (1996). On issues of process and out-comes, see Susskind et al. (1999), Forester (1999a), Innes (2004), Reardon (1993), and note 18 in chapter 1.

4. We are concerned here with governance and planning processes that produce not just better processes but better neighborhoods, places, and spaces, urban or rural, and not just the "right to the city," but the material city required for adequate housing, transportation, infrastructure, and so on. Dealing with differences means dealing materi-ally to satisfy stakeholders' interests, not dealing procedurally simply with "process" or "just talk" (Cochran 2008). In so doing, we subvert facile distinctions between public and private, of course, as critical theory and feminist theory taught long ago. Is global warming in principle any more a public threat than a private one? Is the lack of clean air and drinkable water in principle any more a public threat than a private one? Of course a population's access to clean water, for example, can be contested: but that is the point of the book—not simply to articulate subjectively any one party's claims or "demands," but to assess how to resolve together, politically and intersubjectively, how to share (protect, clean, preserve, etc.) the resources whose control and use might be in dispute. Doing this work practically, not as a matter of symbolic claims alone, but also as matters of mate-rial political and legal claims, is the work of organizing real hope and so real action in the world as well. So these chapters undermine, too, any facile detachment of planning from action, even if the planning conduct at stake here resembles that of the midwife more than the autocrat, the responsive organizer more than the technocrat, the Freireian

educator more than the all-knowing lecturer (cf. Freire 1970, Coles and Hauerwas 2007, Forester 1999a).

5. Here the legacy of philosophical pragmatism finds deep agreement with post-modernists' rejection of grand schemes and master narratives, even of the very notion of *philosophy* detached from practice. William James put this beautifully once when he argued that a landlord about to rent out a flat to a prospective tenant needed to be at least as concerned with the tenant's philosophy as with his or her bank account.

6. On the integration of processes of effective negotiation with those of meaning-ful participation, see Forester (2006e, 2008a). No one has done more to advance the field of public dispute mediation, theoretically and practically, than Lawrence Susskind of MIT's Department of Urban Studies and Planning and the firm he cofounded, the Consensus Building Institute. I will not use the language of *consensus building* here in order to avoid the misunderstandings that *consensus* so often provokes, even as my somewhat reluctant use of *mediation* will lead to other problems, as notes 1, 2, and 8 suggest.

7. For substantial discussions of conflict assessment, see Susskind et al. (1999). For implications of conflict assessment practice for policy analysis more generally, see Laws and Forester (2007a) and cf. Shmueli, Kaufman, and Ozawa (2008).

8. This book approaches these questions by examining strategies and practices in the face of conflict as recounted and considered by community activists, urban planners, lawyers-turned-mediators, management consultants, civic leaders, and others, all of whom have been in the trenches of the work to resolve messy and contentious public disputes. Their good work, we shall see, presents us with practical challenges and opportunities too. The challenges show us the blood and guts, the complexities and the obstacles, the problems of distrust and power imbalances, cynicism and revenge that haunt participa-tory processes when citizens confront one another's real histories of fear and exploita-tion. The opportunities show us openings, chances for learning and reconciliation, for reframing and invention, possibilities of innovation and transformation, of collaboration and surprising joint action that no one thought possible earlier, given everything that's happened in the past (Kolb and Williams 2000, 2003, Laws and Rein 2003; cf. the related view of Anderlini 2007).

9. Susskind and Cruickshank (1987) argue that we might evaluate negotiated (and thus, participatory or collaborative) agreements with respect to simultaneous and inde-pendent criteria of fairness, by which they roughly mean legitimacy or inclusivity, effi-ciency, by which they mean the extent to which joint gains are maximized, stability, and what they call "wisdom," by which they mean the quality of being well-informed or mak-ing use of the best available scientific information. See also Laws and Forester (2007b).

10. For a striking, all too uncommon and cogent discussion of dispute resolution efforts grappling with long legacies of historical injustice and racism, see Chesler (1991). Chesler recognizes the pervasiveness of ethnic and racial injustice as it structures everyday life and contemporary community disputes, and he points to practical steps that dispute resolution practitioners working in the face of such histories of inequality and power relations can take. Cf. Forester (1999a), Ross (2001), Sandercock (2003a, 2003b), Umemoto (2001, 2005).

11. Mediation and facilitative leadership processes should complement—not substitute for—social movement or community organizing, and building power. Mediation offers the possibility that actual negotiations might produce more community benefits than adversarial posturing and rhetoric. Whether that is true in a given case must be examined, not assumed to be true or false. So from the perspective of oppositional parties, large or small, building power and exploring payoffs in mediated negotiations might well go hand in hand as related strategies of action, not either-or choices, as I have argued in related ways in earlier work (Forester 1989, 1999a). For a cogent view showing that mediated negotiation or facilitative leadership might play a role in, but not substitute for, related processes of peacemaking, peacekeeping, and peace building, see Umemoto (2005) and compare Anderlini (2007) and Marks (2000).

Chapter One

1. Thanks to Kieran Donaghy and Bob Beauregard for comments, to Jessica Pitt and David Laws for materials, and to Howard Bellman for the joke. The interviews with the mediators quoted here were conducted by Irene Weiser in the summer of 1995, transcribed by Linda Phelps, and edited by the author, with help as well from Ellen Macnow and Kathrin Bolton.

2. See, e.g., Sandercock (1995: 85) who concludes, "How does this moral vision and political practice translate to the domain of planning? Most obviously, we need to develop ways of planning (and of theorizing planning) which acknowledge and respect difference and reflect diversity."

3. To make matters worse, even if political fashion today suggests that "reality is socially constructed," that "we are all social constructivists now," the truth that some social constructions do not deserve respect, that some are illegitimate, or unjustified, that some are simply untrue, seems difficult for some to swallow. We seem culturally sophisticated, but ethically agnostic. Or worse: if at times we can soar like sharp-eyed descriptive eagles, far too often we seem to be running for cover, a good deal more like evasive normative weasels. Cf. the discussion of gullibility and the used-car-buying problem in the introduction in this volume and Forester (2008b).

4. Beauregard (1991: 193) wrote compellingly: "We are not condemned to toil with a flawed modernist project, nor are we compelled to abandon it for a postmodernism that casts planners as authors of texts, eschews authoritative positions in public debates, succumbs to global forces, and, in a false respect for differences, remains politically silent in the face of objective conditions of inequality, oppression, ignorance, and greed."

5. In Margalit (1993: 70). Cf. Frankfurt (2005).

6. Cf. Postema (1995: 366): "We should not mistake the *theoretical incommensurability* of different systematic conceptions of the good, for the *practical impossibility* of locating moral and political common ground through public discourse" (emphasis added). Postema's observation makes a deep point about the framing of agonistic views of politics. Cf. Mouffe (2005), Norval (2007), Howarth (2008), and Forester (forthcoming).

7. James Fishkin makes this point forcefully (1991: 29): "Without deliberation, democratic choices are not exercised in a meaningful way. If the preferences that determine the results of democratic procedures are unreflective or ignorant, then they lose their claim to political authority over us. Deliberation is necessary if the claims to democracy are not to be de-legitimated."

8. Notice the care with which Sloan distinguishes *accommodation* from *compromise*. In an important sense—the sense of common connotation that has *compromise* mean the betrayal of principle—negotiation and conflict resolution as discussed in this book are simply *not about compromise* at all. When negotiators seek improved relationships, for example, compromise of principle may be irrelevant. When negotiators trade time, "I'd like to use the car [or other resource] sooner rather than later," in return for support or labor, "and in return I'll help you with project X," compromise might also be irrelevant. More technically, in a complex case in which any of us as parties might consider choosing one among several possible agreements we could craft in a zone or space of possible agreements, calling any one of these agreements a *compromise* tells us nothing about what distinguishes a better from worse agreement (as we shall see throughout this book). These points, taken together, suggest that *compromise* misleads us more than it informs us about what conflict resolution, mediation, or negotiation really involve or produce, for these involve primarily improving relationships (being able to act together in various ways—from agreeing to disagree to actually cooperating and coordinating actions) and satisfying diverse interests, certainly not simply achieving mutually poor, lousy compromises. Cf. Menkel-Meadow (2007). I have added the italics for emphasis in these quotes.

9. Sloan elaborated: "In this mediation there were 14 sectors. It was such a big mediation that we organized all of the interests on Vancouver Island, and in fact, way beyond Vancouver Island; they were global in nature. Each sector was defined as a unique perspective on the problem, so that rather than any one organization or one corporation or one government being at the table, we simply had whole perspectives which caused them to have to form constituencies. There was a lot of integration that went on, in terms of organizing participation away from the table. We spent months doing that before the table even convened—about four months in a preparation and pre-table assessment phase."

10. Cf. Michael Walzer's striking, "A Day in the Life of the Socialist Citizen" (1980: 230): "Oscar Wilde is supposed to have said that socialism would take too many evenings. This is, it seems to me, one of the most significant criticisms of socialist theory that has ever been made."

11. See Lax and Sebenius (1987) for an economistic view, Friedmann (1979, 1981, 1987) on social learning, Forester (1999a) and Menkel-Meadow (1995) on public dispute resolution, and Warren (1992: 8), who writes of "a more general failure of standard liberal democracy to appreciate the transformative impact of democracy on the self, a failure rooted in its view of the self as prepolitically constituted." Warren (1992: 8) continues to explore an alternative: "On the expansive view, were individuals more broadly empowered, especially in the institutions that have most impact on their everyday lives (workplaces, schools, local governments, etc.), their experiences would have transformative effects: they

would become more public spirited, more tolerant, more knowledgeable, more attentive to the interests of others, and more probing of their own interests."

12. As Seyla Benhabib reminds us, such learning about the perspectives of the other lies at the core of developing political judgment. Benhabib (1988: 39) quotes Arendt: "The power of judgment rests on a potential agreement with others, and the thinking process which is active in judging something is not, like the thought process of pure reasoning, a dialogue between me and myself, but finds itself always and primarily, even if I am quite alone in making up my mind, in an anticipated communication with others with whom I know I must finally come to some agreement. From this potential agreement judgment derives its specific validity."

13. We explore these issues of anger, venting, emotion, and identity—and mediators' roles with respect to them—at length in the chapters that follow in cases involving health, racism, hate crimes, deep value differences, and sheer political contentiousness. Cf. Forester (1999a, 1999b), Marris (1975), Nussbaum (1990), and Sandercock (2003a, 2003b).

14. As Craig Calhoun (1993: 280) argues, contrary to Habermas, "Participation always holds the possibility not just of settling arguments or planning action but of altering identities. The 'identity politics' common to 'new social movements' is thus a normal and perhaps even intrinsic part of a successful, democratic public sphere. Even the very identity of the political community is a product, not simply a precondition, of the activity of the public sphere of civil society." Cf. Warren (1992) quoted above.

15. As Paolo Freire (1970: 73) brilliantly put it (anticipating and summarizing volumes of work by Michel Foucault and Jurgen Habermas alike: "Any situation in which some ... prevent others from engaging in the process of inquiry is one of violence." As I have argued at length (Forester 1989, 1993)—if not always persuasively—we can usefully understand much of Habermas's work as a meditation upon and deep analysis of Freire's insight here. On humiliation and implications for practice, see Scheff (1994).

16. Cf. Susan Collin Marks (2000: 28) writing about peacemaking in South Africa: "We were learning as we went along, what we could and couldn't do, what worked, what didn't, and why. We discovered that if peacemakers are available, they are likely to be used. A peacemaker's worth depends on community recognition of that role more than on peacemaking skills per se. In Pofadder, Chris Spies found that crisis often provides the opportunity for establishing a peace structure, if peace workers grasp the moment. Another story, from Plettenberg Gay in the Southern Cape, taught us that, by its mere existence, a peace committee or similar structure can itself become the mechanism for conflict resolution, because it provides a safe, neutral, and legitimate place for former enemies to meet, build relationships of trust, discard divisive stereotypes, and approach conflicts as common problems to be solved in common."

17. Cf. Benhabib (1988: 39) quoting Arendt above in note 12. On the crucial importance of narrative interpretation to the understanding of human action, cf. Rorty (1992), Somers (1994), and MacIntyre (1981). Rorty (1992: 7) writes, "Drama reveals the form and point of the protagonist's actions, their sometimes hidden directions and purposes.

In a way, we cannot see what an action really is, until we see it contextualized, embedded in the story of which it is an essential part. Until we see the completed whole in which an action functions, we cannot determine whether it has been well or ill performed, whether it succeeds or fails...."

18. J. Robert Cochran (2008: 205) concludes his recent dissertation by crisply refuting critics who suspect collaborative and negotiated strategies to be merely processual and not substantive: "In the Great Miami River, the trading program generated new water quality information that feeds into setting environmental goals, which would have been impossible without the new relationships formed with farmers during collaboration. In the South Nation River, trading increased the available funds and number of water quality projects implemented compared to what could have happened if organizers had not taken time out to introduce a more inclusive process. In the Minnesota River, trading program design became an avenue for greater cooperation among point sources and the Minnesota Pollution Control Agency. *The common thread running through these examples is that the processes used to frame and design institutions create relationships that enable implementation actions to begin making environmental gains. Process itself also builds institutions that make sure short-term gains are sustained over time. The trust and satisfaction created by these four trading programs in the Midwest came from conscious decisions about collaboration that changed relationships in ways that made success possible"* (emphasis added, jf).

19. Ernst Vollrath (1977: 165) writes, "The main condition for participation within the space of political phenomena is the recognition of participating human beings and their plurality within this space." See also Calhoun (1993, 1994), Gutmann and Taylor (1992), Appiah (1994), Young (1990), Menkel-Meadow (1995), and Forester (1995).

20. See Nussbaum (1990: ch. 2), Benhabib (1992), Sunstein (1991), Elster (1983), and Sager (1994).

21. See Susskind and Cruickshank (1987), Forester and Stitzel (1989), Checkoway (1994), Sherman (2005). Noting planners' possible influence, and thus the point of planning theory, Beauregard (1995: 165) writes, "Democracy cannot exist without a countervailing force to the political economy. People need to be empowered, social philosophies need to be articulated, and a public sphere needs to be nurtured. Planners *can* contribute to each of these tasks..." (emphasis added).

22. Compare LaCapra (1994), Herman (1992), Marris (1975), and Bar-On (1989, 1999). Daniel Yankelovich (1991: 117) finds hope in the midst of processes in which people might nevertheless be grappling with great pain, historical injustice, and traumatic memory (cf. Forester 1999a, ch. 7): "Fortunately, analysis of the working-through process leads to many practical methods of improvement...In discussing the various forms of working through and the obstacles that beset it, we will have reached the heart of our subject, and I believe, one of the keys to the successful practice of democracy in the twenty-first century." For related work in the shadow of apartheid and widespread violence in South Africa, see Marks (2000), and for a cogent discussion of diverse peacemaking efforts by women activists in many countries, see Anderlini (2007). In contrast to the national and multinational treatments of Marks (2000) and Anderlini (2007), here we try to explore what we might call the micropolitics of dealing

with differences—a micropolitics whose elements like storytelling, or the differences between dialogue and debate and negotiation, will of course take differing particular forms in distinctly differing historical settings.

Chapter Two

1. Cf. here Susan Collin Marks's surprising and eye-opening book about mediators' important work under conditions that many would think impossible (Marks 2000). She writes at one point, "'Monitors' became a catchall word for most peace workers, especially on marches, at demonstrations, or in crises. When we were called out to monitor a mass demonstration and ended up mediating, when our presence was enough to prevent violence, whether we were called mediators, observers, or monitors did not matter. We were too busy doing it to think about what we should call ourselves" (Marks 2000: 67).

2. The mediators' "practice stories" we consider here form part of a longer term research project to explore the micropolitics of planners' and mediators' practices in a range of politically contested settings (Forester 1999a, Forester, Peters, and Hittleman 2005). Our oral history interviews focus on accounts of the challenges and opportunities presented by cases and projects; we do not focus upon life histories. Instead, we work to gather the accounts of insider-actors, not outside-spectators. We ask distinctive questions to focus on practice rather than attitude, belief, or espoused theory: we ask not, "What do you *think* about X issue?" but instead, "How in this case did you *handle* X issue?" As a result, we document not full case histories or opinions about issues but rather the practiced sense of engaged intervention of practicing planners and mediators, and we try to examine their accounts not as last words about cases, but as accounts needing triangulation and corroboration as any interpretive evidence does (Forester 2006a).

3. Other students of urban conflict and difference similarly recognize passion, humor, and emotion as central to the story of practical rationality in the face of conflict (Forester 2004b, Sclavi 2006a,b; Sandercock 2003a). We explore these issues even more directly in Chapter 8.

4. On identity conflicts, see Rothman (1997), and on intractable conflicts, for example, see Lewicki, Grey, and Elliott (2003).

5. The classic statement here, no less apt than when first published, is Sherry Arnstein's clear-eyed discussion of the dangers of "we participate, they profit" in her "A Ladder of Citizen Participation" (Arnstein 1969). Bent Flyvbjerg (1998) and Oren Yiftachel (1998) extend Arnstein's warnings by arguing that in settings of political conflict, we can expect the power of rationalization to trump rationality and that much "planning" serves not broader aspirations of diverse publics but hegemonic agendas of spatial control.

Chapter Three

1. Cf. "Grammar tells us what kind of object anything is" (L. Wittgenstein, 1950: 373), and John Austin's (1961) wonderful essay, "A Plea for Excuses."

2. This might help us to understand that humiliating remarks are not about words but about acts, not about antiseptic "communication" but about violence done to our social fabric that makes us, in part, who we are. So we can take a slight from a teacher, police officer, or employer not as mere "words" but as an assault on our identity—and we are likely to forget neither the words nor the assault for a very long time.

3. Warfield's striking example finds echoes throughout this book: astute practitioners, such as cultural translators, mediators, facilitative leaders, organizers, and others, can anticipate and respond practically—if, of course, with real limits—to the ways that race, ethnicity, and power intertwine inseparably (Chesler 1991, Payne 1995, Marks 2000, Umemoto 2005). Warfield also implies that "whiteness" and other attributes of identity (white, male, monolingual, affluent...) can play crucial roles shaping how those playing mediating roles will be seen and treated by others *and* how they will be more or less able to listen astutely and learn what they need to learn.

4. We explore these challenges of respect and taking seriously what may remain unsaid as well as what's announced explicitly in Kahane and Forester (2008).

5. Cf. Marianella Sclavi (2006a,b).

Chapter Four

1. Recall here our opening discussion of gullibility.

2. For an extensive discussion, see the last chapter of Forester (1999a).

Chapter Five

1. I quote the original account approved by Mike Hughes in 1996. A subsequent published version appears in slightly edited form in Susskind et al. 1999.

2. As one reviewer of this manuscript suggested, a central theme of this book concerns the social organization of creativity, not only the psychology of framing and reframing so often discussed in books on problem solving but also the wisdom of recent work on networked intelligence, play, and discovery. See, e.g., Adams 1986, Menkel-Meadow 2001, Nachmanovitch 1990, Innes and Booher 1999, Pinch 2007, Sclavi 2006b, cf. Hajer and Wagenaar 2003.

Chapter Six

1. Here I follow Susskind and Cruickshank (2006)'s characterization of this work as *facilitative leadership*, a characterization I take to be virtually synonymous with *mediation* and suggesting, very usefully, still broader roles. Throughout, as well, I use *interests* almost as a shorthand term for concerns, desires, hopes, fears, worries, preferences, and needs—all of which can matter practically, can be significant, even as, curiously enough, parties can more or less deliberately hide or not even perceive such "interests" clearly.

2. This is not just an essential problem of rational problem solving and decision making; it is also a substantial ethical problem—we can call it "learning about value" (not about values, but about what matters, what's at stake)—even though calling it "the problem of moral salience," as moral theorists do, doesn't make it any easier really. I explore this problem at length in the practical work of deliberation in *The Deliberative Practitioner* (Forester 1999a), drawing heavily from the work of Martha Nussbaum (1990; cf. Flyvbjerg 2001).

3. Learning through practice stories, it should now be coming more clear, enables us to learn through the entanglements and relationships of the racially, politically, and economically structured settings at hand. This book focuses on questions of the *hows* of dealing with differences, the character of the practical judgments required, and the broader lessons we may learn about designing and enacting democratic processes. But much more can be done by looking through the windows of these situated practice stories. See, for example, the related work of Scott Peters (2004, Peters et al. 2005). Cf. Forester 2006a.

Chapter Seven

1. In the face of widely conflicting claims and interests, planners work to shape parties' senses of possibilities, in effect to "organize hope," by asking questions more than by making any claims. They shape possibilities by creating spaces for parties both to "say what needs to be said" and to listen and learn as well, spaces for joint inquiry, consultation, and negotiation of options. They work in between multiple stakeholders— such as neighborhood residents, developers, environmentalists, business owners, agency staff, and activists—with very different agendas to evoke practical proposals. Then, *having crafted those proposals together*, the parties can work to ratify them as mutually acceptable to their narrower and broader interests—even though each party began the process no doubt suspicious, if not already convinced, that the planners were "really on someone else's side"! Cf. note 11.

2. Professor Soo-Jang Lee of Kangnam University has pointed out lucidly (in correspondence) that "the point of departure for collaborative planning is not a collaborative situation but an adversarial one." The same needs perpetually to be said, it seems, for "communicative planning." In the face of power, listening insightfully and critically, sensitively and politically, for example, becomes all the *more* important as posturing and rationalization continually threaten to trump rationality, as Bent Flyvbjerg (1998) argues, and as advocates of conflicting interests compete for advantage (Hillier 2002). Mediation practice, too—the focus of this chapter—neither ignores nor assumes away, but begins with, concerns about power and interdependence, and exemplary mediators work to craft new, unforeseen alternatives. In *Planning in the Face of Power*, I asked experienced planners (to paraphrase), "How do you try to work *with* everyone, when everyone thinks you're partial to someone else?" Their responses revealed several practical strategies—for example, coaching parties, trying shuttle diplomacy, splitting the convening from the

mediating role—that planners can use every day. This chapter continues my research into the possibilities of participatory planning processes fostered by deliberative (here, mediated) practices always working in settings of inequality and difference, conflict and power (Forester 1989, 1999a).

3. Whenever planners and public managers work in between stakeholders to enable their more informed and influential participation, those planners play mediating-like roles and face the diverse challenges of what we can call more generally *mediated participation*. We will see that skillful mediation practices can involve striking and instructive work—transforming real antagonisms into working relationships and practical agreements, not through any magic but through sustained and creative effort—and just when so very few people really think that anyone can do that at all. Cf. notes 11 and 12.

4. See Diepeveen (2005). Bill Diepeveen is coordinator of mediation services for Alberta Municipal Affairs, where he designed and implemented the Municipal Dispute Resolution Initiative. The initiative provides municipalities, regional boards, and regional service commissions with opportunities to use mediation to resolve intermunicipal disputes, training in interest based negotiation techniques, and dispute resolution system design services. Further information on the initiative is available at http://www .municipalaffairs.gov.ab.ca/ms/dispute/mediation/index.cfm.

5. Cf. Dodge et al. (2005). It may be useful to recapitulate our research method here. The interview material that follows comes from an ongoing research effort to use oral history methods and interviews to explore the practice of planners and mediators "in the trenches" (Forester, Peters, and Hittleman 2005, Eckstein and Throgmorton 2003, Portelli 1991). Initially forming the basis for the author's *Deliberative Practitioner* (Forester 1999a), these interviews differ from traditional interviews in several important ways (Forester 2006a,b). They seek to learn from practitioners as actors, not as spectators. They ask planning and mediation practitioners not, "What do you think about (challenge) X?" but instead, variations on the thematic question, "How did you deal with (challenge) X?" They seek not to probe general beliefs or preferences but concrete, messy "practice stories"—not theories or detached histories but enmeshed accounts of the challenges of tough work.

As a result, these practice-focused oral histories produce not fully described case studies, but detailed first-person reflective portraits of the difficulties of practice. In these practice stories, experienced practitioners try to make sense of what they've done and give us, as readers, richly described, emotionally nuanced, and politically revealing portraits of their work (Forester 1999a). These powerful oral history accounts provide no last words, but as they echo other cases and analyses of planning and mediation processes, as they corroborate and triangulate with similar experiences, they provide—like case studies more generally—richly instructive ethnographic material for our study (Nussbaum 1990, Flyvbjerg 2001, Eckstein and Throgmorton 2003).

6. Lisa Beutler is the associate director of the Center for Collaborative Policy, California State University Sacramento. She has worked on numerous state, local, and federal issues involving, among other things, natural resources, correctional reform, and e-government, and she has provided assistance with quality improvement and efficiency

initiatives. Because I will quote her account at length, I will use her first name in what follows.

7. Cf. Beutler (2005). Deborah Chavez and Robert Fitzhenry (2005: 29) describe the background to this case as follows: "In May 2000, the State of California's Department of Parks and Recreation Off-Highway Motor Vehicle Recreation (OHMVR) Division established the Off-Highway Vehicle (OHV) Stakeholders Roundtable and convened a precedent setting series of meetings to address reauthorization of the OHV program and the efforts necessary to develop the optimum off-highway motor vehicle recreation program in California. The purpose of the OHV Stakeholders Roundtable is to enhance the OHMVR Division's ability to provide quality off-highway recreation opportunities in a safe and environmentally responsible manner. The Division and OHMVR Commission consider stakeholder recommendations for incorporation into legislation, regulations, Commission policy and the Division action plan. The Division initially formed the OHV Stakeholders Roundtable to inform and ensure a consensus-oriented process, respecting the needs of all affected parties, and focused on identifying the best methods to manage OHV programs."

8. If we are lucky, we will be able to "learn by example," following Iris Murdoch, who helped us to understand just what that means when she wrote: "Where virtue is concerned, we often apprehend more than we clearly understand and *grow by looking*" (Murdoch 1970: 31, italics in original).

9. Personal conversation with Lisa Beutler, August 6, 2008.

10. I take the clearest exposition of these options to be Larry Susskind's first-person account in Kolb et al. (1994). He has written extensively as well, e.g., in Susskind et al. (1999), Susskind and Cruickshank (1987, 2006).

11. Susskind argues that we should ask mediators not to be "neutral" but rather nonpartisan, for they ought, especially in cases of public disputes, to be committed to, and in part responsible for, protecting the *quality of the stakeholders' negotiated agreements*, thus the quality of not just *the process* but *the outcome* as well. Again, see Susskind's profile in Kolb et al. (1994), but cf. Susskind and Cruickshank (1987). For discussions of the ethics of mediation, cf. Menkel-Meadow and Wheeler (2004). For extensive examples discussed in the first-person voice accounts of diverse mediators of public disputes, see the collection of mediator profiles in Forester (forthcoming). On deliberative practice more generally concerned with both process and outcome, see Forester (1999a).

12. Like the courts or the political process (via votes or the streets), mediation provides no guarantees. Expertise informs knowledge and judgment but provides no guarantees (pace Bengs, 2005; cf. Sager 2005). Religious faith offers strength, but no guarantees. Mediation can provide assistance when interdependent parties need to deal with their differences and with each other—as in many cases, aspiring to some form of inclusive participation. If one party—developer or community leader or environmentalist—has a sure-fire way to get what he or she wants without any negotiation, mediation is unlikely to help. But when these parties do need to deal with their differences, to negotiate practically, mediation can help, as each of our chapters here has shown.

Chapter Eight

1. Bachle, personal correspondence, October 3, 2003. Originally from the Great Plains, Laura Bachle is a planner, member of the American Institute of Certified Planners, and mediator working with Confluence Consulting in Alexandria, Virginia.

2. Personal correspondence, June 26, 2003. Susan L. Podziba, a public policy mediator for 20 years, is currently managing negotiations among government, industry, and civil society representatives to develop worker safety standards for the U.S. Department of Labor, environmental assessment procedures to determine hazardous waste contamination on lands prior to redevelopment for the U.S. Environmental Protection Agency, and a comprehensive strategy for a sustainable dairy farming industry in the state of Wisconsin.

3. Nathan Edelson has been a community planner for 30 years working primarily in Vancouver's new high-density neighborhoods and historic inner-city communities. He has worked with residents, businesspeople, and community organizations to help develop and implement policies on topics ranging from adult entertainment, basement suites, drug treatment, liquor licensing, market housing, public realm improvements, single-room occupancy (SRO) hotels, and transit to Vancouver's commercial developments.

4. Because shared, unexpected, spontaneous laughter often reveals genuine and (strategically) uncalculated responses to a shared situation, laughing together can produce (equally unexpected) moments of intimacy that can be vital to building future relationships. Thanks to Anne Kilgore for this observation.

Thanks also to Ray Lorenzo, a Brooklyn-born, Harvard-trained, Italian-American city planner who promotes, programs, and facilitates participatory planning and design processes in the areas of sustainable urban development, children's rights and friendly cities as he works toward "participatory, democratic Italian planning" (a possible multiple oxymoron, he suggests). Ray offered an apt quote from Victor Borge: "Laughter is the shortest distance between two people." Ray continued, "That's it: the use of humor and laughter (as our Zen masters teach us) brings people closer…physically and conceptually (mediates different opinions)" (personal correspondence, July 2, 2003).

5. Normajean McLaren has been working in the field of diversity, antiracism, and community development for the past 18 years. Her work takes her to small northern communities, to corporate boardrooms, and to staff and client workshops for community agencies—all kinds of communities where inclusivity and healing can become the driving goals. Cf. Forester 2004a.

6. How can this work? Bayard Catron suggests that the playfulness enacted in such humor can "break the tension and open the situation to new possibilities by announcing that a real person has shown up rather than a role-player" (personal correspondence, October 14, 2003).

7. David Boyd is a practicing planner and a member of the American Institute of Certified Planners. His work embraces the idea that all people can make valuable contributions to community decisions and that the role of planners is that of *interpreter*, and not

that of *expert* or *educator*. He invites dialogue with others who are interested in this role for planning, and he may be reached via e-mail at dsboyd@tds.net.

8. In their various television incarnations, Phil Donohue hosted visitors and moderated discussion between the studio audience and his guests. Bob Barker, a game-show host, chose members of the audience to compete for consumer goods and vacation packages, and Jerry Springer invited visitors to share their intrigues with an often astonished, if not also repulsed, audience.

9. Frank Blechman has been involved in public policy in the United States as an advocate and agitator since the 1960s. He designs, manages, and interferes in public policy processes at the local, regional, and national levels.

10. Interview, Honolulu, April 2002, quoted with permission. Puanani Burgess works in the creative field of conflict transformation. The processes she has developed, which she calls "Building the Beloved Community," are rooted in the Hawaiian concept of ALOHA: *Ala* (Awareness), *Lokahi* (Unity), *Oiaio* (Honesty), *Ha'aha'a* (Humility), and *Ahonui* (Patience/Perseverance).

11. I asked, in part, because I recalled that Wittgenstein had famously remarked that much of philosophy could be taught through humor, which I took to mean, through the frame switching of seeing one way and then coming abruptly to see the same thing another way (Wittgenstein 1950, Cavell 1969). Marianella Sclavi (2006a,b) had more recently argued, too, I knew, that good ethnographic work, understanding others especially in situations of conflict and politics (when else?), depended also on the multiperspectival imagination of having a sense of humor, bringing a "humoristic" methodology to bear. Here was Normajean McLaren, too, telling me that she couldn't work in the face of class relations and ethnic inequalities without a sense of humor. I wanted to know how humor could possibly be an essential element of Normajean's work on racism, empowerment, and community building. What was going on here? My speculations could easily be wrong, but if Wittgenstein, Sclavi, and McLaren corroborated each other, then we might learn philosophically, ethnographically, politically, and practically too.

12. We might understand such uses of humor—not joking, not canned, but culturally responsive, politically interactive, emotionally sensitive, mutually attuned—to enact potentially transformative participatory rituals (Forester, 1999a) through which parties both learn about the world and change themselves, change their minds and their relationships. Thanks to Christopher Winship for suggesting connections between irony and humor's "loosening up" of focus and frames and the socially constructed, revisionary spaces of liminality.

13. So the sensitive use of humor may address the uncertainties and threatening anxieties of openings captured so well by Michael Wheeler (2002, 2004): "Openings thus may be especially critical as moments when anticipation meets reality. Ideally, our worst fears are not confirmed. We discover that the people that we encounter are not the wolves and alligators that we fantasized, so we can put our anxieties aside and get to work. Things may not be so clear in other cases, however. Our on-going uncertainty about other people's motives and trustworthiness may deepen our initial fears."

BIBLIOGRAPHY

Abrams, Kathryn. 1991. "Hearing the Call of Stories." *California Law Review* 79(4): 971–1052.

Adams, James L. 1986. *Conceptual Blockbusting: A Guide to Better Ideas*. Reading, MA: Addison Wesley.

Adler, Peter. 2005. "Dispute Resolution Meets Policy Analysis, or Native Gathering Rights on 'Private' Lands? A Profile of Peter Adler." In *Mediation in Practice*, ed. J. Forester, 35–54. Ithaca, NY: Cornell University, Department of City and Regional Planning.

Adler, Peter S., Robert C. Barrett, Martha C. Bean, Juliana E. Birkhoff, Connie P. Ozawa, and Emily B. Rudin. 2000. *Managing Scientific and Technical Information in Environmental Cases: Principles and Practices for Mediators*. Washington, DC: RESOLVE.

Anderlini, Sanam Naraghi. 2007. *Women Building Peace: What They Do, Why It Matters*. Boulder, CO: Lynne Rienner.

Andrews, Clint. 2002. *Humble Analysis: The Practice of Joint Fact-Finding*. Westport, CT: Praeger.

Appiah, Anthony. 1994. "Identity, Authenticity, and Survival: Multicultural Societies and Social Reproduction." In *Multiculturalism and "The Politics of Recognition,"* ed. Amy Gutmann and Charles Taylor, 149–63. Princeton, NJ: Princeton University Press.

Arnstein, Sherry. 1969. "A Ladder of Citizen Participation." *Journal of the American Institute of Planning* 35, no. 4 (July): 216–24.

Austin, John. 1961. *Philosophical Papers*. London: Oxford University Press.

Axelrod, Robert. 1985. *The Evolution of Cooperation*. New York: Basic Books.

Bar-On, Dan. 1989. *The Legacy of Silence*. Cambridge, MA: Harvard University Press.

———. 1998. *The Indescribable and the Undiscussable: Reconstructing Human Discourse after Trauma*. Budapest, Hungary: Central European University Press.

Barrett, Frank. 1998. "Creativity and Improvisation in Jazz and Organizations: Implications for Organizational Learning." *Organization Science* 9(5): 605–622.

———. 2006. "Toward an Aesthetics of Cooperation." In *A Handbook for Transformative Cooperation: New Designs and Dynamics*, ed. S. Piderit, R. Fry, and D. Cooperrider. Palo Alto, CA: Stanford University Press.

Baum, Howell. 1996. "Why the Rational Paradigm Persists: Tales from the Field." *Journal of Planning Education and Research* 15(2): 127–35.

———. 1997. *The Organization of Hope*. Albany: State University of New York Press.

Beauregard, Robert. 1991. "Without a Net: Modernist Analysis and the Post-Modern Abyss." *Journal of Planning Education and Research* 10(3): 189–94.

———. 1995. "Edge Critics." *Journal of Planning Education and Research* 14(3): 163–66.

Bengs, C. 2005. "Planning Theory for the Naive?" *European Journal of Spatial Development*. http://www.nordregio.se/EJSD.

Benhabib, Seyla. 1988. "Judgment and the Moral Foundations of Politics in Arendt's Thought." *Political Theory* 16, no. 1 (February): 29–51.

———. 1989–1990. "In the Shadow of Aristotle and Hegel: Communicative Ethics and Current Controversies in Practical Philosophy." *Philosophical Forum* 21(1–2): 1–30.

———. 1992. *Situating the Self: Gender, Community and Postmodernism in Contemporary Ethics*. New York: Routledge.

———. 1995. "Cultural Complexity, Moral Interdependence, and the Global Dialogical Community." *Women, Culture, and Development*, ed. Martha Nussbaum and Jonathan Glover, 235–255. New York: Oxford University Press.

Beutler, Lisa. 2005. "From Nightmare to National Implications: A Profile of Lisa Beutler." In *Mediation in Practice*, ed. J. Forester, 224–42. Ithaca, NY: Cornell University, Department of City and Regional Planning.

Blechman, Frank. 2005. "From Conflict Generation through Consensus-Building Using Many of the Same Skills: A Profile of Frank Blechman." In *Mediation in Practice*, ed. J. Forester, 1–17. Ithaca, NY: Cornell University, Department of City and Regional Planning. (Edited from original interview, January 21, 1993.)

Bollens, Scott. 2002. "Urban Planning and Inter-Group Conflict: Confronting a Fractured Public Interest." *Journal of the American Planning Association* 68(1): 79–91.

———. 2007. *Cities, Nationalism and Democratization*. New York: Routledge.

Briggs, Xavier de Sousa. 2008. *Democracy as Problem Solving*. Cambridge: MIT Press.

Brown, Michael, and R. Rosecrance, eds. 1999. *The Costs of Conflict*. Lanham, MD: Rowman and Littlefield.

Bush, Robert Baruch, and Joseph Folger. 1994. *The Promise of Mediation*. San Francisco: Jossey-Bass.

Calhoun, Craig. 1993. "Civil Society and the Public Sphere." *Public Culture* 5(2): 267–80.

———. 1994. *Social Theory and the Politics of Identity*. Cambridge, MA: Blackwell.

Carpenter, Susan, and William Kennedy. 1988. *Managing Public Disputes*. San Francisco: Jossey-Bass.

Cavell, Stanley. 1969. *Must We Mean What We Say?* New York: Scribner's.

Chasin, R., M. Herzig, S. Roth, L. Chasin, C. Becker and R. Stains. (1996). "From Diatribe to Dialogue on Divisive Public Issues: Approaches Drawn from Family Therapy." *Mediation Quarterly* 13 (Summer): 4.

Chavez, Deborah, and R. Fitzhenry. 2005. "California Off-Highway Vehicle Stakeholders Roundtable." In *Off-Highway Vehicle Use and Collaboration: Lessons Learned from Project Implementation*, ed. Lawrence Fisher. Tucson, AZ: U.S. Institute for Environmental Conflict Resolution.

Checkoway, Barry, ed. 1994. "Paul Davidoff and Advocacy Planning in Retrospect." *Journal of the American Planning Association* 60, no. I (Spring): 139–61.

Chesler, Mark. 1991. "Racial/Ethnic/Cultural Issues in Dispute Resolution." Working Paper 28, Program on Conflict Management Alternatives, University of Michigan.

Churchman, C. West. 1968. *The Systems Approach.* New York: Delacorte Press.

Cobb, Sara. 2006. "A Developmental Approach to Turning Points: 'Irony' as an Ethics for Negotiation Pragmatics." *Harvard Negotiation Law Review* II: 147–97.

Cochran, J. Robert. 2008. "Giving Process Its Due: Can Collaboration Help Environmental Markets Succeed?" PhD diss., Portland State University.

Coles, Robert. 1989. *The Call of Stories.* Boston: Houghton Mifflin

Coles, Romand, and Stanley Hauerwas. 2007. *Christianity, Democracy, and the Radical Ordinary: Conversations between a Radical Democrat and a Christian.* Eugene, OR: Wipf and Stock.

Corburn, Jason. 2005. *Street Science: Community Knowledge and Environmental Health Justice.* Cambridge, MA: MIT Press.

Crocker, Chester, F. A. Hampson, and P. Hall, eds. *Herding Cats.* Washington, DC: United States Institute of Peace.

Dale, Norman. 1999. "Cross-Cultural Community-Based Planning: Negotiating the Future of Haida Gwaii (British Columbia)." In *The Consensus Building Handbook: A Comprehensive Guide to Reaching Agreement,* ed. Lawrence Susskind, S. McKearnan, and J. Thomas-Larmer. 923–950. Thousand Oaks, CA: Sage.

Dewey, John. 1927. *The Public and Its Problems.* New York: Henry Holt.

Diepeveen, William. 2005. "From Environmental to Urban to Inter-Municipal Disputes: A Profile of Bill Diepeveen's Mediation Practice." In *Mediation in Practice,* ed. J. Forester, 341–82. Ithaca, NY: Cornell University, Department of City and Regional Planning.

Dodge, Jennifer, Sonia Ospina, and Erica Gabrielle Foldy. 2005. "Integrating Rigor and Relevance in Public Administration Scholarship: The Contribution of Narrative Inquiry." *Public Administration Review* 65, no. 3 (May–June): 286–300.

Dryzek, John. 1990. *Discursive Democracy: Politics, Policy, and Political Science.* Cambridge: Cambridge University Press.

———. 1995. "The Informal Logic of Institutional Design." In *The Theory of Institutional Design,* ed. Robert Goodin, 103–25. Cambridge: Cambridge University Press.

———. 1996. "From Irrationality to Autonomy: Two Sciences of Institutional Design." In *The Constitution of Good Societies,* ed. Stephen Elkin and Karol Soltan. University Park: Pennsylvania State University Press.

———. 2000. *Deliberative Democracy and Beyond: Liberals, Critics, Contestations.* Oxford: Oxford University Press.

———. 2003. "Alternatives to Agonism and Analgesia: Deliberative Democracy in Divided Societies." Draft for the conference on Deliberative Democracy and Sensitive Issues, Amsterdam, March 25–26.

Dukes, Frank, Marina Piscolish, and John Stephens. 2000. *Reaching for Higher Ground.* San Francisco: Jossey-Bass.

Dundes, Alan. 1987. *Cracking Jokes*. Berkeley, CA: Ten Speed Press.

Eckstein, Barbara, and James Throgmorton, eds. 2003. *Stories and Sustainability: Planning, Practice and Possibility for American Cities*. Cambridge, MA: MIT Press.

Edwards, Mencer D. 2006. Classroom presentation to City and Regional Planning 546, Cornell University, Ithaca, NY, November 2.

Ehrmann, John R., and Barbara L. Stinson. "Joint Fact-Finding and the Use of Technical Experts." 1999. In *The Consensus Building Handbook: A Comprehensive Guide to Reaching Agreement*, ed. Lawrence Susskind, S. McKearnan, and J. Thomas Larmer, 375–99. Thousand Oaks CA: Sage.

Elster, Jon. 1983. *Sour Grapes*. Cambridge: Cambridge University Press.

Fay, Brian. 1996. *Contemporary Philosophy of Social Science*. Cambridge, MA: Blackwell.

Fisher, Roger, and William Ury. 1991. *Getting to Yes: Negotiating Agreement without Giving In*, 2nd ed. New York: Penguin.

Fishkin, James. 1991. *Democracy and Deliberation*. New Haven, CT: Yale University Press.

Flyvbjerg, Bent. 1998. *Rationality and Power*. Chicago: University of Chicago Press.

———. 2001. *Making Social Science Matter: Why Social Inquiry Fails and How It Can Succeed Again*. Cambridge: Cambridge University Press.

Forester, John. 1989. *Planning in the Face of Power*. Berkeley: University of California Press.

———. 1993. *Critical Theory, Public Policy, and Planning Practice*. Albany: SUNY Press.

———. 1994. "Lawrence Susskind: Activist Mediation and Public Disputes." In *When Talk Works: Profiles of Mediators*, ed. Deborah M. Kolb and Associates. San Francisco: Jossey-Bass.

———. 1995. "Response: Toward a Critical Sociology of Policy Analysis." *Policy Sciences* 28: 385–96.

———. 1999a. *The Deliberative Practitioner*. Cambridge, MA: MIT Press.

———. 1999b. "Dealing with Deep Value Differences: How Can Consensus Building Make a Difference?" In *The Consensus Building Handbook: A Comprehensive Guide to Reaching Agreement*, ed. Lawrence Susskind, S. McKearnan, and J. Thomas Larmer, 463–494. Thousand Oaks CA: Sage.

———. 2004a. "Community-Building Challenges of Listening, Humor, and Hope: A Profile of Normajean McLaren." Profiles of Practitioners Project. Cornell University, Department of City and Regional Planning, Ithaca, NY, Interview, March 2003.

———. 2004b. "Planning and Mediation, Participation and Posturing: What's a Democratic Planner to Do?" *Interaction: Journal of the Canadian Dispute Resolution Network* 17, no. 1–2 (September): 5–8, 40–41.

———. 2004c. "Critical Moments in Negotiations: On Humor, Recognition and Hope," *Negotiation Journal* 20. No. 2 (April): 231–38.

———. 2005. *Mediation in Practice: Profiles of Facilitators, Mediators, Coalition- and Consensus-Builders*. Ithaca, NY: Cornell University, Department of City and Regional Planning. (Typescript.)

———. 2006a. "Exploring Urban Practice in a Democratizing Society: Opportunities, Techniques, and Challenges." *Development South Africa* 23, no 5 (December): 569–86.

————. 2006b. "Policy Analysis as Critical Listening." In *Oxford Handbook of Public Policy*, ed. M. Moran, M. Rein, and R. Goodin, 124–51. New York: Oxford University Press.

————. 2006c. "Making Participation Work When Interests Conflict: From Fostering Dialogue and Moderating Debate to Mediating Disputes." *Journal of the American Planning Association* 72, no. 4 (Fall): 447–56.

————. 2006d. "Rationality and Surprise: The Drama of Mediation in Rebuilding Civil Society." In *Engaging Civil Societies in Democratic Planning and Governance*, ed. Penny Gurstein and Nora Angeles, 118–40. Toronto: University of Toronto Press.

————. 2006e. "Challenges of Deliberation and Participation." *Les Ateliers de l'ethique* 1, no. 2 (Fall): 19–25.

————. 2008a. "Participation as Dialogue, Debate, and Negotiation: Entangled Promises and Practices." In *Governance Reform under Real World Conditions: Citizens, Stakeholders, and Voice*, ed. Sina Odugbemi and Thomas Jacobson, 209–218. Washington, DC: International Bank for Reconstruction and Development/World Bank.

————. 2008b. "Are Collaboration and Participation More Trouble than They're Worth?" Editorial for *Planning Theory and Practice* 9, no. 3 (December): 299–304.

————. Forthcoming. "Learning through Conflict." *Journal of Critical Policy Analysis*.

Forester, John, and David Stitzel. 1989. "Beyond Neutrality: The Possibilities of Activist Mediation in Public Sector Conflicts." *Negotiation Journal* (July): 251–64.

Forester, John, and Irene Weiser, eds. 1996. *Making Mediation Work: Profiles of Community and Environmental Mediators*. Typescript, Cornell University, Department of City and Regional Planning, Ithaca, NY.

Forester, John, Scott Peters, and Margo Hittleman, eds. 2005. "Profiles of Practitioners: Practice Stories from the Field." http://instruct1.cit.cornell.edu/courses/practicestories/.

Fowler, Anne, et al. 2001. "Talking with the Enemy." *Boston Globe*, January 28. http://www.publicconversations.org/pcp/resources/resource_detail.asp?ref_id=102.

Frankfurt, Harry. 2005. *On Bullshit*. Princeton, NJ: Princeton University Press.

Freire, Paulo. 1970. *The Pedagogy of the Oppressed*. New York: Seabury Press.

Freud, Sigmund. 1960. *Jokes and Their Relation to the Unconscious*. New York: Norton.

Friedmann, John. 1979. *The Good Society*. Cambridge, MA: MIT Press.

————. 1981. *Retracking America*. Emmaus, PA: Rodale Press. (Orig. pub. 1973.)

————. 1987. *Planning in the Public Domain*. Princeton, NJ: Princeton University Press.

————. 1995. "Teaching Planning Theory." *Journal of Planning Education and Research*. 14(3): 156–62.

Friedmann, John, and Michael Douglass, eds. 1998. *Cities and Citizens: Planning and the Rise of Civil Society in a Global Age*. New York: Wiley.

Fuller, Boyd. 2005. "Trading Zones: Cooperating for Water Resource and Ecosystem Management When Stakeholders Have Apparently Irreconcilable Differences." PhD diss., MIT Department of Urban Studies and Planning.

Fung, Archon. 2004. *Empowered Participation: Reinventing Urban Democracy*. Princeton, NJ: Princeton University Press.

————. 2005. "Deliberation before the Revolution: Toward an Ethics of Deliberative Democracy in an Unjust World." *Political Theory* 33(2): 397–419.

Fung, Archon, and Erik Olin Wright. 2003. *Deepening Democracy: Institutional Innovations in Empowered Participatory Governance*. London: Verso.

Gauthier, David. 1993. "Constituting Democracy." In *The Idea of Democracy*, ed. D. Copp, J. Hampton, and J. Roemer, 314–34. Cambridge: Cambridge University Press.

Glendon, Mary Ann. 1996. "Civil Service: A Review of Michael Sandel's *Democracy's Discontent: America in Search of a Public Philosophy*," *New Republic* (April 1): 39–41.

Greig, Michelle Robinson. 1997. Interview by Kristen Grace. Profiles of Practitioners Project. Cornell University, Department of City and Regional Planning, Ithaca, NY.

Grossman, David. 1989. *The Yellow Wind*. New York: Delta.

Gurevitch, Z. D. 1989. "The Power of Not Understanding: The Meeting of Conflicting Identities." *Journal of Applied Behavioral Science* 25(2): 161–73.

Gutmann, Amy, and Charles Taylor. 1992. *Multiculturalism and "The Politics of Recognition."* Princeton, NJ: Princeton University Press.

Gutmann, Amy, and Dennis Thompson 1996. *Democracy and Disagreement: Why Moral Conflict Cannot Be Avoided in Politics, and What Should Be Done About It*. Cambridge, MA: Harvard University Press.

Habermas, Jurgen. 1996. "Three Normative Models of Democracy." In *Democracy and Difference: Contesting the Boundaries of the Political*, ed. Seyla Benhabib, 21–30. Princeton, NJ: Princeton University Press.

Hajer, Maarten, and Hendrik Wagenaar, eds. 2003. *Deliberative Policy Analysis*. Cambridge: Cambridge University Press.

Hanson, Norwood Russell. 1961. *Patterns of Discovery*. Cambridge: Cambridge University Press.

Healey, Patsy. 2006 (1997). *Collaborative Planning: Shaping Places in Fragmented Societies*. London: Macmillan.

Heifetz, Ronald, and Martin Linsky. 2002. *Leadership on the Line*. Boston: Harvard Business School Press.

Herman, Judith. 1992. *Trauma and Recovery*. New York: Basic Books.

Herzig, Maggie, and Laura Chasin. 2006. *Fostering Dialogues across Divides*. Watertown, MA: Public Conversations Project.

Hillier, Jean. 2002. *Shadows of Power*. London: Routledge.

Hoch, Charles. 1994. *What Planners Do*. Chicago: American Planning Association, Planner's Press.

————. 2006. "Emotions and Planning." *Planning Theory and Practice* 7(4): 367–82.

Honneth, Axel. 1994. "The Social Dynamics of Disrespect: On the Location of Critical Theory Today." *Constellations* 1(2): 255–69.

Horton, Myles, and Paulo Freire. 1990. *We Make the Road by Walking*. Ed. Brenda Bell, John Gaventa, and John Peters. Philadelphia: Temple University Press.

Howarth, David. 2008. "Ethos, Agonism and Populism: William Connolly and the Case for Radical Democracy." *British Journal of Politics and International Relations*. 10:2. May. 171–193.

Howell, Philip. 1993. "Public Space and the Public Sphere: Political Theory and the Historical Geography of Modernity." *Environment and Planning* 11(3): 303–22.

Hughes, Michael, with John Forester and Irene Weiser. 1999. "Facilitating Statewide HIV/AIDS Policies and Priorities in Colorado: A Profile of Mike Hughes." In *The Consensus Building Handbook: A Comprehensive Guide to Reaching Agreement*, ed. Lawrence Susskind, S. McKearnan, and J. Thomas-Larmer, 1011–30. Thousand Oaks CA: Sage.

Huxley, Margo, and Oren Yiftachel. 2000. "New Paradigm or Old Myopia? Unsettling the Communicative Turn in Planning Theory." *Journal of Planning Education and Research* 19(3): 101–10.

Innes, Judith. 1995. "Planning Is Institutional Design." *Journal of Planning Education and Research* 14(2): 140–43.

———. 1996. "Planning through Consensus-Building." *Journal of the American Planning Association* 62, no. 4 (Autumn): 460–72.

———. 2004. "Consensus-Building: Clarifications for the Critics." *Planning Theory* 3(1): 5–20.

Innes, J. E., and Booher, D. E. 1999. "Consensus Building as Role Playing and Bricolage: Toward a Theory of Collaborative Planning." *Journal of the American Planning Association* 65(1): 9–26.

———. 2003. "Collaborative Policy Making: Governance through Dialogue." In *Deliberative Policy Analysis: Governance in the Network Society*, ed. Maarten Hajer and Henk Wagenaar, 33–59. Cambridge: Cambridge University Press.

Jackstreit, Mary and Adrienne Kaufmann. 1995. *Finding Common Ground in the Abortion Conflict: A manual*. Washington, D.C.: Common Ground Network for Life and Choice, Search for Common Ground.

Kahane, David, and J. Forester. 2008. "Propositional and Performative Argumentation: Lessons from the Field." In *Realizing Deliberative Democracy*, ed. D. Kahane, D. Leydet, D. Weinstock, and M. Williams, ch. 11. Vancouver: University of British Columbia Press.

Kolb, Deborah, and Associates. 1994. *When Talk Works*. San Francisco: Jossey-Bass.

Kolb, Deborah, and Judith Williams. 2000. *The Shadow Negotiation: How Women Can Master the Hidden Agendas That Determine Bargaining Success*. New York: Simon & Schuster.

———. 2003. *Everyday Negotiation: Navigating the Hidden Agendas of Bargaining*. San Francisco: Jossey-Bass.

Kressel, Kenneth, Dean Pruitt, and Associates. 1989. *Mediation Research: The Process and Effectiveness of Third Party Intervention*. San Francisco: Jossey-Bass.

Krumholz, Norman, and J. Forester. 1990. *Making Equity Planning Work*. Philadelphia: Temple University Press.

LaCapra, Dominick. 1994. *Representing the Holocaust: History, Theory, and Trauma*. Ithaca, NY: Cornell University Press.

Laws, David, and John Forester. 2007a. "Public Policy Mediation: From Argument to Collaboration." In *Handbook of Public Policy Analysis*, ed. Frank Fischer, Gerald J. Miller, and Mara S. Sidney, 513–36. Boca Raton, FL: CRC Press.

———. 2007b. "Learning in Practice: Public Policy Mediation." In *Critical Policy Analysis*, (1), 4, 2007: 342–371.

Laws, David, and Martin Rein. 2003. "Reframing Practice." In *Deliberative Policy Analysis: Governance in the Network Society*, ed. Maarten Hajer and Henk Wagenaar, 172–206. Cambridge: Cambridge University Press.

Lax, David, and James Sebenius. 1987. *The Manager as Negotiator*. New York: Free Press.

LeBaron, Michelle. 2002. *Bridging Troubled Waters*. San Francisco: Jossey-Bass.

———. and N. Carstarphen. 1999. "Finding Common Ground on Abortion." In *The Consensus Building Handbook: A Comprehensive Guide to Reaching Agreement*, ed. Lawrence Susskind, S. McKearnan, and J. Thomas-Larmer, 1031–1049.

Lederach, John Paul. 1995. *Preparing for Peace*. Syracuse, NY: Syracuse University Press.

———. 2003. *The Moral Imagination*. New York: Oxford University Press.

Lewicki, Roy, B. Gray, and M. Elliott. 2003. *Making Sense of Intractable Environmental Conflicts*. Washington DC: Island Press.

Lowry, Kem, Peter Adler, and Neal Milner. 1997. "Participating the Public: Group Process, Politics, and Planning." *Journal of Planning Education and Research* 16: 177–87.

Lynch, Owen. 1998. "Kitchen Antics: Humor in Organizations." Master's thesis, Texas A&M University, Department of Speech Communication.

MacIntyre, Alasdair. 1981. "The Virtues, the Unity of a Human Life, and the Concept of a Tradition." In *After Virtue*, 190–209. London: Duckworth.

Margalit, Avishai. 1993. "Prophets with Honor." *New York Review of Books* 40, no. 18 (Nov. 4): 66–71.

Marks, Susan Collin. 2000. *Watching the Wind: Conflict Resolution during South Africa's Transition to Democracy*. Washington, DC: U.S. Institute for Peace Press.

Marris, Peter. 1986. *Loss and Change*. London: Routledge and Kegan Paul.

Marris, Peter, and Martin Rein. 1973. *Dilemmas of Social Reform: Poverty and Community Action in the United States*, 2nd ed. Chicago: Aldine.

McCreary, Scott T., John K. Gamman, and Bennett Brooks. 2001. "Refining and Testing Joint Fact-Finding for Environmental Dispute Resolution: Ten Years of Success." *Mediation Quarterly* 18(4): 329–48.

Menkel-Meadow, Carrie. 1995. "The Many Ways of Mediation: The Transformation of Traditions, Ideologies, Paradigms, and Practices." *Negotiation Journal* (July): 217–42.

———. 2001. "Aha? Is Creativity Possible in Legal Problem Solving and Teachable in Legal Education?" *Harvard Negotiation Law Review* 6: 97–144.

———. 2007. "The Ethics of Compromise." In *The Negotiator's Fieldbook*, ed. Andrea Kupfer Schneider and Christopher Honeyman, ch. 18. Chicago: American Bar Association.

———, and Michael Wheeler. 2004. *What's Fair: Ethics for Negotiators*. San Francisco: Jossey-Bass.

Mitchell, Christopher. 2000. *Gestures of Conciliation*. New York: St. Martin's Press.

Moore, Carl. 2002. Interview with author. Cambridge, MA.

Moore, Mark. 1995. *Creating Public Value*. Cambridge: Harvard.

Mouffe, Chantal. 2005. *On the Political*. London: Routledge.

Murdoch, Iris. 1970. *The Sovereignty of Good*. London: Ark.

Myerhoff, Barbara. 1988. "Surviving Stories: Reflections on *Number Our Days*." In *Between Two Worlds*, ed. Jack Kugelmass, 265–94. Ithaca, NY: Cornell University Press.

Nachmanovitch, Stephen. 1990. *Free Play: The Power of Improvisation in Life and the Arts*. New York: Putnam.

Needleman, Martin and Carolyn Needleman. 1974. *Guerrillas in the Bureaucracy*. New York: Wiley.

Norval, Aletta. 2007. *Aversive Democracy: Inheritance and Originality in the Democratic Tradition*. Cambridge: Cambridge University Press.

Nussbaum, Martha. 1990. *Love's Knowledge*. New York: Oxford.

Payne, Charles. 1995. *I've Got the Light of Freedom: The Organizing Tradition and the Mississippi Freedom Struggle*. Berkeley: University of California Press.

Peters, S. J. 2004. "Educating the Civic Professional: Reconfigurations and Resistances." *Michigan Journal of Community Service Learning* 11(1): 47–58.

Peters, S. J., N. R. Jordan, M. Adamek, and T. R. Alter, eds. 2005. *Engaging Campus and Community: The Practice of Public Scholarship in the State and Land-Grant University System*. Dayton, OH: Kettering Foundation Press.

Pinch, Trevor. 2007. "Between Technology and Music: Distributed Creativity and Liminal Spaces in the Making and Selling of Synthesizers." Society for the History of Technology NSF Workshop on the Animating Passions of the History of Technology, Washington DC, October 18.

Podziba, Susan. 1995. "Collaborative Civic Design in Chelsea, Mass.: A Profile of Susan Podziba." In *Mediation in Practice*, ed. J. Forester, 203–31. Ithaca, NY: Cornell University, Department of City and Regional Planning.

Portelli, Alessandro. 1991. *The Death of Luigi Trastulli and Other Stories: Form and Meaning in Oral History*. Albany: State University of New York Press.

Postema, Gerald J. 1995. "Public Practical Reason: Political Practice." *Nomos XXXVII: Theory and Practice*, ed. Ian Shapiro and Judith Wagner DeCew. New York: New York University Press. 345–85.

Putnam, Linda. 2004. "Transformations and Critical Moments in Negotiations." *Negotiation Journal* 20(2): 275–95.

Putnam, Robert, R. Leonardi, and R. Nanetti. 1992. *Making Democracy Work*. Princeton, NJ: Princeton University Press.

Reardon, Ken, with John Welsh, Brian Kreiswirth, and John Forester. 1993. "Participatory Action Research from the Inside: A Profile of Ken Reardon's Community Development Practice in East St. Louis." *The American Sociologist* 24, no. 1 (Summer): 69–91.

Reich, Robert. 1988. "Policymaking in a Democracy." In *The Power of Public Ideas*, ed. R. Reich. Cambridge, MA: Ballinger.

Richardson, Henry. 2003. *Democratic Autonomy*. New York: Oxford University Press.

Rivkin, Malcolm. 1977. *Negotiated Development: A Breakthrough in Environmental Controversies*. Washington, DC: Conservation Foundation.

Rogers, Mary Beth. 1990. *Cold Anger*. Denton: University of North Texas Press.

Rorty, Amelie. 1992. "The Psychology of Aristotelian Tragedy." In *Essays on Aristotle's Poetics*, ed. A. Rorty. 1–22. Princeton, NJ: Princeton University Press.

Ross, Marc Howard. 2001. "Psychological Interpretations and Dramas: Identity Dynamics in Ethnic Conflict." *Political Psychology* 22(1): 157–78.

————. 2004. "Ritual and the Politics of Reconciliation." In. *From Conflict Resolution to Reconciliation*, ed. Yaacov Bar-Siman-Tov, 197–223. New York: Oxford University Press.

Rothman, Jay. 1997. *Resolving Identity Based Conflict*. San Francisco: Jossey-Bass.

Sager, Tore. 1994. *Communicative Planning Theory*. Aldershot, UK: Avebury.

————. 2005. "Communicative Planners as Naive Mandarins of the Neo-liberal State?" *European Journal of Spatial Development* (December). 9 pgs.

Sandercock, Leonie. 1995. "Voices from the Borderlands: A Meditation on a Metaphor." *Journal of Planning Education and Research* 14(2): 77–88.

————. 1998. *Making the Invisible Visible: A Multicultural Planning History*. Berkeley: University of California Press.

————. 2000. "When Strangers Become Neighbors: Managing Cities of Difference." *Planning Theory and Practice* 1(1): 13–30.

————. 2003a. "Dreaming the Sustainable City: Organizing Hope, Negotiating Fear, Mediating Memory." In *Stories and Sustainability*, ed. Barbara Eckstein and Jim Throgmorton, 142–64. Cambridge, MA: MIT Press.

————. 2003b. *Cosmopolis II: Mongrel Cities in the 21st Century*. New York: Continuum Books.

Sarkissian, Wendy. 2005. "Stories in a Park: Giving Voice to the Voiceless in Eagleby, Australia." *Planning Theory and Practice* 6(1): 101–28.

Scheff, Thomas J. 1994. *Bloody Revenge: Emotions, Nationalism, and War*. Boulder, CO: Westview Press.

Schön, Donald. 1983. *The Reflective Practitioner: How Professionals Think in Action*. New York: Basic Books.

Schön, Donald, and Martin Rein. 1994. *Frame Reflection: Toward the Resolution of Intractable Policy Controversies*. New York: Basic Books.

Schram, Sanford. 1995. "Against Policy Analysis: Critical Reason and Poststructural Resistance." *Policy Sciences* 28(4): 375–84.

Schutz, Alfred. 1970. *Alfred Schutz on Phenomenology and Social Relations*. Ed. Helmut Wagner. Chicago: University of Chicago Press.

Sclavi, Marianella. 2006a. "Postface: Why Understanding the Bronx Requires the Humorist's Touch: The Art of Listening, Thick Descriptions, and Layered Emotions." Translated by Henry Martin, 2002. In *La Signora va nel Bronx*, 3rd ed. Milan: Bruno Mondadori.

————. 2006b. "The Place of Creative Conflict Management in Intercultural Communications: A Study of Conflict in a Non-linear World." Prepared for the Environment and Public Policy Conference of the Association for Conflict Resolution, Cambridge, MA, June 28–30.

Segal, Jerome M. 1997. "Negotiating Jerusalem." *Report from the Institute for Philosophy and Public Policy* 17(4): 21–27.

Sherman, Laurence. 2005. "Mediation and Collaboration in Architecture and Community Planning: A Profile of Larry Sherman." In *Mediation in Practice*, ed. J. Forester, 103–124. Ithaca, NY: Cornell University, Department of City and Regional Planning

Shmueli, Deborah, Sanda Kaufman, and Connie Ozawa. 2008. "Mining Negotiation Theory for Planning Insights." *Journal of Planning Education and Research* 27(3): 359–64.

Sloan, Gordon. 2005. "Facilitating the Land-Use Planning Process for Vancouver Island: A Profile of Gordon Sloan." In *Mediation in Practice,* ed. J. Forester, 55–80. Ithaca, NY: Cornell University, Department of City and Regional Planning.

Smith, William P. 1985. "Effectiveness of the Biased Mediator." *Negotiation Journal* (October): 363–72.

Somers, Margaret R. 1994. "The Narrative Constitution of Identity: A Relational and Network Approach." *Theory and Society* 23: 605–649.

Sorensen, Eva and J. Torfing. 2005. "Network Governance and Post-liberal Democracy." *Administrative Theory and Praxis.* 27:2. 197–237.

Stone, Deborah. 1997. *Policy Paradox: The Art of Political Decision Making.* New York: Norton.

Storper, Michael, and Sayer, Andrew. 1997. "Ethics Unbound: For a Normative Turn in Social Theory." Guest editorial essay. *Environment and Planning D: Society and Space* 15: 1–17.

Sunstein, Cass. 1991. "Preferences and Politics." *Philosophy and Public Affairs* 20, no. 1 (Winter): 3–34.

Susskind, Lawrence, and J. Cruikshank. 1987. *Breaking the Impasse.* New York: Basic Books.

———. 2006. *Breaking Roberts Rules.* New York: Oxford University Press.

Susskind, Lawrence, and Patrick Field. 1996. *Dealing with an Angry Public.* New York: Free Press.

Susskind, Lawrence, S. McKearnan, and J. Thomas-Larmer, eds. 1999. *The Consensus Building Handbook: A Comprehensive Guide to Reaching Agreement.* Thousand Oaks, CA: Sage.

Susskind, Lawrence, and Jennifer Thomas-Larmer. 1999. "Conducting a Conflict Assessment." In *The Consensus Building Handbook,* ed. Lawrence Susskind, Sarah McKearnan, and Jennifer Thomas-Larmer, 99–136. Thousand Oaks, CA: Sage.

Thom, Stephen. 1997. Interview by Kristen Grace. Profiles of Practitioners Project. Ithaca, NY: Cornell University, Department of City and Regional Planning.

Townsend, Jon. 2005. "Explosion and Redemption in Community Mediation (or, When Neighbors Aren't Neighborly): A Profile of John Townsend." In *Mediation in Practice,* ed. J. Forester, 81–102. Ithaca, NY: Cornell University, Department of City and Regional Planning.

Umemoto, Karen. 2001. "Walking in Another's Shoes: Epistemological Challenges in Participatory Planning." *Journal of Planning Education and Research* 21: 17–31.

———. 2005. "Dispute Resolution and Deliberation and Racial Violence: A Profile of Karen Umemoto." In *Mediation in Practice,* ed. J. Forester, 291–312. Ithaca, NY: Cornell University, Department of City and Regional Planning.

———. 2006. *The Truce.* Ithaca, NY: Cornell University Press.

Ury, William, Jeanne Brett, and Stephen Goldberg. 1988. *Getting Disputes Resolved.* San Francisco: Jossey-Bass.

Vollrath, Ernst. 1977. "Hannah Arendt and the Method of Political Thinking." *Social Research.* 44, no. I (Spring): 160–82.

Wagenaar, Hendrik. 2002. "Value Pluralism in Public Administration: Two Perspectives on Administrative Morality." In *Rethinking Administrative Theory: The Challenge of the New Century,* ed. J. S. Jun, 105–30. Westport, CT: Praeger.

Walzer, Michael. 1980. "A Day in the Life of a Socialist Citizen." In *Radical Principles,* 128–39. New York: Basic Books.

Warfield, Wallace. 2005. "Joint Problem Solving and the Challenges of Cultural Translation: A Profile of Wallace Warfield." In *Mediation in Practice,* ed. J. Forester, 268–91. Ithaca, NY: Cornell University, Department of City and Regional Planning.

Warren, Mark. 1992. "Democratic Theory and Self-Transformation." *American Political Science Review* 86(I): 8–23.

———. 1996. "Deliberative Democracy and Authority." *American Political Science Review* 90, no. I (March): 46–60.

Weisbord, Marvin, et al. 1992. *Discovering Common Ground.* San Francisco: Berrett-Koehler.

Wheeler, Michael. 2002. *Anxious Moments: Openings in Negotiation.* Working draft, October 21. Cambridge, MA: Harvard Business School.

———. 2003. *Notes on Improv, Creativity, Intuition and Presence of Mind.* NCDD-03 class, January 30. Cambridge, MA: Harvard Business School.

———. 2004. Editor's introduction. *Negotiation Journal* 20.

———, and Gillian Morris. 2001. *A Note on Critical Moments in Negotiation.* Cambridge, MA: Harvard Business School.

White, Stephen, ed. 1995. *The Cambridge Companion to Habermas.* Cambridge: Cambridge University Press.

Winship, Christopher. 2006. "Policy Analysis as Puzzle Solving." In *Oxford Handbook of Public Policy,* ed. Michael Moran, Robert E. Goodin, and Martin Rein, 109–23. New York: Oxford University Press.

Wittgenstein, Ludwig. 1950. *Philosophical Investigations.* Oxford: Blackwell.

———. 1984. *Culture and Value.* Chicago: University of Chicago Press.

Yankelovich, Daniel. 1991. *Coming to Public Judgment: Making Democracy Work in a Complex World.* Syracuse, NY: Syracuse University Press.

———. 2001. *The Magic of Dialogue.* New York: Touchstone.

Yanow, Dvora and Peregrine Schwartz-Shea, ed. 2006. *Interpretation and Method: Empirical Research Methods and the Interpretive Turn.* Armonk, N.Y.: M.E. Sharpe.

Yiftachel, Oren. 1998. "Planning and Social Control: Exploring the 'Dark Side.'" *Journal of Planning Literature* 12(2): 395–406.

Young, Iris Marion. 1990. *Justice and the Politics of Difference.* Princeton, NJ: Princeton University Press.

Zartman, I. William. 2000. *Traditional Cures for Modern Conflicts.* Boulder, CO: Lynne Rienner.

Index

acknowledgment
  and difference, 3, 20, 22,43, 47, 69–70, 78, 84, 88, 100, 108, 141, 147, 152, 153, 158–163, 171–173, 185
  and traumatic memory, 20
Adler, Peter, 118–120, 124–127
advocacy
  and conflict, 41, 56, 90, 97, 108
  and justice, 3, 5, 187
agreements
  and accommodations, 3–5
  continent on negotiation strategies, 82–85
  and joint gains, 34, 52–53, 74, 90, 195n9
  mediated, 14, 19, 22, 26, 51–53, 83, 90, 100, 104, 106, 109, 111, 133, 138–139, 152–153, 185, 186
  negotiated, 15, 40, 69, 111, 192
  not thought possible, 3–5, 7–9, 25, 40–41, 45–50, 72–73, 75, 78–79, 101, 103, 140–141, 147, 176–178, 180, 184
  See also mediation; negotiation; outcomes
anger
  channeled toward substance, 144, 148–150, 198n13
  and contentiousness, 4, 44–45, 95–111, 136–138, 148–150, 152
  and dismissing values, 83–86, 96–98, 109
  and environmental disputes, 10 148–150
  energy for change, 11, 144, 148–150, 152, 182, 183, 190

and fury, 7, 64
and humor, 161
and less adversarial relations, 143–144
and mediation, 27–29, 137–153
and resentment, 38, 61–64
and surprising possibilities, 54
assessment, 1, 3, 7, 8, 13, 14, 23, 25, 35, 45, 50, 54, 75, 85, 106, 108, 113, 120, 125, 128, 138, 140, 145, 178, 180–182, 189, 195n7, 197n9
  and interdependence, 181
  See also interest analysis

Bachle, Laura, 156, 205n1
Beauregard, Robert, 20, 196n4, 199n21
Bellman, Howard, 196n1
Beutler, Lisa, 4, 10, 11, 137–152, 203n6, 104n7, 204n9
Blechman, Frank, 4, 41, 44–46, 50–53, 161–163, 167, 178, 206n9
Boyd, David, 160–161, 205n7
Burgess, Puanani, 72–76, 163, 206n10

capacity building, 35, 37. 74, 75, 81, 83, 148, 155, 156, 160, 165, 172
  See also empowerment; power; presumptions of others; recognition
Catron, Bayard, 205n6
Chavez, Deborah, 146

219

cooptation, 61
civil society, 19–23, 25–26, 34, 36, 38,
    198, 205
civic friends, 33, 170, 205
collaboration, 4, 12–16, 31, 33, 35, 42,
    66–67, 76, 90, 99–100, 104, 109,
    115, 134, 137, 143, 147, 150–152,
    161, 163–173, 176, 195, 199
    collaborative learning, 33, 35, 76,
        95–106, 169
    not compromising values, 95–103
    and cooperation, 51–53, 164–165
    developing from adversarial relationships,
        31, 104, 150, 202n2
    not about harmony, 103–104, 164–165
    and the need to learn, 90, 108
    and participation, 12–15, 66, 95–105,
        202n2
    and pragmatism and power, 42
    and processes of dialogue, debate, and
        negotiation, 15, 66
    and reconciliation, 66, 76, 150
    not reconciling beliefs, 100–104, 106
    satisfying interests when values conflict,
        49–51, 100, 104
    See also dealing with differences; hope;
        humor; mediation; participation
conflict
    acknowledging and learning, 100, 107, 146
    apparently irreconcilable, 49, 53, 196n6
    and caring for more than we say, 56,
        164–165
    and deep value differences, 6, 77–81, 95
    exploiting differences, 90, 107
    and history, 61–71
    and interdependence, 37, 135
    and identity, 41, 47, 60–73, 77, 95–108,
        162, 200n4, 201n2
    not erasing, 33, 99, 100–103
    and problem wars, 116–117
    surfacing not suppressing, 99, 100–104
    See also interdependence; interest analysis;
        negotiation
compromise
    and accommodation, 24, 26, 98–101
    confusing and vague, 9

    and deal-making, 81
    joint gain agreements, 34–35, 90,
        107–109, 142, 196n8
    lose-lose, 34–35, 38, 40, 84, 107–109,
        121, 142
    neither compromise nor betrayal of
        values, 3, 80, 90, 103–109, 139,
        142–143
    suspicion of betraying values, 79–82,
        100–101
convening, 4, 7, 8, 14, 23, 27, 33, 46, 54,
    63, 75, 95, 106, 108, 179–182,
    190, 202
    and argumentative bait, 69
    when conflict See also ms irreconcilable,
        52, 54
    create the setting, 67, 75, 106, 180
    deeply opposed parties, 51–52, 182–183
    and ground rules, 27–29, 32, 46
    and personalities, 98–99, 105
    and representation, 25, 95–99, 196n9
consensus building, 193n2, 195n6
    and conflict generating, 42,
    and facilitative leadership, 14
    and practical agreement, 4, 8, 41–42, 45,
        66, 88, 95–96, 98, 103, 136, 151
    and self interest, 42
    and suspicion, 79–80
critical analysis, 11, 21
    for activist realists, not resigned cynics, 36
    and bullshit, 21
    and complaint, 11, 200n5
    and creativity, 54, 201n2, 203n3
    and critical pragmatism, 15, 22–23, 36,
        195n5, 198n15, 100n5
    expect obstacles, respond practically, 123
    failure of theory to address posturing, 121
    and hope, 20, 49
    of power, 11, 49, 199n21
    and practical reconstructive vision, 33, 121
    resisting grandiose ideal conditions, 33
    and self reflection when values conflict,
        49–50
    and surprise, 40
    See also hope; interest analysis; mediation;
        power

cultural differences, 3, 15, 19, 20, 30, 32, 34, 37–40, 44, 54, 58–63, 66, 84–89, 98, 104, 115, 117, 151, 163–164, 170, 182, 186, 196, 201, 206

Dale, Norman 88
dealing with differences, 16, 34–35, 41, 44, 52–55, 186
  and deep values, 77–91, 96–99
  exploring differences, 90, 107
  goal of participation, 37, 95, 155
  inadequacy of procedural solutions, 80
  and incommensurability, 196n6
  and the need to learn, 90, 106, 117, 186
  and presuming less, learning more, 54, 76, 89, 106, 186
  probe more, presume less, 91, 146, 186
  and raiding the impossible, 40, 186
  and reconciliation, 64–67, 76
  and ritual, 55, 64–65, 68–73, 75–76, 146–147, 151
  via serious humor, 155–173, 200n3
  specify, don't generalize, 104
  and stories, 29–35, 62–68, 70–73, 76, 86–88, 126
  trap of misplaced abstraction, 105–107
debate
  argumentative bait, 69–71, 74, 106, 146, 151–153
  displacing dialogue, 3, 66, 73–74, 106, 115, 128, 152–153, 184
  distinct from dialogue, 6, 7, 13, 33, 60, 66, 71, 73–75, 106, 115, 128–129, 143–148, 151–153, 175–187, 184–185
  distinct from negotiation, 6, 13, 76, 146–148, 152–153, 184–185
  internal to negotiations, 68–70
  and problem wars, 116–117
  and "rebut mode", 63, 66, 73–74, 146
deliberation
  bridging not erasing differences, 33, 64–71
  and critical pragmatism, 21

deliberative rituals and political imagination, 33, 56, 81
democratic, 5, 23, 25, 197n7, 198n14, 202n2
  and evaluation, 15, 194n4, 199n18
  and fury, 64
  informal taking different forms, 70
  and learning, 21, 26, 46, 64–67, 68–71, 72–76, 95–109, 120, 126
  and participation in civil society, 19, 63–68
  and political design, 34, 63–65
  and processes of dialogue, debate, and negotiation, 6, 15, 76
  and ritual, 32, 64, 70, 151
  and transformative learning, 35
  See also dialogue; debate; negotiation; participation
deliberative practitioner, v, 202n2
designing participatory processes, 19, 34–35, 52, 63–67, 81–82, 95–98, 106–109, 114–117, 146–147, 151–153, 176, 197n11
  detail not doctrine, 107, 108
  distinguish dialogue and debate, 63–64, 69, 74, 106, 125, 133–153
  and education before negotiation, 145, 147–148
  failures of, 119, 152, 171, 176, 179–180
  guts on the table, 72
  and humor, 155–177, 206n12
  informal fora, 69–70, 198n16
  learning and reframing, 139, 145
  looking beyond core issues, 52, 117, 148
  and pain, 64–66, 119
  and safety, 46, 106, 119, 125, 128
  slowing argument, 146–148
  using indirection, 146–147, 198n16,
  and value differences, 60, 63, 72–76, 81–82, 95–108
  See also convening, ground rules, learning
dialogue, 6, 7, 13, 15, 18, 20, 26, 28, 33–34, 38, 55, 60, 63, 71, 74, 88, 96, 117, 141, 152, 184–185, 187, 200
  and face to face meeting, 48, 66, 69–70, 96, 128, 141, 151

dialogue (*continued*)
   and fellowship circles, 65
   and ground rules, 34, 96
   and naïve optimism, 5
   and surprise, 72–73, 140 157–158
   and thoughtful discourse, 63–68, 128
   versus debate and negotiation, 13, 55, 60,
     63–64, 67, 69, 70, 73–76, 114–116,
     128, 146–148, 184–185
   See also trust and distrust; debate,
     negotiation
Diepeveen, William, 135, 136, 142, 147,
   152, 203n4
drama of mediation, 7–8, 40,49, 50, 89,
   107, 111, 138, 139–141, 155, 198n17
   and non-negotiable issues, 50
   and past suffering, 149–150, 199n22
   realism blinding us, 49
   and struggle for discovery, 89
   and unexpected results, 49, 139, 141, 148
   See also presumptions of others; wisdom,
     practical

Edelson, Nathan, 157, 161, 205n3
Edwards, Mencer D., 123, 176, 181
Eliot, T. S., 40
empowerment, v, 4, 35, 43, 108, 116, 160,
   162 167–173, 187, 197, 199, 206
   and coalition building, 42
   and inequality, 35
   obstacles to, 119–120, 168–169,
     172–173
   obstructing agreements, 42
   See also participation; power; mediation;
     negotiation
escalation, 68–71, 74
ethics, 34, 38, 39, 74, 121, 204
   learning about value, not values, 35, 202n3
   See also agreements; justice; outcomes
evaluation, 12, 13, 15
   See also agreements; ethics; justice;
     outcomes
expertise, 4, 5, 15, 25, 33, 39, 91, 107, 135,
   145, 148, 156, 168, 169, 171, 180,
   184, 186, 191, 204n12, 206n7

facilitative leadership, 4, 14, 111–113,
   151–152, 172–173, 175–179, 180,
   182–190,193n1, 193n2, 193n3,
   194n3, 196n11, 201n1, 201n3,
   and facilitation, 7, 13
   and integrating participation and
     negotiation, 175, 179–180
   and interdependence, 14, 152, 201n3
   and learning about interests, 111–113, 152
   less misleading than consensus building,
     14, 200n1
   and mind-mapping, 142–144, 151
   and multi-voting, 143
   no panacea, 14, 204n12
   and traps of negotiation, 14, 152
fear, 24, 26, 28, 41, 44, 46, 54, 69, 74, 78,
   86, 106–107, 114–116, 117–129,
   134, 146, 151, 161, 183, 190, 195,
   201n1, 206n13
Fitzhenry, Robert, 146
Frankfurt, Harry, 21

Grieg, Michelle Robinson, 42–43, 53
groundrules, 27–29, 32, 34, 75, 97–98, 100,
   104–106, 183, 190
   and safe spaces, 34–35, 46, 97–98,
     164–165, 183
gullibility, 5, 12, 20, 54, 56, 70, 83–84, 91,
   187, 196n3, 201n1
   and listening critically, 54, 69–70
   and realism, 52–54
   See also interest analysis; presumptions of
     others; recognition

Hanson, Russell Norwood, 50
hope, 5, 6, 10, 20, 22, 32, 36, 38, 43, 49, 3,
   56, 63, 73, 112, 122–123, 140, 147,
   149, 150, 155–172, 175–179, 194n3,
   194n4, 199n22, 201n1, 202n1
   or complaining cynicism, 20
   and deep differences, 38, 150, 166–167,
     202n1
   facing apparently irreconcilable conflicts,
     49–55, 150

and mediators' responses, 123, 167
  modest, incentive to learn, 140
  to reduce suffering, 150
  and seductive cynicism, 38
  and surprise after cynicism, 49, 72–73,
    166–167
Hughes, Mike, 4, 95–106, 201n1
humor, 155–173, 200n3, 205n4, 206n11,
    206n12
  and anger, 42–43, 200n3
  dismantling presumptions, 155–173
  and irony, 4, 155
  and judgment, 156, 173
  and possibility, 20–22, 43, 76, 160, 163,
    168–169, 173, 206n12
  and recognition, 43, 155–177
  and reframing, 158, 163, 169
  and respect, 157, 159, 160, 163
  serious and freeing, 43, 76, 156, 158,
    160, 163
  and surprise, 157–158, 169
  and vulnerability, 159, 164–165
  and ways of *See also*ing, 43, 76, 155–156,
    173, 206n11
  and Wittgenstein, 206n11

implementation, 7, 25, 42, 80, 102, 105, 109,
    171, 179, 180, 199n18, 203n4, 205n3
  and obstruction, 41–42
improvisation
  and argumentative bait, 69, 74
  creating deliberative spaces, 74, 95, 98,
    166–167
  debate less, learn more, 106–108
  humor, 156, 160, 166, 170–171, 173
  and informal discussions, 69, 150, 151
  and judgment calls, 35, 150
  to learn and satisfy interests, 56, 98, 106,
    146–148
  not anything goes, 101
interdependence, 9, 12, 15, 37, 39, 42, 56,
    66, 147, 152, 158, 177, 178m 180,
    181, 189, 203n1, 202n2, 204n12
  and ambiguity, 56, 69–71, 157–158
  and deliberation, 15, 38

and difference, 37, 54
  and mediation, 38–39
  and place, 66
  and presuming less and learning more, 54
  requiring collaborative pragmatism, 42,
    199n18
  and the shadow of the future, 70–71,
    116–117, 148–150
  and shared vulnerability, 9, 135, 152
  and traps of negotiation, 9, 135, 152
  See also negotiation; mediation
interest analysis, 3, 26, 69, 87, 111–129,
    145–146, 148, 152, 176
  acknowledging passionately divided
    interests, 45
  and compensation, not grief, 81–82
  facing exaggeration and posturing, 111–121
  and identities, 34, 49, 61–67, 77, 87
  in negotiation, 112–129, 145–148
  positional bargaining, 112–113
  and priorities, 26, 34, 77, 90, 95, 104,
    121, 124, 142, 143, 145, 147, 178,
    182, 183–186, 190–192
  and relationships, 121–123, 148
  and self interest, 42, 145
  and substance, 121–123, 148
  and values, 35, 49, 59, 67, 77, 87
  when values conflict, 49, 67, 107
irreconcilability, 16, 39, 49, 56, 67, 76, 79,
    90–91, 181
  danger of presuming, 49, 85–86, 90–91
  See also values, dealing with differences;

justice, 3, 5, 11, 12, 15, 27, 29, 41, 62, 121,
    148, 149, 187, 195n10, 199n22
  and complaint, 11
  and critical analysis, 11, 187

Kilgore, Anne, 205n4

learning
  ambiguity as invitation, 71
  detail not doctrine, 106

learning (*continued*)
  and emotion, 28–29, 95–99, 127, 198n13
  about interests, 35, 50–51, 63–70, 87,
    111–129
  by indirection, 72–76, 88–89, 193n1,
    206n12
  when interests conflict, 50–54, 111–129,
    145–146, 180
  via interviews, 46
  listening, learning and acting, 33–35,
    52–54, 63–68, 70, 75, 141
  and orientation sessions, 26
  parties learning about themselves, 25, 26, 88
  probe more, presume less, 91, 108,
    116–118
  and the promise of democracy, 25–26
  soft structures and safe processes, 71, 88,
    96–99, 180–186, 191
  and storytelling, 27–28, 31–32, 63–68,
    70–74, 76, 88, 95–108, 126
  and surprise, 40, 54, 72–73, 75, 78,
    87–88, 106, 18–119
  transformative, 35, 145, 197n11, 206n12
  about value, 35
  and value conflicts, 6, 9, 39, 41, 44, 63,
    77–91, 95–109, 184, 187
  See also dialogue; negotiation; mediation;
    trust
Lederach, John Paul, 3, 5, 187
listening, 12, 22, 29, 31, 34, 41, 54, 55, 68,
    82, 86–90, 101, 108, 113, 117, 121,
    123, 145, 176, 183, 186, 190, 193n1,
    202n2
Lorenzo, Raymond, 205n4

McLaren, Normajean, 159, 161, 164–171,
    205n5, 206n11
mediation
  and alternatives, 136, 196n11
  ambiguity as opportunity, 55–56, 62, 97,
    100, 173
  and conflict assessment, 7, 193n2
  and convening stakeholders, 7, 25, 27–29,
    46, 51–52, 95, 196n11

defined, 14, 193n2
  and difference, 21, 25, 30, 39–55,
    95–101
  distinct from facilitation, 7, 13, 128,
    185, 187
  distinct from moderating, 7, 13, 128,
    185, 187
  and facilitative leadership, 14, 193n1,
    193n3, 196n11, 201n1, 201n3
  ethical challenges, 22, 33, 34, 38, 39,
    43–44, 55, 71, 74, 111, 156, 196n3,
    202n2, 204n11
  and justice, 3, 5, 6, 11, 12, 15, 27, 29, 62,
    121, 148, 149, 187, 195n10, 199n22
  mediation within a mediation, 98–100
  and mind-mapping, 142–144, 145,
    151, 183
  and multi-voting, 143, 145
  not anything goes, 101, 148, 204n12
  not magic but hard work, 8, 176
  not merely process, 148, 204n11
  not persuasion, 101
  not reconciling beliefs, 100
  and safe space, 27–29, 32, 97–98
  searching for practical strategies, 38–43,
    49–52, 100, 144, 202n2
  and traps of lose-lose agreements, 40, 142
  See also facilitative leadership; interest
    analysis; learning; negotiation
mediators
  activist mediators, 5, 19
  as canaries in the mine, 39
  as cultural interpreters, 61–62, 201n3
  and dealing with differences, 19–22, 34
  and facilitators, 3, 13, 200n1, 201n1
  facing interdependence, 9, 144
  and giving up too soon, 39, 52–54
  not judges, not bureaucrats, 25
  lessons from, 8, 23, 39, 180–187
  mediating vs. facilitating vs. moderating,
    13, 128, 152
  like midwives, 26, 138, 175, 194n4
  profiles of practitioners, 10, 22–23,
    39–40, 195n8
  See also king qualities of agreements, 14

wisdom of, 8, 40, 123
  See also also assessment, convening, learning,
    negotiating,
metaphor, 61, 62, 65, 143
moderating, 7, 13–15, 60, 74, 124, 128,
    133, 147, 152–153, 161, 176,
    184–185, 206
Moore, Carl, 116–117, 119–121, 127
multiculturalism, 20, 38, 164

negotiation
  acting with non-negotiable values, 104
  and apparent irreconcilability, 47–53,
    77–80
  and deceptive realism, 5, 52–54
  and deep value differences, 6, 47, 50–54,
    77–91, 95–104
  and good agreements, 186, 192
  and identity, 47, 162, 195n10, 198n13
  integrated with participation, 6, 14, 142,
    175–189, 192, 195n6, 196n11
  and learning, 46–54, 63–72, 95–107,
    133–153
  and lose-lose traps, 13, 14, 34, 40, 84,
    107, 121, 142, 152, 177
  and surprise, 54, 158
  traps of, 9, 14, 16, 20, 40, 83–86, 90,
    105–106, 121, 124, 152, 170
  zero-sum, 41, 55, 134, 136
  See also interest analysis; learning;
    mediation
negotiator's dilemma, 121–123
networks, 14, 15, 44, 78, 177, 178, 180,
    186, 201n2
  and collaboration, 14
  and governance, 14–15
  See also interdependence
neutrality of mediation, 4, 19, 26, 30–32,
    35, 47, 61–62, 74, 80, 183, 190,
    198n16, 204n11
  fiction, of 35
  and moderation, 74
  and suspicion, 80
  and false promises, 80

outcomes
  beyond process, 148, 194n4, 199n18,
    204n11
  and expertise, 148
  joint gains, mutually beneficial, 34, 38, 52,
    83, 90, 107, 148, 152
  lose-lose, 14, 38, 83, 121, 152
  missing, when values conflict, 49, 83,
    105–107
  and new possibilities, 40, 49–52
  possible value irreconcilability, 91
  quality of, 7, 15, 26, 108, 112, 148, 177,
    195n9, 196n8, 199n18, 204n11
  qualities of agreements, 14, 152, 195n9,
    196n8, 199n18, 204n11
  and successful negotiations, 9

participation
  and alternatives, 136
  constructive criticism vs complaint, 11
  facile rhetorical claims, 12, 111, 133,
    200n5
  and identity, 37, 77, 95, 147–148
  integrated with negotiation, 6, 14, 147–148,
    175–180, 197n10, 203n3, 206n12
  and not so civil civil societies, 34, 63,
    96, 134
  and posturing, 4–7, 20, 71, 83–84, 105,
    109, 111–129, 134, 152, 170, 181,
    183, 190, 196n11, 202n2
  and representation, 6, 95, 99, 104, 200n5
  surfacing proposals, 147–150
  threatened by fear and anger, 44, 96, 134
  and voice, 20, 120, 147–148, 179–180
  See also dialogue; debate; deliberation;
    learning; mediation; negotiation
peacemaking, 196n11, 198n16
place, 6, 13–16, 22, 27, 29, 30, 31, 37, 39,
    48, 55, 59, 64–68, 70, 72, 75–76, 98,
    194n4, 197n11
  deliberative placemaking, 67, 194n4
  pain and interdependence, 66
  and stories, 64–65, 76, 126
  and identity, interests and values, 67

planning, v, 6–8, 12, 14, 15, 23, 29, 33, 36, 41,
    42, 44–46, 66, 72, 73, 77, 86, 88–89,
    100, 111–121, 133–138, 148–153,
    155–159, 160, 168, 177, 194n3,
    194n4, 196n2, 198n14, 199n21,
    200n5, 202n2, 203n3, 203n5, 205n4
  defined, 6, 193n1, 194n4, 202n1
  enhancing deliberative spaces, 33, 199n21
  and evaluation, 12, 13, 15,
  incorporating skilled facilitation and
    mediation, 33
  knowledge displacing action, 13
  looking beyond discouragement, 45
  and process design, 4, 13, 19, 32, 34–35,
    44–46, 199n18
  promoting welfare of parties, 33
  spatial, 14–16, 116, 139, 200n5
  threatened by anger, 44–46
planning in the face of power, v, 193n1,
    202n2
possibility
  and constructive criticism vs complaint, 11
  and critical analysis, 21–23, 36, 49, 123
  and fallible claims, 21
  and giving up too soon, 39, 52–54, 177
  and hope, 6, 10, 20–21, 73, 161–163,
    202n1
  and humor, 21–22, 76, 155–173
  and impossibility, v, 3–6, 8, 16, 41,
    49–55, 177
  not prescribed, 160
  and raiding the impossible, 40, 53–55, 177
  of satisfying interests when values conflict,
    49–55
  and surprise, 40, 49, 50, 53–54, 72–76,
    155–160, 165
  and vulnerability, 21, 159, 168–170
  See also humor; irreconcilability
Podziba, Susan, 156
power, v, 3, 6–22, 32, 36, 41–43, 47, 49,
    52, 61–66, 89–90, 97–98, 108, 117,
    134, 151, 155, 159, 161–162, 165,
    167–169, 172, 177, 186, 193n3,
    195n8, 195n10, 196n11, 199n21,
    200n5, 201n3, 202n2, 206n11

  and collaboration, 42, 164–166, 202n2
  and critical analysis, 36, 196n4, 196n11,
    199n21
  and deceptive realism, 38, 49, 52–53, 151,
    202n2
  and differences, 19
  disciplinary, 32
  and emotion, 41, 64, 148–151
  and humiliation, 32, 62, 165, 198n15
  and humor, 155–173
  to implement, 42
  and possibility, 11, 16, 21, 151, 160,
    165–166, 193n1
  and problem-framing, 117, 139–140, 143
  and reconciliation, 64, 167–169
  and stories, 9, 10, 27, 31, 32, 34, 37,
    41, 53, 61–69, 74–76, 88, 96–108,
    128–129
  and systematically distorted
    communication, 32, 62, 165, 198n15
  and voice, 20, 193n1
practice stories, v, 10, 22–23, 40–41, 74,
    121, 136, 187, 195n8, 198n17 200n2,
    202n3, 203n5, 204n8
presumptions of others, 5, 8, 10, 15, 16, 25,
    31, 34–35, 38–39, 49–50, 53–56,
    61–62, 78–91, 104–109, 114,
    117–118, 122–126, 129, 134, 151,
    159, 167–169, 172, 176, 180–181,
    186, 206n13
  hold us captive, 56, 86, 88–89,
    125, 181
  and humor, 159, 161
  and ineradicable conflict, 15–16
  and mediators' need to learn, 54
  and missing possibilities, 16, 38, 181
  and narrowing vision, 50, 55
  and possibilities, 123, 161–165
  and probing not presuming, 89, 108,
    117–118, 123, 146, 151, 181
  and stories, 62–68, 127–129, 151
  and supposed irreconcilable conflicts, 49,
    85–86
  See also learning; recognition; surprise; trust
    and mistrust

problem-solving, 27–29, 61, 75, 80, 82,
    98, 108, 109, 113, 115, 117, 138,
    141–142, 151–152, 201n2, 202n2,
    and bounding problems, 61
    and musicians' search, 76
    solving the wrong problems, 113
    See also deliberation; mediation;
        negotiation
profiles of practitioners, v, 4, 9–10, 19, 29,
    31, 34–35, 41, 50, 59, 74–75, 78, 86,
    160, 163, 169, 171–172, 176, 193n2,
    195n8, 198n17, 200n2, 201n3,
    202n3, 203n5

racial and ethnic disputes, 4, 5, 15, 22, 38,
    40, 50, 60, 61, 95, 97, 114, 116, 129,
    151, 162, 163, 170, 195n10, 201n3,
    202n3
rationality of deliberation, 19, 25, 35, 39,
    76–78, 89, 106, 117, 177, 200n3,
    200n5, 202n2
    See also designing participatory processes;
        interest analysis
realism, 5, 21, 38, 49, 52–55, 81, 84, 181
    and critical pragmatism, 15, 22, 36
    deceptive, 38, 52–53
    as a source of failure, 52–53
    wrongly presuming impossibility, 40, 52–53
Reardon, Kenneth, 175
recognition, 4, 15 24, 31, 33, 34, 43, 54, 59,
    62, 64, 70, 75, 76, 82, 90, 97, 100,
    101, 108, 109, 113, 149, 152, 155,
    159, 160, 164, 165, 170, 172, 183,
    190, 193n1, 198n16, 199n19
    and humor, 155–177
    See also learning; presumptions of others;
reconciliation, 63–67, 76, 79, 195n8
respecting differences, 4, 19–22, 29, 33,
    35, 37–38, 43–48, 54–55, 59–65,
    69–71, 74–75, 78–85, 95–108, 152,
    155–173, 196n2, 196n3
    bridging not erasing differences, 33, 38,
        71, 96–99, 100–103
    not compromising values, 103

and double vision, 69–71
and identity, 38, 68, 72, 95–108
and recognition, 33, 97
respect persons, question claims, 20,
    82–85
and ritual, 55, 63–71
and traumatic memory, 35, 168–169
and voice, 20, 68
Roberts, Rules of Order, 30, 32
Ross, Dennis, 68–71, 73–74, 76

Sarkissian, Wendy, 119–121
Sclavi, Marianella, 206n11
Sloan, Gordon, 23–26, 31–35, 86, 89
Sobel, Gregory, 27–29, 31–35
social capital, 44
Solomon, Shirley, 3, 29–35, 63–69, 71,
    73–74, 76, 88
surprise, 5, 8, 12, 25, 31, 34, 37, 40, 49, 54,
    60–61, 71–72, 88, 106, 158, 161,
    169, 176,
    See also learning; possibility; presumptions
        of others
Susskind, Lawrence, 14, 88, 107, 136,
    137, 147, 152, 179, 195n6, 204n10,
    204n11

Thom, Stephen, 41, 47–49, 53
Townsend, Jon, 87, 89, 112–113
trauma
    and the commisertation trap, 170–171
    and grief, 65–67, 96–99, 115, 149,
        166–167, 170–171
    and memory, 35, 61–62, 135, 149, 166,
        199n22, 201n2,
    and racial conflict, 114–116, 164–165,
        198n15, 199n22
    revealed in stories, 6–74
    seriousness cycles down, 166
    and unmitigated seriousness, 167
    and working through, 35, 64, 96–99, 115,
        149–150, 164–167, 170–171, 193n1,
        199n22

trust and distrust, 3, 7. 9, 24, 29, 35, 40, 44,
    46, 55, 72, 78, 80–83, 99, 104, 105,
    112–113, 117, 126–127, 134, 136,
    141, 152–153, 158, 161, 163–165,
    171, 172, 175, 177, 179, 181, 182,
    183, 189, 190, 194n3, 195n8,
    198n16, 199n18, 206n13

Umemoto, Karen, 114–116, 121, 126–127

values, 3, 37–56, 59–75, 77–91, 95–103
    and ambiguity, 60, 62, 70–71, 97–99
    conflict, and satisfying interests, 49–51
    and deep value differences, 4, 6, 38–40,
        41, 63–67, 68–76, 77–91
    differences as irreconcilable abstractions,
        39, 67, 78, 96
    differing from interests, 59, 77, 85–87
    differences presumed non-negotiable, 39,
        67, 70, 76, 78–79, 85
    and identity, 60, 62–67, 72–76, 77, 85
    irreconcilability as product not
        premise, 90
    and not so civil society, 34
    and parallel conversations, 71
    pro-life and pro-choice forces, 51–52
    and resignation, 78–79
    and sacred land, 47–48, 77
vulnerability, 4, 9, 21, 117, 141, 142, 155,
    158–159, 165, 172, 183, 194n3

enabling joint learning, 126, 144, 183
as opportunity for joint work, 142, 144
recognized with humor, 159
See also dealing with differences; racial and
    ethnic disputes; respecting differences

Warfield, Wallace, 60–62, 64–65, 68–69, 71,
    73–74, 76
Weiser, Irene, 196n1
Wilde, Oscar, 25
wisdom, practical, 5, 8, 41, 71, 100–103,
    105–109, 117, 123–129, 145–148
    act creatively, honor values, 101–103,
        155–177
    climb down, cook together, 101, 168–169
    detail not doctrine, 107
    facing posturing and gamesmanship, 112,
        123–129
    focus on options not doctrine, 100–109
    and growing by looking, 40
    and judgment, 35, 198n12, 200n1
    listening beyond words, 71, 144–145,
        201n4
    of mediators, 7–8
    options not value systems, 100–106
    and practice stories, 10, 41, 95–102
    traps of misplaced abstraction, 105–107,
        196n6
    windows onto the world, 34, 157
    See also also dialogue; mediation;
        problem-solving